THE ENERGY WORLD IS FLAT

THE ENERGY WORLD IS FLAT

Opportunities from the End of Peak Oil

Daniel Lacalle
Diego Parrilla

WILEY

Library of Congress Cataloging-in-Publication Data

Lacalle, Daniel.
  The energy world is flat : opportunities from the end of peak oil / Daniel Lacalle, Diego Parrilla.
      pages cm
  Includes index.
  ISBN 978-1-118-86800-3 (cloth)
  1. Energy security. 2. Energy consumption. 3. Petroleum reserves. 4. Petroleum industry and
trade. 5. Energy industries. I. Parrilla, Diego, 1973– II. Title.
  HD9502.A2L3325 2015
  333.79–dc23

                                                                                  2014044969

Cover image: ©shutterstock.com/Madlen
Cover design: Wiley

Set in 11/15pt in ITC Garamond Std by Laserwords Private Limited, Chennai, India

Dedication

From Daniel Lacalle

To all my colleagues in the energy sector and decades of hard work looking for a better world, and in particular to those who passed away during geopolitical conflicts and terror attacks. We will never forget you.

To Patricia, Jaime, Pablo and Daniel, my parents, my brother, and his family. To all my uncles, aunts, and cousins who give and share so much joy. To all of them, my never ending source of energy.

From Diego Parrilla

To my wife, Gema, and my children, Yago, Lucas, and Carmen. My life and purpose in life.

To my father, Paco, and my mother, Nieves, my role models.

To my brother Paco, the best brother I could have wished for. My inspiration.

To my sisters Nieves and Marta, the geniuses of the family.

And, of course, to our sister Belen, our Guardian Angel.

Contents

Disclaimer

The opinions expressed in this book by Daniel Lacalle and Diego Parrilla are strictly personal and do not in any way reflect the opinion, strategy or philosophy of the firms they work or have worked for, nor should be taken as buy or sell recommendations

CHAPTER ONE

THE MOTHER OF ALL BATTLES. THE FLATTENING AND GLOBALIZATION OF THE ENERGY WORLD

There is nothing permanent, except change.

Heraclitus

At 2.46 pm on the 11 March 2011, the largest earthquake in the history of Japan triggered a giant tsunami wave that would change the energy world forever.

I was on a conference call in my office when the prices of the Japanese yen started to swing wildly. Something had happened. Shortly after, the news was hitting the wires: "Massive 9.0 Earthquake Hits East Coast of Japan. Tsunami Warning Issued". While Japan had a long history of earthquakes, such as the Unzen earthquake and tsunami in 1792 that left a death toll of over 15,000,[1] a tremor of 9.0 on the Richter scale was at a whole new level, and would make this earthquake the largest in the history of Japan and the fifth largest globally since records began in 1900.

Within minutes, a series of giant tsunami waves reached Fukushima Daiichi power plant. More than twice as high as the protective seawalls, the waves flooded the power station and damaged the back-up generation and cooling systems. The situation was out of control, and radiation was eventually released, making Fukushima the worst nuclear accident since Chernobyl in 1986, both rated level 7 on the International Nuclear Event Scale.

Nuclear politics

I immediately recognized Fukushima as yet another "black swan", an event that has a very large impact that no one had anticipated before the fact, but that everyone viewed as obvious after the fact. The scale of the earthquake and the unfortunate series of events were unique to Fukushima, but lessons would be learnt and new processes and security measures would be put in place, as has always been the case when accidents and natural disasters have occurred.

But within days, and despite decades of safe nuclear power, countries around the world were closing down nuclear plants and rethinking their plans of extending the life of existing plants and building new ones. Politicians had taken over and were reshaping the future of nuclear power.

But not all countries reacted the same way. Fukushima did not change the position of France, which produces over 75% of its own energy needs from nuclear power. And it did not change the position of China either, which maintained its plans to build up to 70 new nuclear plants by 2020.

The nuclear world was polarized, but I was optimistic that common sense would prevail and that short-term knee-jerk reactions would give way to long-term constructive solutions and even safer power generation across the world.

There is, however, no doubt in my mind that Fukushima was a critical milestone towards the end of OPEC's dominance. Let me tell you why.

The sustained spike in natural gas prices

The close down of all nuclear capacity in Japan left a large gap in power generation that had to be filled by coal, natural gas, and crude oil.

The seaborne coal market was able to absorb the increase in Japanese demand with relative ease, but the much smaller market of seaborne liquefied natural gas (LNG) suffered a severe shock that sent prices skyrocketing.

Prices of natural gas in Asia more than doubled reaching over \$20/MMBtu, equivalent to over US\$110 per barrel of oil equivalent (USD/boe).[2]

Fukushima impacted other large Asian consumers, such as Korea, Taiwan, and China, who also rely on natural gas for their current and future power generation mix, reinforcing the perception that Asia would buy "unlimited amounts of gas, at unlimited prices".

The imbalances could not be resolved easily, and the price of LNG for delivery to Japan stayed at an extremely high level for several years in order to direct any available LNG towards North East Asia.

In March 2014, three years after the Fukushima accident, and after extensive political debate in Japan, Japanese Prime Minister Abe announced his pledge to gradually restart nuclear reactors towards the end of the year, which will most likely ease the demand and domestic tightness of natural gas in the region.

However, the sustained high prices and optimistic demand expectations have been a major incentive to the development of new production and liquefaction capacity around the world. The list of producing countries and investments is long.

Look at Australia, for example, investing over half a trillion dollars in new LNG infrastructure to unlock large stranded reserves.

Or Mozambique, where local engineers in the mid-1990s were telling me how desperate they were to prove the large potential of the country, but where the perception among politicians was that it was not worth exploring. Ten years later, with the incentives of high prices and cooperation with international investors and companies, the country made some of the most important gas discoveries and infrastructure development in the region.

Or, even Cyprus and Israel, where large discoveries are putting them on the energy map . . . as producers!

Fracking and the collapse in US natural gas prices

While Fukushima created a demand shock and sharply higher global LNG prices, a *quiet revolution* had been taking place in North America for over a decade that had transformed the supply and drastically reduced prices of domestic US natural gas.

For decades, engineers knew about the vast amounts of natural gas resources that were trapped inside shale formations, but had not found a way to extract them commercially on a large scale. But the supply revolution which had started quietly in the Barnett Shale, Texas, in the early 2000s changed that.

"Not sure I told you before", a senior member of one the largest sovereign wealth funds in the world told me, "I have a degree in nuclear engineering. My first job during the 1970s was to research the application of nuclear technology to extract natural gas from shale formations. It has taken a few decades, and a different technology, but I guess my fellow engineers have finally won".

Indeed, production engineers had found a solution to unlock the gas trapped inside shale rock formations thanks to the combination of horizontal drilling and hydraulic fracturing. And the potential was massive.

The United States, once thought to be in critical shortage of natural gas, was now enjoying an abundance with enough supply to cover over 100 years of demand.

I remember the first time I heard "US energy independence is real". It was in 2006, and I was meeting large oil and gas producers in Houston. I had endless debates about decline rates, lack of commerciality, environmental risks, the impossibility to replicate the success of the Marcellus Shale elsewhere in the United States, and other considerations. At that time the view was that shale gas would not be economical below $8/MMBtu and that decline rates would make the "fad" disappear soon.

But the reality turned out to be quite different.

By April 2012, following the unusually warm winter in North America, the price of US natural gas had fallen to $2/MMBtu,[3] levels not seen for over a decade. The words of a good friend resonate in my head: "never bet against human ingenuity".

The divergence in prices between North America and Asia had indeed been extraordinary. Exactly the same molecules of natural gas were trading at a 1000% premium across the world. The implications are deep, and go beyond energy markets.

Access to abundant, cheap, and cleaner energy has been an important contributor to the recovery and enhanced competitiveness of the United States relative to the rest of the world. On the other hand, expensive energy has had a negative impact on the Japanese economy and competitiveness.

Looking forward, the combination of political and logistical constraints may keep these extraordinary differentials for several more years, but this will not last forever. The markets are sending strong signals, and the response is simply a matter of time.

US tight oil

The shale gas revolution is not just about natural gas. It is also about crude oil.

The engineering feats of horizontal drilling and fracking have been applied with great success in the extraction of crude oil from shale-like formations.

The impact of this "tight oil" is very significant, and has contributed to the growth towards record domestic production in North America.

I was in Moscow in 2006 when a senior executive of a large national oil multinational told me "shale oil is a bluff". I started talking about the rapid development in technology and reduction in the cost curve, and how the trend would make tight oil economical within three years at above \$70/bbl. I could see he was getting agitated. "I will not see shale oil reach a meaningful level of production, and neither will my children nor my grandchildren". And four years later, during a debate in Spain with some peak oil defenders who had never seen an oil field in their lives, I was told again "shale oil is a bluff". Yet, during that time, the production in North Dakota had increased threefold,[4] twice as much as what doomsayers said would be "the peak", contributing to the record US production, now as high as Saudi Arabia. Yet, still today I hear the occasional "shale oil is a bluff".

Geopolitics and high crude oil prices

The oil embargo in 1973 had taken everyone by surprise, changed the energy world forever, and shaped international politics and economics.

Energy security became a top strategic priority for governments around the world, who were using any tool at their disposal to reduce their dependency on Middle East oil.

The high prices of the 1970s displaced crude oil from power generation and industrial uses in favour of coal, natural gas, nuclear, and other alternatives.

But crude oil managed to maintain its monopoly over the transportation sector. Gasoline, diesel, and jet fuel are all derived from crude oil and have *so far* faced limited competition from other fuels such as natural gas and electric cars.

Consumers have tried to find cheaper and more reliable alternatives, but until recently they have not been available on a large and commercial scale. But things are changing, and quickly.

In the meantime, geopolitics has remained a major source of volatility and uncertainty, giving consumers an incentive to find alternative solutions.

In 2011, around the same time as the Fukushima disaster was changing the nuclear and natural gas markets, North Africa was involved in a geopolitical tsunami that would become known as "the Arab Spring".

The events that started in Tunisia quickly spread across the region – Egypt, Libya, Syria, Bahrain, Algeria – in what seemed like an unstoppable geopolitical domino that would eventually reach the core of the Middle East.

I was supposed to fly to Riyadh in Saudi Arabia around those dates. During my career in the oil industry I have travelled to many live conflict areas – Sierra Leone, Nigeria, Colombia, Venezuela, and Jordan – and from the airport to the hotel to the meeting to the hotel and back to the airport, I have always been accompanied by bodyguards and a convoy of armoured cars. Sometimes it felt a bit excessive, but time would prove them right. During those trips I had numerous scares. Perhaps the worst one happened at the Sheraton in Ikeja, Nigeria, when we were woken in the middle of the night by gunfire as a mob was trying to assault the premises. Luckily the situation was kept under control, yet, as scary as it was, we had our morning meetings at the hotel the day after as if nothing had happened. However, this time, for some reason, it felt different.

The developments in North Africa sent crude oil prices sky-rocketing in response to both actual and potential supply disruptions.

But the consumer world was better prepared this time and started to trigger its defence mechanisms. The US Energy Information Administration (EIA) coordinated the release of 60 million barrels from its global strategic petroleum reserves, helping to calm and stabilize the nervous markets.

Luckily the situation was contained, and the largest producers such as Saudi Arabia were not impacted, and despite the ongoing disruptions in North Africa, prices moved to what felt like an unstable equilibrium at high but moderate prices.

What is important to note is that events that perhaps create the perception that the energy world is not flat, such as geopolitics, supply concentration, and the dependence on oil, are actually strong flattening forces that destroy those imbalances.

How? Well, for every geopolitical event and every issue of security, consumers have always reacted by building buffers and making contingencies, from storage, to demand destruction, to new discoveries, to developing new technologies.

In 2014, despite the ongoing supply disruptions from Libya, oil sanctions in Iran, ongoing conflicts and disruptions from Sudan and Syria, and a drastic reduction in Iraq volumes, the price of crude oil had a very moderate response.

Yes, geopolitics can result in higher prices in the short term, but invariably result in lower prices in the longer term. The net result: a flatter energy world.

Expensive oil, cheap natural gas

In 2012, the price of crude oil in North America was almost 10 times more expensive than natural gas in energy equivalent terms. Never before had the ratio between crude oil and natural gas been so wide.

The reason for such extreme divergence is that there is no direct mechanism of *short-term* substitution between them. As discussed, crude oil is mostly used for transportation, and natural gas for power generation and residential and industrial uses.

But how about the *longer term*? Is there a mechanism for substitution? Why continue to rely on Middle East oil? Why continue to feed our cars with petrol? Or with corn-based ethanol? Why not use natural gas for transportation? Exactly!

In North America, the abundance of natural gas reserves, a surge in production, and a steep price discount are incentivizing consumers to develop and implement technologies that use less oil and more natural gas.

The substitution is starting to be evident and will have major implications for the crude oil market.

I am amused when I hear people say that crude oil is untouchable or that the shale revolution will only impact North America. The revolution is global and has deep implications across energy sectors with many winners and losers, OPEC among them.

The market does not attack, it defends itself

One of the first lessons I learnt when I got involved in the world of commodities is that prices are both signals and incentives.

Prices signal imbalances and incentivize economic behaviour, as the market "defends itself". For example, Fukushima created a positive premium that incentivizes the transport of natural gas to Japan. On the other hand, shale gas has created a negative premium for US domestic producers, while incentivizing the demand via the substitution of coal for power generation, or attracting petrochemical businesses back to North America.

The large price differentials across crude oil and regional natural gas are incentivizing the development of new infrastructure capacity such as liquefaction plants, pipelines, and storage.

Energy infrastructure is very capital intensive, and can take many years to complete. A new LNG project can easily cost from $5 billion to $10 billion, and take 5 to 10 years to complete. But once the barriers to entry are removed and the investment decisions are triggered and completed, the capacity increases inexorably, perhaps slowly, but surely.

And the greater the barriers to entry, the greater the price signal and incentives needed, often creating "super-cycles" or multi-decade round trips from shortage to glut and back to shortage.

Winners and losers

We are currently living through an extraordinary phase in the energy world.

History books will look back at this period of transformation, which will ultimately transcend into a new world order.

Those who depend on commodity price inflation to survive or justify long-term returns are in trouble, but a flatter energy world is not a one-way "price inflation versus price deflation bet". The dynamics are complex and reach beyond energy markets.

But before we dive into the energy revolution, the flattening of the energy world, and its winners and losers, I would like to review the recent history of the internet revolution and dot-com bubble and the important lessons and parallelisms it can show for the energy markets.

NOTES

1. National Geophysical Data Center.
2. Conversion factor from 1 million British thermal units (MMBtu) to crude oil barrel (bbl) is 5.8 MMBtu/bbl.
3. Bloomberg and NARECO Advisors.
4. US Energy Information Administration.

CHAPTER TWO

LESSONS FROM THE INTERNET REVOLUTION AND THE DOTCOM BUBBLE

Of all the things I have lost, the one I miss the most is my memory.

Mark Twain

He who knows how will always work for he who knows why.

David Lee Roth

I finished reading *The World is Flat*[1] shortly after it was published. Four years had passed since the internet bubble had burst, and the word "dotcom" still carried very negative connotations. Many investors were left with a bitter taste.

It was easy to lose perspective of the bigger picture of what the internet revolution had done. It was easy to get lost in bubbles and valuations. But Thomas Friedman was an eye opener for me. His "post-mortem" analysis brought a new dimension.

The dotcom bubble had *accelerated* the impact of the internet revolution, and with it, the flattening of the world.

The internet has revolutionized the way we do business. But in the energy sector, not many things have changed. I suffered a few episodes of kidnap scares and terror threats when I was in the oil industry. We had to travel with an army of bodyguards and various vehicles and still, at least on three occasions, we were attacked by professional kidnappers aiming at the funds of the energy industry. One day, after a violent episode in Caracas, a colleague said "in a few years all will be done by video call and there will be no need for this". Twenty years later, the energy business is still about meeting face to face . . . But technology and efficiency are gradually eroding peak pricing power.

The bubble path

This flattening, or equalization, of the world happened in two phases.

First was the "boom phase", which took place during the 1990s, as a technological revolution led by internet, mobile, and broadband, had a major impact on productivity and growth expectations. Valuations were going up exponentially, based on growth expectations, not on profits. Traditional valuation methods, such as PE ratios, were largely ignored. A venture capital mentality had developed, where the potential winners would more than offset the losers in the portfolio. The cash piling in was used to acquire smaller promising businesses, feeding into the frenzy. Everyone wanted to participate and large amounts of capital flowed into the new industry. Pretty much overnight, the world was "wired" with fibre optics. High return expectations had attracted capital from other industries. A gradual build-up that might have taken decades, happened instead in a few years. The bubble had accelerated a process.

Second, and equally importantly, was the "bust phase". Valuations had gone too far, supply had increased beyond realistic expectations. Bad news for profits. Valuations collapsed and many companies went bankrupt. The "paper valuations" disappeared, but the assets, such as fibre-optic wires, stayed. And thanks to the write-offs, they were now available at very low prices, pretty much free. The investor party was over, but the consumer party had only started.

During the following decade, consumers were the main beneficiaries of the IT revolution. Outsourcing on a large scale became a reality. Our IT specialist was now able to support clients in Los Angeles, with lower cost and faster turnaround.

The world was becoming more equal. It was becoming flatter. For the first time in history, talent had become more important than geography. The brain drain from emerging markets was reduced, in fact, it reversed, as many experienced emigrants returned to their roots and developed successful businesses at home that took advantage of the new opportunities.

The dotcom bubble had played an important role after all.

Technological revolutions that increase supply. The "game changers"

The technological revolution of internet, mobile, broadband, and other technologies of the dotcom revolution has changed our lives. There was a "before" and "after". No question about it.

Likewise, the energy revolution of fracking, horizontal drilling, and other aspects are "game changers" that produce a "quantum leap" in the supply of oil and gas reserves and production.

The energy revolution is already a reality in North America, but its reach is global.

The demise of peak oil theories and doomsday predictions are clear side effects of the energy revolution.

Not only has the United States become one of the largest producers in the world with 11 million barrels per day, but also global oil production today is more abundant and diversified than ever.

The "call on OPEC" (the barrels needed from OPEC to balance the market) has remained at 29 million barrels per day for years with spare capacity exceeding 2.5 million barrels per day.[2]

With shale oil and oil sands, the reliance on imported oil has shrunk to decade lows, the supply–demand balance is stronger, and the geopolitical risk premium attached to oil prices has been dramatically cut.

Think about 2013. Despite large disruptions in Libya, sanctions on Iran, Syrian unrest, and Iraqi cuts in supply, oil prices barely moved more than $10/bbl from bottom to peak, averaging $104/bbl[3] despite global recovery in economic growth.

In the rest of the world, public opinion and governments are divided about the energy revolution exemplified by fracking. Some countries in the European Union started out by banning fracking, and many others are still ignoring the full implications and potential of the energy revolution, or perceive it as an irrelevant force.

Part of the scepticism comes from environmental concerns. But think about the early days of offshore drilling. In the early 1990s, ultra-deep-water drilling faced fierce critics from the media and environmentalists. The debate then was very similar to today's debate for shale. The oil industry learned from the accidents and offshore drilling is now a safe and major contributor to world oil and gas production. Likewise, fracking and horizontal drilling are and will continue to grow in a safe and environmentally friendly way.

High expectations attract large amounts of capital

During the dotcom revolution, equity valuations of many companies implied exponential growth. The word "dotcom" had a "Midas touch". Capital was flowing in, and new ideas, technologies, and infrastructure were able to raise funding with extreme ease, as investors and "venture capital" looked for the next golden investment.

As the "tide was rising" everything looked good. The internet revolution was a game changer. Some of the more established firms like Microsoft were in a strong position, but there were many small start-ups, such as Google, Amazon, and eBay, that have become large multinationals and showcase the reality of the new economy. But some others became major "flops", such as pets.com in North America or boo.com in Europe. With the benefit of 20/20 hindsight, it is easy to see why the winners won, and why the losers lost.

The "euphoria" of the markets was no excuse to get involved in the wrong company or business, but also no excuse to miss out on the good companies and businesses. The opportunities then, and today, are enormous.

In the energy space, the energy revolution is facing similar dynamics. On the one hand, it has the potential to be a game changer, but not everything that goes up with the tide will be winners in the long run. Today's *current* extreme price differentials across regions and across fuels offer very attractive returns on investment. And the capital is flowing in and supporting large investments in infrastructure of supply, from exploration through distribution. Annual capital expenditure exceeds \$750 billion.[4] Look at exploration, with major discoveries in Kazakhstan, Israel, Cyprus, Uganda, Ghana, Mozambique, Brazil and Colombia, to name a few. Or LNG with major investments in Australia, West Africa, and Yamal (North East Siberia). Or look at the pipelines, expanding all across Europe and Asia. Or storage and trading hubs, such as Shanghai and Singapore. The "invisible hand" is responding to the incentives.

In the energy revolution, just like the internet revolution, there will be large winners and losers. There are some "energy Googles" and "energy pet.coms" out there. We do not have the benefit of 20/20 hindsight, but we do have the tools to analyse and understand the forces and dynamics at play.

As a senior member from the Central Bank of Spain once told me, "Trading is not a *science*. It is an *art*. But it helps to know a lot of science!" Very true.

Excessive expectations for demand growth result in overcapacity

During the dotcom revolution, expected returns were largely driven by assumptions of exponential demand growth. From telephone landlines to mobile phones. From shops to e-commerce. From regional to global. The potential for growth seemed unlimited. Invariably, many sectors built significant overcapacity. Among them, fibre-optic broadband infrastructure was one of the most critical.

Similarly, in the energy world, investment decisions are predicated on a view of "world energy demand growth". Demand forecasts are based on "diplomatic" assumptions about global growth (which tend to be revised down more often than not) and where important forces such as efficiency or substitution are often underestimated or ignored. We know from the past that overcapacity is often the result of overly optimistic assumptions about the future. As Jim Steinman wrote, "the future ain't what it used to be". Well, today's demand expectations seem to imply that "Asia will buy unlimited amounts of gas at an unlimited price". Is the writing on the wall?

Furthermore, think about the impact of shortages in energy and infrastructure: "black-outs", "brown-outs", or simply long queues at the petrol station. Not good news for the economy. Worse news for politicians. The overcapacity of energy supply is therefore a desired state for consumers, which explains why, in addition to "private" investors, there is a strong centralized, planned, and strategic process driven by governments and state-owned enterprises. Look at China . . .

Efficiency is also proving to be a game changer, acting as a source of "demand destruction", and often ignored in demand growth estimates. Think of global industrial output for example, which has increased by 2% per annum with flat energy consumption growth since 2005.[5] The world is producing more with less energy. In the US gasoline demand has fallen every year since 2007 thanks to efficiency, as the light duty vehicles went from 20 miles per gallon to 24. The IEA estimates that improving efficiency to 34 miles per gallon could reduce global oil demand by 4%.

According to the International Energy Agency (IEA), greater energy efficiency could cut the growth in global energy demand by half. The accrued resources or "savings" from efficiency gains could facilitate a gradual reorientation of the global economy to higher added value investments and a gross domestic product (GDP) that is led more by the consumer than industry.[6]

We will continue to hear and read optimistic assumptions about energy demand growth. It hasn't happened since 2005, yet many anticipate that the "big demand growth" will come. These expectations are missing a key point: the change we are seeing is not cyclical, it's structural. The new economy, even in China, is less about large industries and massive construction.

Think "against the box"

One of the main traps for investors in the energy markets is to follow consensus.

The energy world is driven by extremely optimistic assumptions of demand growth, and downward revisions of estimates tend to be shrugged off as "noise" always looking at the elusive long-term perspective. This "growth mirage" that we will discuss later is best exemplified by the average adjustment in demand growth from the IEA and OPEC.

According to my analysis, every year demand growth estimates are revised down an average of 15–20% from the January estimates. Since 1998, only one year, 2012, has seen meaningful upward revisions from initial estimates.

My experience in the past years as an analyst and a portfolio manager has taught me to use forward guidance from companies and agencies with extreme caution. This has helped me to avoid the constant stream of profit warnings and to keep a moderated view about the supply–demand picture, which has proven to be right. We have not seen a supply shock or a demand boost. This philosophy of not just thinking "outside the box" but also understanding that the compilation of data made to support forward guidance is tainted by diplomacy.

Governments are always optimistic about GDP, and always overestimate the correlation between GDP and energy demand. A correlation that has been broken since 1998, where strong economic growth does not necessarily imply industrial and energy demand rising. The best way to add value and make money is precisely to question and understand the intricacies of forward-looking guidance, put under scrutiny the details, and always know that it will be better to err on the side of caution, rather than let ourselves be guided by consensus. As an investor one must know that none of the companies' executives, analysts at agencies or brokers will suffer professionally from providing optimistic guidance. It will always be justifiable with "unexpected one-off" events. The same happens with doomsday predictions, as we have already seen with peak oil.

The assumption of ever-rising prices due to supposed depletion and alleged energy shocks has been what we call in the financial world "a widow maker" as an investment strategy.

The strategic premium results in overcapacity

During the early 2000s, the telecom industry continued to push the boundaries with the new 3G technology. But governments controlled the licenses, and were determined to maximize the amount of money they could raise from them. To keep the competitive pressure, they offered fewer licenses than the number of operators likely to bid. A similar auction had been applied in the United States and had to be re-run when the winners defaulted on their bids. Yet, and despite the potential harm to the telecoms future competitiveness, the European governments proceeded with the blind auction and sealed bids.

Telecoms were in a difficult position. If they lost the auction, they felt they would miss out on the next technological phase of the business. Many assigned a strategic premium and made high bids, often financed via debt. The result was staggering. The UK auctions raised £22.5 billion. The German auctions raised around £30 billion. To put this in perspective, this was 10 times more per megahertz than the television companies were charging at the time for national broadcasting.[7]

A similar dynamic where majors are investing "not to miss out" is also taking place across the energy markets.

Investments "to be there" throughout a possible game-changing environment are typical of the energy industry. It's called "position rent". The economic decision to devote large amounts of money in energy investments comes not only from the possibility of generating solid returns on an equity investment, but also from the opportunity that technology gives to higher asset value and strategic position of the company in a country. Out of the hundreds of billions of capital investments made every year in energy around 5% to 10%, looking at the plans of the large integrated companies, will likely be in "strategic opportunities" or "security of supply" where returns are unclear, but companies feel the need to be involved. These figures are higher when we look at national companies of the calibre of Gazprom or PetroChina. A very significant amount that unwillingly helps the flattening process.

Certainly, these strategic decisions can play an important role in the future competitiveness and solvency of these companies. Whether in a real estate boom, or internet boom, or energy boom, paying too much to stay ahead may well be the kiss of death. The corporate graveyard is full of companies that paid too much at the top.

The "strategic premium" and "geopolitical risk positioning" are eroding peak demand pricing with incremental supply, both from new capacity and new technologies. The erosion of peak pricing has been instrumental in improving the economic outlook of countries, because it reduces the shocks and undesired effects of uncertain and volatile pricing.

Another important consideration is the "venture capital" approach, supporting new technologies via the deployment of "risk capital" through a diversified portfolio.

During the dotcom revolution, it was clear that many new technologies and start-ups would not make it. But the mindset was that "we just need one winner". It was impossible to "guess" who the winner would be, so investors were diversifying and spreading their bets, reaching to a much larger number of projects.

In the transportation world, several technologies are looking to break the crude oil monopoly. In addition to the more widely known and accepted compressed natural gas (CNG), LNG (for trucks, trains, and ships), electric car vehicles (ECVs), and hybrid vehicles (HVs), during the 2013 Motor Show in Tokyo, Toyota shocked the transportation world wih the announcement of the commercial launch of a fuel cell vehicle (FCV).

Yet, there are powerful forces that can delay change.

In 2009, my analysis "against the box" indicated that the expectations from the EU and US governments for electric vehicle sales were totally unrealistic and simply impossible. Five years later, the electric vehicle has turned out to be a much smaller alternative than these governments had anticipated. But, ironically, the penetration of the electric car was not "killed" by the oil companies or energy lobbies, as many people think. The list of "murder suspects" for the delay in electric cars is quite long, and includes those governments who were seemingly trying to promote the electric car industry in the first place.

Start with the bailouts of the car companies. The industry was deemed "too big to fail" in the United States and Congress worked out a $25 billion loan and by December 2008 the US government became the majority shareholder of General Motors.

In this environment, it is not surprising that the subsidies from EU and US governments to buy a new "conventional combustion engine car" (and help reduce the brutal inventory of unsold vehicles) exceeded by six to one the amount devoted for the development of electric cars. Anecdotally, 2010 turned out to be the year of highest sales of SUVs since 2006,[8] as the government subsidies strongly incentivized the absorption of inventory and accelerated the renewal of the fleet, reducing significantly the potential for electric cars for years.

There are other important factors that have slowed down the development of electric cars, which we will discuss in more detail in Chapter 14. One of them is pricing. An electric car, which seeks to replace a combustion engine vehicle, cannot succeed if it sells at an average of 50% higher than the alternative. This concept of promoting expensive alternatives does not make for a realistic economy. Alternatives will only exist if they are more attractive, cheaper, and efficient. Another factor is taxation. The EU collects €250 billion a year in taxes from petrol and diesel (taxes on petrol range between 40% and 65%).[9] So, if the electric vehicle took a significant percentage of market share, governments may be forced to "transfer" the gasoline/diesel tax to the power sector. In fact, subsidies to power, including renewables, but also coal and gas, have resulted in a higher average cost of electricity across the EU.

Overcapacity eventually reprices assets and the cost of services

Following an extremely volatile period, the dotcom bubble finally burst in 2001. Equity valuations had collapsed across the board. Many companies went bankrupt. Others were not worth much more than the cash they had raised from investors. There were many winners too, who took advantage of the situation and expanded through acquisitions. Among them was Apple, who in 2000 acquired SoundJam MP and its team of developers.

Apple simplified the user interface, added the ability to burn CDs, removed its recording feature and skin support, and renamed it iTunes. In October 2001, Apple launched the first iPod as "one thousand songs in your pocket".

But for internet and broadband, competition and overcapacity made them available at a fraction of what had been anticipated. Bad news for the telecoms industry. Good news for consumers.

The future of the energy world is highly uncertain, but it is not unthinkable (in fact it is our base case) that the large development of "parallel" infrastructure will lead to a similar situation.

Commodity assets and prices are driven by marginal economics. Large imbalances between supply and demand can result in sharp swings in valuations, as producers know well.

The current energy revolution is relevant. Previous oil crises were largely "just about oil". This time it is not only oil supply and demand forces competing against each other. This time we have new dimensions as natural gas, renewables, and other fuels become real threats to crude oil's relevance. With more options available, the impact of price spikes and peak pricing is eroded, preventing economic shocks. As such, despite constant global conflicts, the "oil burden" (the amount of money devoted by OECD countries to pay for imported oil) has not surpassed the "tipping point" of 5.5% of GDP.[10]

New technologies displace older and more expensive ones

The internet revolution was a game changer. It opened a whole universe of new opportunities that (for most people) were unimaginable, even at the peak of the market in 2001.

The success of the internet, Apple, and Facebook has left a long list of direct and indirect casualties across industries. Look at Blackberry or Nokia for example, once upon a time leaders in their sector, today at risk of disappearing. Or look at music-buying patterns. CD shops are history. Or think about the impact on the advertising industry, increasingly dominated by companies like Google and Facebook. Many newspapers are struggling as their advertising revenues via digital are a fraction of the print. Who would have said that 10 years ago?

The needs of the consumers are being addressed but they are being served and consolidated with superior and new technologies. The old and expensive technologies are dead (even if they don't know it yet).

New technologies increase competition and create deflationary forces

Thanks to the development and overcapacity in broadband, wireless, and applications like FaceTime or Skype, I am now able to have a live high-definition videoconference (voice and image) with someone across the Atlantic pretty much "for free". Yet, a telephone call (voice only) would cost me an arm and a leg. "This must go down in history as a major inconsistency", I keep thinking to myself. "I can eat and smell a cake, cheaper than just smelling it. This is crazy. Something has to give", and it does not take a genius to figure out who the losers in this battle will be.

In the energy world, the "shale revolution" has already had a major impact in North America across many industries. And the implications do not stop there. They are global and are already feeding through the energy system, flattening the world.

Look for example at US coal. The surge in US natural gas production and cheap prices resulted in a significant displacement of coal demand. Power generation used more natural gas and less coal. The displacement of coal did not only result in lower prices within the United States, but also made more and cheaper coal available for export. Producers outside of North America felt the impact too. In March 2010, in search for new markets and responding to strong incentives and regional premiums, Colombia shipped a cargo of coal over 10,000 miles, all the way to China.[11] Some of the switching is very "price sensitive", and may flip back into coal as and when the economics make sense. But in the long run, the availability of more environmentally friendly natural gas (as a rule of thumb, coal pollutes three times more than natural gas for a given unit of energy produced) may result in the retirement of coal-fired power plants. The impact is therefore more global and more permanent than what the large majority believes today.

Another example is the renaissance in the fertilizers and petrochemical industries in North America. A version of what is being called as "re-shoring" (the reversal of "offshoring"), as industries return to North America.

Perhaps most importantly, over the medium and longer term, the energy revolution has the potential to change the transportation industry and challenge crude oil's monopoly. Cheaper electricity and natural gas provide a strong incentive to switch away from oil. This process is already happening and faster than many people think. And, just like coal, the impact will be more global and more permanent than what the large majority believes today.

Yet another example is how solar has impacted the electricity market and taken over peak capacity in countries like Germany. See Chapter 14 for more details.

The effect of these forces and competition ultimately results in winners and losers. And along the process, perhaps the major beneficiary of the flatter energy world is the consumer. Just like the internet revolution.

The bubble accelerated the impact of the revolution

As discussed before, the bubble played an important role in the development of new technologies, the overcapacity, and the availability at cheap prices. But bubbles are complex processes. When do they accelerate, when do they peak, what triggers the burst?

"We are fine. We do not need to be bailed out"[12] said the Finance Minister of Portugal in 2009. And it may have well been true, when, at that time, Portuguese credit spreads were at 2% and they could finance themselves. Under those market conditions, Portugal was solvent.

But not everyone believed it, and investors in Portuguese debt started demanding higher and higher returns for the risk they were taking. Downgrades by rating agencies such as Standard & Poor's, Moody's, and Fitch compounded the problem. The cost of borrowing increased, and servicing the debt started to become a problem. Portugal was still solvent, but the pricing dynamics were quickly deteriorating the "fundamentals" of the country. The process started to accelerate into a "vicious cycle" that fed on itself. Higher credit spreads resulted in higher servicing costs, which in turn would push credit spreads higher, until, eventually, the yield of the 10-year bond reached 8%, a level regarded by many as the "tipping point" when a country's finances become unsustainable. The price of the bonds collapsed as the yield exploded above 15% within just a few weeks.[13] Prices had impacted fundamentals. Portugal was no longer solvent.

"We have agreed to a bailout package", said the same Finance Minister. Was he lying a few months before when he said the country did not need a bailout? Well, not necessarily. Portugal was solvent, but vulnerable to higher rates and refinancing needs. Should the price path had been different, Portugal might have not needed to be rescued. But the reality was different.

And the "domino effect" that had "knocked out" Iceland, Greece, Ireland, and then Portugal, repeated itself once again and brought Spain and Italy to the brink of collapse. It took decisive action by Mario Draghi, President of the European Central Bank (ECB) to support the euro "by all means possible" and the introduction of the LTRO (Long Term Repurchase Obligation) programme to contain the negative spiral.

Once under control, the process reversed and through a virtuous cycle, the 10-year Spanish bond, having been at 7.5% in the summer of 2012, reached historical low levels in December 2014. Enough to swing a government from solvency to insolvency.

These reflexive relationships also exist in the energy markets.

The "quiet revolution" in North America, the Fukushima nuclear crisis, ongoing geopolitical tensions in North Africa and the Middle East, and monetary easing have all contributed to the large price divergences that act as the catalyst for change and impact fundamentals.

Look at the super-spike in oil prices in 2007. In previous times when oil prices have risen dramatically, panic takes over. Even if the disruptions are expected to be short-lived, the mind-set impacts governments, consumers, and of course, the media. People dust off Hubbert's peak oil theories (even if they have been debunked many times over) and subsidies and incentives are provided to guarantee the security of supply. To respond to the situation, the investment machine takes over. In Europe, between 2007 and 2010 around 3% of the Eurozone GDP was devoted to large infrastructure and energy projects based on "security of supply". In parallel, oil-producing countries devoted another 2% of their GDP to new sources of generation.[14] Combined, the expansion results in overcapacity and excess power generation to meet expected growth and needs until well over 2020.

How much capacity will be built this time? Where? How fast? The answers will shape the future of energy prices, not only from a cyclical point of view, but also on a more structural and permanent basis. Just like the 1970s resulted in the displacement of crude oil from power generation forever.

Timing: there is no such thing as a crystal ball

In the early stages of the subprime crisis in North America, as Alan Greenspan and others were dismissing the potential impact of the crisis, I came across a very interesting poll that asked mutual and hedge fund managers "Which inning are we in?", a baseball analogy in reference to "are we closer to the beginning, middle, or end, of the crisis?" The answers were very polarized. Some believed we were at the eighth inning (closer to the end), while many others thought we were at the second inning (closer to the beginning).

Yet, the crisis went on to unfold into one of the global recessions in modern history, much further than many had anticipated, showing how market participants and industry experts can disagree on basic issues as "which inning are we in?" With the benefit of 20/20 hindsight, everyone today is familiar with the magnitude and main reasons for the crisis. But back then it was not so obvious.

If we did a poll today about the impact and timing of the energy revolution, we are likely to have a very polarized view too. Many are dismissive of the impact. Others believe we are undergoing a major structural change. Time will tell, but it will likely take years for the full impact of the energy revolution to be understood.

My view, going back to the sporting analogies, is that we are at somewhere around the fourth inning in baseball, or towards the end of the first half in soccer, or near the end of the 1990s in the dotcom revolution. The revolution has had an undeniable impact already, arguably as a positive contributor to the economic recovery in North America, but also globally, as the energy world is responding to the signals and incentives and capital flowing into the development of new infrastructure across key energy sectors and regions.

The opportunities are in front of our eyes. The potential is huge. There is plenty of match ahead. And, just like in sports, "anything can happen".

Investors must avoid the growth mirage and value traps

A stock is considered to be a "value trap" when it *appears* to be cheap because it trades at low multiples of earnings, cash flow, or book value, but in reality it is not. Such stocks tend to attract investors who are looking for a bargain, but the low valuation may imply that the company or the entire sector is in trouble. Often, a value trap appears to be such a good deal that investors become confused when the stock fails to perform.

In the energy sector, just like the dotcom bubble, overly optimistic assumptions for growth, profit margins, and cash flows can lead to disappointment. And when reality catches up and the bubble bursts, "value traps" often emerge with a "growth mirage" that tends to justify the high multiples based on elusive targets and unrealistic expectations.

I had been working in an integrated oil company for almost a decade, reading about why the large telecoms had become value trap investments and why the energy sector was different. I kept hearing about "value", "growth", "next year will be different", and "market perception is unjustified". Large discounts to net asset value, opportunities to create synergies, and vast amounts of detailed analysis from corporate bankers led to enormous mergers in oil, gas, and utilities . . . all the way to 2007. But the actual results of these giant mergers and acquisitions would only become evident over time, after many years of justifications and excuses. Growth had disappointed year after year but capital expenditure (capex) had continued to rise, eroding the benefits from higher commodity prices. The sector was "running to stand still".

The utilities sector is another clear case of "growth mirage" and "value trap".

The European power sector has handed the keys to the reserve margin management and investment decisions in new generation capacity to its governments, who are delighted to see overcapacity. The sector invests hundreds of billions per annum for 25-year projects, but where the rules of the game change every four or five years. The only companies that are doing well are the ones showing financial discipline, focusing on return on capital employed (ROCE) and their core-strong business.

These issue of "value trap" will be discussed in full detail in Chapter 14, but be wary of promises of value based on estimates of "sum-of-the-parts". Because it ends as a text-book case of "value trap" with good businesses subsidizing bad businesses.

Focused strategies should be welcomed. At the end of the day a company is not a non-governmental organization (NGO). It is a "capital allocator" which should review its portfolio mercilessly and focus on profitability. Size does not matter unless it creates value.

Lessons not to forget

The energy revolution is set to be a game changer.

And just as the dotcom bubble *accelerated* the impact of the internet revolution, and with it, the flattening of the world, the current market dynamics, signals, and incentives have the potential to accelerate the flattening and equalization of the energy world, with important changes in the world order.

The process is driven by flattening forces, or "flatteners", that we will present and discuss in the following chapters along with the opportunities and expected winners and losers.

Yet, to make money, the analysis needs to be implemented correctly. There are just too many examples when good ideas fail because of the wrong implementation, with particular focus on avoiding mistakes.

As I tend to say, in investing, just like golf, the best way to improve your scorecard is by "avoiding double bogies", not by "making more eagles".

Some of the points may become quite technical, but that is the nature of game and cannot be ignored.

NOTES

1. Thomas L. Friedman (2005). *The World is Flat*. New York: Farrar, Straus & Giroux.
2. US Energy Information Administration. http://www.eia.gov /cfapps/ipdbproject/IEDIndex3.cfm?tid=5&pid=53&aid=1
3. Bloomberg and NARECO Advisors.
4. Barclays Equity Research (9 December 2013). *Global 2014 E&P Spending Outlook*. http://www.pennenergy.com/content/dam /Pennenergy/online-articles/2013/December/Global%202014%20 EP%20Spending%20Outlook.pdf
5. Enerdata (2013). *Global Energy Statistical Yearbook 2013*. http:// knoema.com/GESY2013/global-energy-statistical-yearbook-2013
6. *IEA World Energy Outlook*. http://www.iea.org/newsroomand events/pressreleases/2012/november/name,33015,en.html
7. Paul Klemperer (2002). How (not) to run auctions: the European 3G telecom auctions. *European Economic Review*. http://www .nuff.ox.ac.uk/users/klemperer/hownot.pdf
8. *Wall Street Journal* (3 March 2009). *Market Data Center – Auto Sales*. http://online.wsj.com/mdc/public/page/2_3022-autosales.html
9. European Commission. *Taxation and Customs Union*. 25 July 2012.
10. Ronald Stoeferle (12 March 2012). *Economic Consequences of the High Oil Price*. http://oilprice.com/Energy/Oil-Prices/Economic -Consequences-of-the-High-Oil-Price.html
11. Javier Blas (2010). A market ee-emerges. *Financial Times*, 14 April.
12. Bruno Waterfield and Robert Winnett (2010). Euro under siege after Portugal hits panic button. *The Telegraph*, 15 November. http://www.telegraph.co.uk/news/worldnews/europe/portugal /8135686/Euro-under-siege-after-Portugal-hits-panic-button.html
13. Bloomberg, Portuguese Government Bonds – 10 Year.
14. US Energy Information Administration. http://www.eia.gov /cfapps/ipdbproject/IEDIndex3.cfm?tid=5&pid=53&aid=1

CHAPTER THREE

THE 10 FORCES THAT ARE FLATTENING THE ENERGY WORLD

Growth is not a coincidence, it is the result of many forces acting together.

JCPenney

Is the energy world flat?

Today's energy world is not flat. In fact, it is very far from it.

What I mean by "flat" is that the availability and cost of energy around the world varies significantly across regions and commodities. Look at the extraordinary differentials between crude oil and natural gas across North America, Europe, the Middle East, and Asia.

Historically, the availability and cost of natural resources in general, and energy in particular, has been a critical factor in the wealth and poverty of nations both across developed and developing economies. Energy has often been the constraint for the growth and development of countries such as China, where the one-child policy would most certainly not be in place if China had unlimited natural resources.

The debate about the scarcity of natural resources has been discussed at length for centuries, from the days of Thomas Malthus "population grows geometrically, but resources grow linearly", to more recent theories such as Hubbert's "peak oil".

There is no scarcity of energy. There is concentration, but no shortage. I remember when I visited Ghawar, the largest oil field in Saudi Arabia. At that time, some industry commentators were questioning decline rate and production capacity, and how they thought it was "technically impossible" for Saudi Arabia to produce more than 8.5 million barrels per day by 2012. My good friend Mufti said to me "we are the central bank of oil, if it's needed we will produce more". If it's *needed*. How true a statement. At the end of the day, oil countries are not NGOs. They produce when needed. In 2013 Saudi Arabia was producing 11 million barrels per day, according to the EIA.

In the energy world, where we are witnessing the mother of all battles, technology and security of supply are the weapons of consumer countries, resources and global reach are the weapons of producers.

The future is unknown and is path dependent. There are many forces at play, but the engineering feats in the Barnett Shale, Fukushima's natural disaster, and the nuclear politics response around the world, have set a path to a flatter energy world, where consumers ultimately benefit from the tug of war between technology and resources as we slowly but inexorably move towards a flatter energy world.

As discussed, we are currently living in an extraordinary phase in the energy world.

Similar to the internet revolution and the dotcom bubble, the current energy revolution and the sustained divergence in prices will lead to a more globalized, equalized, and flatter world, where energy will be an enabler and less of a constraint.

The dynamics are complex, driven by the "invisible hand" of the markets as well as the "visible hand" of governments and regulation.

But with the invaluable help of history, *the teacher of life*, as the Latin saying goes, I have identified the top 10 forces that in my view are shaping and flattening the energy world.

These 10 "flatteners" work together, in parallel, and often reinforcing each other, and will be discussed in detail in the following chapters.

Flattener #1 – Geopolitics: The Two Sides of the Energy Security Coin

Flattener #2 – The Energy Reserves and Resources Glut

Flattener #3 – Horizontal Drilling and Fracking

Flattener #4 – The Energy Broadband

Flattener #5 – Overcapacity

Flattener #6 – Globalization, Industrialization, and Urbanization

Flattener #7 – Demand Destruction

Flattener #8 – Demand Displacement

Flattener #9 – Regulation and Government Intervention

Flattener #10 – Fiscal, Monetary, and Macroeconomic Flatteners

These flatteners are at full force today, shaping the world in front of our eyes, perhaps much faster than we realize.

The bets and implications are huge, and will leave large winners and losers.

Let's start with geopolitics, and the two sides of the energy security coin.

CHAPTER FOUR

FLATTENER #1 – GEOPOLITICS: THE TWO SIDES OF THE ENERGY SECURITY COIN

The bad guy is the good guy of his own movie.

Mike Myers

On no one quality, on no one process, on no one country, on no one route, and on no one field must we be dependent. Safety and certainty in oil lie in variety and variety alone.

Winston Churchill, speaking to Parliament in July 1913.

The oil weapon

"With great power comes great responsibility" goes the saying. And this is certainly true for the Persian Gulf, which according to EIA data, holds over 60% of proven reserves and produces more than 25% of world oil output. The extraordinary concentration of cheap reserves has made it very influential in the world economy and politics.

During the colonialism era, from 1900 to 1960, the United States and the OECD countries relied upon cheap oil for economic growth by exerting political control on the producing countries, through "managed" regimes or direct colonialism. The creation of the Anglo-Persian Oil Company (Iran, 1908) and the discovery of Ghawar, the largest oil field in the world, in Saudi Arabia, are key milestones that fuelled the dependence on foreign cheap oil of Western economies. But the policy of extracting resources in one country to generate economic prosperity in another created the seed for resource nationalism and independence.

Eventually producing countries decided enough was enough, and aware of their power, founded OPEC in 1960, nationalized natural resources, displaced puppet regimes . . . and became the price setters.

The oil weapon became a powerful political and economic threat, and was eventually successfully unleashed in 1973 in the form of an oil embargo, which was followed by prolonged conflicts between producers and authoritarian regimes, from the Arab world to African large producers and in Latin America. The Iran–Iraq war that followed the Iranian Revolution in 1979 extended through the whole decade and had a deep and lasting impact on the infrastructure of both countries.

Elsewhere, the curse of the petro-state – enjoying vast revenues from oil but failing to deploy those extraordinary resources for development, democracy, and economic freedom.

The shocks of the 1970s caught the West by surprise, but were followed by a strong response from the consuming nations. Technological developments across exploration and production opened large new producing areas such as the North Sea, government policies resulted in significant increases in energy efficiency and demand destruction, while the creation of the EIA and strategic petroleum reserves provided additional lines of defence. Those measures, combined with the pure market forces, resulted in a swing from shortage to glut that sent prices collapsing in 1986. The world seemed awash with oil, and consumer countries remained heavily dependent on the Middle East to deliver cheap oil.

In 1991, Saddam Hussein was on the offence again. This time against Kuwait. But a military intervention by the United States named "Desert Storm" was a quick success. Saddam lost the war, but somehow managed to stay in power.

I visited Baghdad a few times in the 1990s while Saddam Hussein was in power. It was heralded as the most Western city in the Arab world. And it was. Yet anyone that spent a few days there and spoke with the people would have understood that all was not well. "We don't want Western values, we want our own values" said one of my bodyguards. At that very moment I thought "this will not last long". "Oil is our weapon" he said, "the weapon of the people, not of one ruler". This was the biggest example of "free speech" I witnessed in my trip to Saddam's Baghdad.

As had been the case in the 1970s, the oil weapon of the early 1990s raised prices too far and too quickly. The world economy suffered from stagflation (synchronous recession and inflation), the Asian economies suffered a severe crisis, and prices collapsed towards $10/bbl, leading to Russia's moratorium (technical default) on its external debt.

I remember vividly the pessimism of the industry. I was experiencing the first bear market during my own career. The energy industry had to shrink to survive. In 1998, I was working for a large investment bank. "We are a bank. We lend money. Why are we involved in commodities?" would ask the Board. Very few CEOs had the courage, vision, or means to defend the business. Most of the "weak longs" got out, as the industry consolidated. "Bull markets are more fun than bear markets" a colleague of mine told me a few years later. How true!

The following years, the internet revolution was attracting capital into the "new economy". Indeed, the lack of investment was planting the seeds of the next bull market.

The revenge of the oil economy

I remember when oil broke through $50/bbl in 2005 and a Goldman Sachs analyst raised the possibility of a "super-spike" towards $105/bbl.

What back in 2005 looked like a "crazy forecast" for many, would turn out to be quite conservative just two years later. Reality had, once again, beaten fiction, and by July 2008 crude oil was above $140/bbl and jet fuel above $200/bbl.

For the first time in decades, the spike in crude oil prices was not driven by geopolitics. Peak oil theory was very much at its peak.

Yet, to the surprise of many, inventories of crude oil remained ample. There was no shortage of crude, but prices were rallying strongly. How was it possible?

The answer was the bottleneck in refining capacity. Consumers wanted refined products, such as gasoline, diesel, and kerosene. Heavy sour crude oil was in ample supply, but there was not enough refining capacity to produce the lighter and clean products demanded.

Of course, many people were quick to blame the *speculators*. "What has changed over the last few years that justifies such a large price move?" they would ask me. "The demand and supply have not changed that much since last year. It must be the speculators!" I would hear. Yet, most of the people I spoke to had not changed their energy consumption habits because of the higher prices. In the meantime, China, India, and other emerging markets were aggressively looking to increase their car-driving habits.

Something had to give. And due to the very low price elasticity of demand (no one wanted to stop driving in response to the higher prices), the only channel of adjustment was higher prices.

Refiners were finally in the "driving seat". Consumers wanted to buy clean refined products (such as gasoline, diesel, and kerosene) but the existing refining capacity was not enough to cope with the demand. Refineries were operating at maximum capacity.

Producers were pumping as much oil as they could. Which producer would not at $140/bbl? Well, the Saudis did not. And not because they did not want to or they could not physically pump more. The problem was that the global refinery system could not process the excess heavy sour Saudi crude into the clean products consumers wanted. Saudi crude had saturated the refinery system. Bottlenecks limited the ability to process heavy sour crude oil, and any increase in Saudi production would result in a larger glut of residual fuel oil and lower prices for Saudi crude oil. This dynamic, to the surprise of some, forced Saudi Arabia to "cut production", which contributed to the spike later on. Yes, Saudi was acting in its own self-interest. Anyone surprised?

The balance of power had shifted from the producers to the refiners, but not for long.

The large differential between light and heavy crudes created a strong incentive to create "upgrading" refinery units, which would convert heavy sour into clean products. These upgrading units were completed fast.

The other major contributor to the spike was price subsidies across emerging markets, such as China, India, and Indonesia. The original purpose of the subsidies was to control inflation and protect consumers against the volatility in energy prices. But the fixed price unfortunately was giving the wrong message to consumers: "Do not worry about oil prices. You can afford a motorbike or a car. We, the government, will take care of any price issues".

These policies created large problems over the long run. Emerging market consumers were "hooked" on cheap oil prices. The size of these subsidies got out of control and governments could no longer afford them, however, the removal of these subsidies created significant inflation and social unrest. The consuming governments were in a difficult position.

In the Western world there are no subsidies, but there are high taxes. And these high taxes also have a perverse effect of making consumers less price sensitive. At the end of the day, a large proportion of the price they pay at the pump is taxes. Therefore, increases in oil prices would have a smaller percentage impact. They made the consumer inelastic.

But the spike in prices of refined products was already straining the global economy.

The blame for the global financial crisis (GFC) has been attributed to the credit bubble fuelled by securitization and loose regulation, which at the end of the day was the result of a gross misallocation of capital. The credit bubble was fuelled by cheap credit, much coming from emerging markets themselves as they accumulated foreign exchange reserves and "parked" them in US treasuries instead of investing in commodity infrastructure.

As the credit bubble burst, crude oil prices collapsed from the highs of $140/bbl towards $30/bbl but stabilized and recovered thanks to aggressive OPEC production cuts.

However, geopolitics would soon resurface again as a driving force of oil prices.

The Arab Spring

In December 2010, protests across North Africa quickly spread across the entire Arab world, fuelled by internet and social networks, removing regimes that had been in power for decades and resulting in large supply disruptions.

In Egypt, Hosni Mubarak, who had ruled Egypt for 30 years, gave up power on 11 February 2011. In Syria, protests against the Assad government have developed into a multi-year civil war. In Libya, protests against Gaddafi developed into a civil war, but the US and European forces, operating under UN and NATO authorization, intervened on the side of the rebels. By March 2011, virtually all of Libya's oil production was cut, and severe disruptions are expected to last for several years.

The Arab Spring was spreading across the Arab world. Brent crude oil prices rallied towards $130/bbl on actual cuts and fears of contagion into the core of the Middle East, which, combined with the release of 60 million barrels from the global strategic petroleum reserves, helped to contain the situation and gradually lower oil prices.

While conflicts have remained a norm, the interdependence has changed thanks to technology, globalization, and the different strategies and political objectives of OPEC, divided into hardliners (Iran, Venezuela) and the consumer-friendly nations, led by the "central bank of oil", Saudi Arabia.

Despite these positive developments, geopolitics remains a big risk, not only in North Africa and the Middle East, but also in Africa and Latin America.

Iraq 2014, the crisis that brought prices . . . down!

By July 2014, Iraq was producing 3.3 million barrels per day, above the peak of the 1980s.

But the situation of the country had recently turned from bad to worse. The emergence of ISIS (Islamic State of Iraq and Syria), a jihadist group that even has an annual report of its sinister achievements,[1] was a very worrying development that had been triggered by the departure of US and foreign forces. With the benefit of hindsight, the United States and the rest of the OECD placed too much trust on the unstable government of Nouri al-Maliki, the appointed Prime Minister after the demise of Saddam Hussein. This was a very similar mistake to what happened in Libya and Egypt after removing a dictatorship regime. US troops were being removed and the industry seemed to be recovering. It looked as if everything was on track, but the risk had not gone away.

I recommend you read *The Clash of Civilizations* by Samuel Huntington[2] and *The Lesser Evil* by Michael Ignatieff.[3] In the West we are reluctant to understand the culture and customs of these countries, which are very far away from our idea of democracy. Accepting the lesser evil of maintaining a military presence is much more logical than closing our eyes in the hope that the world will move according to our wishes.

The exit of the United States is understandable. Over the past few years, the situation for the United States has dramatically changed. As of July 2014 it was already independent in natural gas, and has become the largest producer of oil ahead of Saudi Arabia and surpassing its own 1970s peak. Why incur the military spend and political burden?

Contrary to popular belief, oil in Iraq does not belong to international companies, much less American. All is state-owned fields where international, American, Russian, Italian, Chinese, and British companies work with contracts for service, and they are paid to maintain or increase production. That is, the state benefits from international companies' experience in improving productivity, and therefore has no interest in seeing these companies leaving. This type of productivity contract is what has led to Iraq recovering its pre-war peak production so quickly.

When I travelled to Iraq people used to say: "Baghdad is a city covered in gold, but the south is where the real gold is". Oil. Indeed, most of Iraq's production, 80%, is exported and more than 77% comes from fields in the south, where terrorist ISIS has limited reach.

By the end of July 2014 terrorists had taken Mosul, the second largest city in Iraq, Tikrit, Tal Afar, and Dhuluiya, Yathrib. However, they had not taken any of the large fields north of the country, especially the giant Kirkuk oil field in the Kurdistan region. The people I knew in the area called this field "the passport of Kurdish independence", which in 2014 already produced 260,000 barrels a day.

By the end of 2014, oil prices had fallen to four year lows despite the crisis. The future is unclear and there are proposals to divide Iraq into three (Kurdistan, a Sunni north and a Shiite south).

There was plenty of noise and potential disruptions. Yet the oil price did not rise. Such was the comfortable level of supply.

The Venezuelan Spring

I was in Venezuela in 2013 when President Chavez died. The television was completely taken by propaganda and messages of support for their leader, but even in a completely biased "debate" between a few young revolutionaries I could hear a revealing sentence. "We, the revolutionary people, must understand that oil is not our weapon anymore". The times of cutting supply and hurting customer countries had gone. At that time the supply disruptions in Libya and around the Middle East were still ongoing, but had somewhat limited impact on the oil market. Threats from Venezuela to "stop exporting to the United States" were shrugged off. The producers need the oil revenues to balance their budget. Producers need their customers.

Milton Friedman once said that "if we let the government in charge of the desert, we would run out of sand in a few years". The track record of the Chavez regime closely resembles that remark. Venezuela missed the opportunity generated by its natural resources and created a cronyism subsidized system instead of a modern developed economy. In 2014, despite having the largest proven heavy oil reserves in the world ahead of Saudi Arabia, and being the fifth largest oil exporter, Venezuela is suffering from 56% inflation and shortages of food and commodities.

When analysing the supposed "achievements" of the Chavez–Maduro regime, it is important to remember that the country has benefited from an increase in oil prices from $18/bbl to $108/bbl. Yet, irresponsible economic policy with huge subsidies, political donations, and grants to friendly countries have been squandering the extraordinary revenues generated by oil.

The case of Petróleos de Venezuela (PDVSA), the national oil company, is worth analysing in detail. Prior to the arrival of Chavez, PDVSA was widely regarded as one of the most advanced and efficient companies in the sector, but has since seen its workforce increase from 40,000 employees to 121,000, while reducing its production by 16%, and its debt balloon from $7.1 billion in 1998 to $43.3 billion in 2013, according to PDVSA official statements.[4]

Far from becoming less dependent on oil, as its government promised, Venezuela is now almost exclusively dependent on its revenues (of every $100 received in the country, $94 come from oil exports),[5] as other industries decline or report losses due to massive intervention. As a result, the Venezuelan government, along with Iran, need the highest oil prices to balance their budgets (over $100/bbl).

Over the last 14 years, the economic growth in Peru, Chile, and Brazil expressed in real terms (excluding inflation, which in Venezuela reaches double-digit rates) has been three times larger than Venezuela. Recently, following the wild Maduro devaluation, the GDP per capita has plummeted[6] from $13,000 to $9000, back to early 2000s level, adding to the seven devaluations in 10 years.[7]

During the first few months of 2014, after years of massive inflation, constant devaluations, and impoverishment throughout the Chavez regime, the people of Venezuela took to the streets and became more vocal: "enough is enough".

The level of repression reached unprecedented heights generating daily headlines around the world. In just two months, Venezuela recorded more than 2000 homicides[8] with paramilitaries and the National Guard officially causing 21 deaths during that period.

"What we will never forgive is how this guy has divided the country", a senior member of the Banco Central de Venezuela told me during a visit to Caracas in 2003. "You know, Venezuela has been blessed by oil, gas, metals, and agriculture, and through the generations we have been richer and poorer, just like many of our Latin American cousins, but the people were always united as one country. Today we are divided and we will never forgive him for that". Clearly, the situation has become much worse since.

Time will tell, but I fear this state of affairs is simply unsustainable and the oil weapon is no longer there to pay for the inefficiencies of government.

Reserve nationalism and barriers of entry

For decades, producing governments have directly or indirectly prevented the development of known existing resources across the Middle East and around the world.

In some cases the nationalism reflects itself in war, terrorism, and ongoing disruptions caused by different factions. Look at Iran or Iraq for example. Their sizeable oil and gas reserves are well known, but have been underdeveloped and underexploited. Conflicts have damaged existing infrastructure and limited the investment and development of new productive capacity. Today's supply curve might look very different without those conflicts.

Or look at Mexico, a country with large energy reserves where the oil and gas industry has been closed to foreign investment since the 1940s,[9] when the government gave Petróleos Mexicanos (Pemex), the Mexican state-owned petroleum company, the mandate to preserve reserves for domestic consumption.

I was in Mexico when the Mexican government presented a bill designed to end the 75-year monopoly in the oil and gas sector. There were union adverts on television demanding "our national treasure" to remain in the hands of the government.

But the move towards efficiency and joint ventures was unavoidable. It was a response to the changing world following the energy revolution in North America, which can add to the flattening forces that at the same time substantially increase foreign direct investment (FDI), strengthen Mexico's fiscal and external accounts, and lift its potential growth and employment.

All these nationalistic barriers have encouraged the exploration and development of "non-OPEC resources", which, added to the large known OPEC resources, reinforces the long-term flattening power of geopolitics.

Geopolitics has been and remains a major risk to oil prices.

The general perception is that consumers face that risk, but the reality is that geopolitics also creates large downside risks to prices and therefore to producers.

Consumers defend themselves via overcapacity, a cost they are willing to pay to protect against potential shortages and price spikes. Energy security is a top priority.

Producers are heavily dependent on oil revenues and are exposed to the risk of a glut in production and collapse in prices. Producers have their own version of energy security, in this case security of demand.

Now while geopolitics can result in higher prices in the short term, lower prices invariably result in the longer term and ultimately a flatter energy world. And the higher the price spike, the greater the response.

So far the response has been somewhat temporary. OPEC has always been able to cut production and tighten the market. But there is a point, not that far away, when OPEC can no longer afford to cut production. It is then that OPEC compliance will break and producers will scramble towards market share, resulting in pushing prices even lower. A dangerous vicious cycle.

Bad news for OPEC is that several of the flatteners are pushing towards that critical point.

"This time is different"

The big question is whether OPEC will be able to "do it again" and rebalance the market. My view is that the fracking revolution and energy broadband are dramatically changing the supply–demand balance of crude oil, and will eventually result in a flatter energy world, subject to the competitive forces of the market, and not the oligopolistic forces of the cartel.

In my view, the end of OPEC's influence is a matter of when, not if. In November 2014 this was proven by the decision of OPEC not to cut production despite oil prices falling 30% to $76/bbl. A cut would have shown to the world and oil consumers that OPEC is not the low cost, reliable supplier. And a cut to defend price would further anchor the shale revolution in the US. Damned if you do, damned if you don't. Oil fell to the lowest level in five years after that meeting.

The gas weapon

If you press the spring too hard, it will snap back.

Vladimir Putin

Russia versus Ukraine and the west?

Geopolitics is not just about oil. Russia and Ukraine have an extremely complex relationship with historical, political, and economic interests mixed up around natural gas.

Ukraine had been part of the Russian Empire ever since the Russian State was created in 1648, but after gaining independence in 1991 the country became increasingly split between the pro-Russia Eastern Ukraine and the pro-European Western Ukraine.

The supply of natural gas, the tariffs, and the control of the crucial pipeline to Europe remained as major issues of contention.[10]

In 1970, West German Chancellor Willy Brandt signed the first Soviet gas deal and a new pipeline passing through Ukraine was built. Soviet gas was flowing into Europe for the first time and created dependence in both directions. For the Soviets, the gas was a major and crucial source of hard currency. And Germany was dependent on Russia for its critical energy imports.

To address the issue of energy dependence, the ratio of Soviet gas was capped at 25% and alternative sources such as Norway's Troll field were contracted. Currently, the European gas supply is in political balance. Domestic European production represents 39%, Russian gas 26%, Norway 16%, Algeria 10%, and the remaining 10% from other sources, largely LNG.[11]

In January 2006, in the middle of winter, and after months of failed negotiations, Russia decided to cut natural gas deliveries to Ukraine.[12] The cuts were supposed to affect only Ukraine, but were also felt across Central Europe.

The conflict was resolved within days, but the lack of trust between both parties resulted in a campaign of diversification.

Russia started to look for new commercial opportunities with China, and additional pipeline routes to Europe.

Europe, on the other hand, built stronger links with alternative suppliers, and reinforced its domestic energy sources, with particular focus on renewables.

As a result, a short-lived crisis had important long-term implications as both sides looked for diversification . . . and overcapacity. Both strong flatteners.

The situation is further complicated by the outstanding debt, pricing of contracts, and compensation of transit of gas to Europe:

- As of January 2014, Ukraine had an outstanding debt to Gazprom of $2 billion[13] which in principle gives Russia some bargaining power. Europe and the IMF are coming into the picture with potential funding.

- Ukraine is paying a discounted price of \$256/mcm in exchange for its imports being maintained. As Ukraine is distancing itself from Russia, the Kremlin has indicated that the price could rise to \$400/mcm.[14] As of writing there is no agreement and this effectively jeopardizes the supply to Ukraine, and could impact Europe as it did in 2006.
- Most of the pipelines going from Russia to Europe pass through Ukraine, which receives a compensation for the transit. Ukraine relies on these payments from Russia to meet its obligations. In 2013, Europe received 25% of its crude oil from Russia and 33% of gas, with c.50% of this piped through Ukraine.[15]
- The commissioning of Nord Stream (September 2011), which runs from Vyborg in Russia to Greifswald in Germany, is an important supply alternative that bypasses the Ukraine.

Ukraine shale gas

Ukraine is heavily dependent on Russian gas at the moment, but recent discoveries indicate that Ukraine's shale gas reserves are the third largest in Europe,[16] only behind Russia and Norway.

In response to the discoveries, Ukraine has quickly developed strategic relationships with US majors to explore and develop the vast shale gas reserves.

This is very bad news for Russia.

First, an energy independent Ukraine means Russia will need to find new markets for the lost Ukrainian demand.

Second, Ukraine has the potential to become a large net exporter to Europe, another major blow for Russia, given the large reserves, the regional proximity to key consuming markets in Europe, and increasing political ties.

The annexation of Crimea

The crisis between Ukraine and Russia escalated again in early 2014, with both Russia and Europe trying to bring Ukraine closer through financial and political incentives.

Ukraine seemed to be moving closer to Europe, but the relationship took a sudden turn towards Russia, which led to protests on the streets. The escalation of the conflict led to the death of hundreds on both sides, and finally, the Parliament voted to oust the President in a clear move towards Europe. This puts Ukraine in a difficult financial position because Russia removed its financial support and exposed Ukraine to a potential default.

The move closer to Europe alienated Russia, who in March 2014 annexed the Peninsula or Crimea and the important harbour of Sebastopol in the Black Sea. The annexation happened without any armed conflict, but was viewed as a breach of Ukraine's sovereignty and led to economic and political sanctions towards Russia.

At the time of writing, the conflict in Eastern Ukraine is at full force.

Europe needs Russia's gas . . . but for how long?

It is important to understand that Russia's position is a bilateral trade dependence with Europe.

Russia would not do much without Europe, because it does not have so much domestic gas demand. Additionally, the threat of shale gas in Ukraine or Poland, added to lignite and renewables, reduces the dependence massively.

Also note that the European dependence on Russian gas is declining.

In the short term, the interdependency is balanced, however, in the long term, I believe Moscow needs Europe more than many people think.

Countries like Qatar, Russia, and Algeria are all producing countries willing to negotiate down the long term as producers face weaker demand, greater competition from renewables, and an increase in diversified sources of LNG.

With the development of domestic gas resources, Ukraine may be able to be truly independent from Russia for ever, and this would be a massive blow to Russia's gas exports to Europe.

There is therefore more at stake than the "political" battle that meets the eye.

The behind-the-scenes "energy" battle is a key driver and has very large economic and strategic implications. Ukraine, Russia, Europe, and the United States know it well.

However . . . the impact of the crisis on natural gas prices made it seem like nothing truly relevant had happened. Resource nationalism and the use of gas as a threat had put in place enough alternatives to make supply available, as we mentioned before.

Despite their strong flattening impact over the long run, geopolitical forces, resources nationalism, the threat of supply disruption and volatility, have created an impression of scarcity of energy supply, which is not true. The world is blessed with abundant energy resources, including crude oil!

NOTES

1. http://azelin.files.wordpress.com/2014/04/al-binc481-magazine -1.pdf
2. Samuel Huntington (1998). *The Clash of Civilizations*. New York: Simon & Schuster.
3. Michael Ignatieff (2004). *The Lesser Evil*. Princeton, NJ: Princeton University Press.
4. PDVSA official statements.
5. http://www.noticierodigital.com/forum/viewtopic.php?t=960279 &view=previous&sid=fb57afe09e77186b0716a2281d532195
6. http://www.el-nacional.com/economia/Ingreso-per-capita-cayo -devaluacion_0_136189075.html
7. http://www.notitarde.com/Economia/Siete-devaluaciones-en-10 -anos-de-control-cambiario-en-Venezuela-/2014/01/18/297841

8. http://www.infobae.com/2014/03/07/1548427-en-apenas-dos-meses-venezuela-ya-registra-2841-homicidios

9. Antonio Rojas (1953). Exploration work in Mexico. *Geophysics*, 18(1), 188–200.

10. http://www.infoplease.com/country/ukraine.html

11. Michael Ratner, Paul Belkin, Jim Nichol and Steven Woehrel (20 August 2013). *Europe's Energy Security: Options and Challenges to Natural Gas Supply Diversification*. Congressional Research Service.

12. BBC News (1 January 2006). *Ukraine Gas Row Hits EU Supplies.* http://news.bbc.co.uk/1/hi/world/europe/4573572.stm

13. Neil Buckley (2014). Gazprom cannot afford another supply shut-off to Ukraine. *Financial Times,* 23 April.

14. Jon Henley (2014). Is Europe's gas supply threatened by the Ukraine crisis? *The Guardian,* 3 March.

15. Rakteem Katakey (25 March 2014). *Crimea Crisis Pushes Russian Energy to China from Europe.* http://www.bloomberg.com/news/2014-03-25/russian-oil-seen-heading-east-not-west-in-crimea-spat.html

16. *BP Statistical Review of World Energy – June 2013.* http://www.bp.com/content/dam/bp/pdf/statistical-review/statistical_review_of_world_energy_2013.pdf

CHAPTER FIVE

FLATTENER #2 – THE ENERGY RESERVES AND RESOURCES GLUT

We are not going to run out of oil any time in my lifetime or yours. The resource base is enormous and can support current and future demand.

Rex Tillerson, Exxon CEO

In the early 1990s, I had just finished my postgraduate degree and was ready to look for a job.

"There are only 40 years of reserves left. Why would you want to join the oil industry?" my best friend asked me. "Never bet against an engineer", I replied half-jokingly. The world would need a lot of energy and a lot of oil to continue to grow, and the optimist inside of me believed we somehow would find a way forward, just like we did in the past. "If you give enough time and money to an engineer, he will eventually find a solution". Technology has been, is, and will be king.

What energy scarcity?

Hydrocarbons are very abundant.

Coal reserves exceed 50+ years of current demand. Resources are even larger and would become available if and when prices increase.

Natural gas reserves exceed 100+ years of current demand. Resources are even larger and would become available if and when prices increase.

Even crude oil reserves exceed 50+ years of current demand. Resources are even larger and would become available if and when prices increase.

And it does not end there. The "new frontier" of methane hydrates (also known as "frozen methane" or "fire ice") are ice crystals with natural methane gas locked inside. They are formed through a combination of low temperatures and high pressure, and are found primarily on the edge of continental shelves where the seabed drops sharply away into the deep ocean floor.

According to the British Geological Survey, "estimates suggest that there is about the same amount of carbon in methane hydrates as there is in every other organic carbon store on the planet".[1] That is, there is more energy in methane hydrates than in all the world's oil, coal, and natural gas put together!

It is worth reminding ourselves that shale gas and tight oil were known to exist, but had been dismissed as not commercially viable. And look where we are today!

The state-backed Japan Oil, Gas and Metals National Corporation (JOGMEC) has recently announced the production of methane hydrates off the coast of Japan, but any impact may not come until beyond 2020.

With or without frozen methane, what is clear is that there is no scarcity or shortage of hydrocarbon resources on planet Earth.

But, as one of my bosses once told me, "perception is reality" and consumer governments around the world, often influenced by geopolitics and other considerations, have created a perception of energy reserves scarcity.

The world is also addicted to hydrocarbons, and ever since the industrial revolution, economic growth has been closely linked to energy demand growth. Coal, natural gas, and crude oil have been at the core of the globalization, industrialization, and urbanization. Other non-hydrocarbon sources of energy such as nuclear, hydro, solar, and wind power have also contributed to energy growth, but at a much lower scale.

To better understand the reality, there is no better place to start than exploring the pricing and technological dynamics of reserves and resources.

Reserves and resources

According to the EIA, the world has produced about 1 trillion barrels of oil since the start of the industrial revolution in the nineteenth century. The extraction took place as prices and existing technology made it commercially viable. It would have stayed underground otherwise!

The world has another 1.5 trillion barrels of proven plus probable reserves that are both technically and economically recoverable at current prices.[2]

And there are another 5+ trillion barrels of crude oil that are known to exist, but that are not commercially viable at *current* prices or with *current* technology.[3]

The cut-off point between reserves and resources is a function of prices and technology. It is not static. As prices go up, resources become commercial reserves. As prices go down, reserves may become uneconomical resources. The frontier is changing all the time.

New technologies can increase reserves via "quantum leaps". In 2003, the EIA[4] revised Canadian reserves from 5 billion barrels to 180 billion (a 3600% increase) thanks to improvements in the extraction technology of oil sand. The revision catapulted Canada to the top three in the world, along with Saudi Arabia and Venezuela.

On the other hand, of course, reserves suffer a constant grind via consumption. Effectively, every barrel of oil consumed is one less barrel of oil available.

Replacing production and decline rates is one of the fundamental jobs of the oil industry. The replacement is achieved via a combination of new discoveries and additions to existing fields, both of which are challenging and require enormous investment . . . and time.

Crude oil concentration, but no shortage

Most people agree that the Middle East has vast resources of conventional oil and gas. I say "most people" because there are some conspiracy theories that question the real size and potential of the Middle East in general, and Saudi in particular. But I guess there are also some conspiracy theories that say Fort Knox does not hold any gold either. I suppose that would make it even, as the United States has enjoyed a great advantage of being the reserve currency of the world for decades. Yes, the value of the US dollar is an act of "faith" (that's what a fiduciary currency means), but people take great comfort in the large amount of gold held by the United States. Well, it is true that the US government is the largest gold holder in the world with over 250 million ounces, but it is worth noting that the gold is worth "just" $325 billion assuming $1300/oz.[5] Very large, but certainly not enough to support a total debt of $17 trillion,[6] or quantitative easing of $85[7] billion per month for years.

Beyond the Middle East and any controversy, most people agree that there are also vast conventional and unconventional resources in the United States, Canada, Mexico, Venezuela, Brazil, Russia, and even China.

Historically, the main problem was not the size or existence of the reserves. The main issue has been the asymmetric distribution of the conventional ("cheap") proven reserves, with more than half of the "low hanging fruit" of cheap oil in the Middle East.

The high concentration of reserves opened the door to OPEC oligopolistic behaviour and nationalistic barriers of entry. Further constraints, such as geopolitical conflicts or embargoes, have exacerbated the impact even further. These dynamics have shaped the world of crude oil as we know it.

Already, the energy revolution is diluting the issue of "concentration of reserves", thus reducing the world's dependence on Middle East oil and gas. Shale oil and tar sands are a reality and are already eroding the impact of geopolitical conflicts. The United States alone has over 24 billion[8] barrels of recoverable shale oil, and is on track for full energy independence by 2020. Many other countries, such as Brazil, are also expanding their productive capacity and are expected to surpass many of the traditional major oil exporters by the end of the decade.

Furthermore, everyone agrees that other energy resources such as global natural gas and coal are also enormous. And that, unlike crude oil, these resources are more evenly distributed around the world. Concentration risk is not a major problem. There is natural gas pretty much everywhere. Even in Israel and Cyprus!

OPEC almighty

The Organization of the Petroleum Exporting Countries (OPEC) was created in 1960 as a permanent, intergovernmental organization, with the objective to "co-ordinate and unify petroleum policies among Member Countries, in order to secure fair and stable prices for petroleum producers; an efficient, economic and regular supply of petroleum to consuming nations; and a fair return on capital to those investing in the industry".[9]

It is ironic that OPEC was born as a defensive mechanism from the producers against the glut of oil. The creation occurred at a time of transition in the international economic and political landscape, with extensive decolonization and the birth of many new independent states in the developing world. The international oil market was dominated by the "Seven Sisters" multinational companies, largely separate from the former Soviet Union (FSU) and other centrally planned economies (CPEs).

The large concentration of reserves is, as we say in mathematics, "a necessary, but not sufficient condition" for a successful oligopoly, but peak oil defenders often forget that OPEC is a cartel aiming to provide a "steady income to producers and a fair return on capital for those investing in the petroleum industry".[10] Peak oil defenders assume that the oil industry is an NGO that needs to "prove" growth to consumers at any price or return.

OPEC took control de facto in 1973, when the "oil weapon" was successfully unleashed for the first time, as its Member Countries took control of their domestic petroleum industries and acquired a major say in the pricing of crude oil on world markets. Since then, OPEC has operated one of the most successful oligopolistic cartels in history, effectively capturing a significant share of the economic rent away from consumers and refiners.[11]

But, following the oil shocks of the 1970s, crude oil was largely displaced from the industrial and power generation sectors by cheaper and more reliable sources, such as coal, natural gas, and nuclear. Since then, as discussed, crude oil has been mainly an input to transportation fuel, and with residual applications to other industries such as petrochemicals, while remaining as a "fuel of last resort" for power generation.

Since 1999, OPEC has kept an average of 25 million barrels per day production quota, with only moderate changes to adapt to price hikes.[12] Despite the quota system, OPEC has consistently produced above it, and we must not forget that the quota system allows for a "cheat" buffer, preventing countries from exceeding much more than 20%[13] cheat on targets.

And OPEC may be set to lose control on both ends of the spectrum.

When prices are low, because by default there is excess supply, they are forced to cut their own production and, with it, the revenues that fall from it. They have done it in the past, but there is a limit to how much and how long, as we saw in 1986 when Saudi Arabia "folded" and was moved into a volume maximization in search of market share.

When prices are too high, there is a strong incentive for demand destruction, substitution, and exploration. The 1970s saw the displacement of crude oil in the power generation sector. Once the forces come into play, the response tends to create a glut. Saudi knows the limits and threats well.

Reserve protectionism

Most of the Middle East and many other countries around the world have put in place barriers to entry to investment that have prevented them reaching their full potential.

But some of these countries are slowly opening up.

Look at Mexico, for example, where over the past 75 years Pemex has kept a monopoly in the oil and gas sector. The industry was effectively closed to foreign investment since 1938[14] as the government aimed to preserve reserves for domestic consumption.

In December 2013, the Mexican government presented a bill designed to change the constitution that would open the hydrocarbon and energy sectors to private and foreign investment. A revolutionary step that will in my view substantially increase foreign direct investment (FDI), strengthen Mexico's fiscal and external accounts, and lift its potential growth and employment. The reserves of Mexico are huge, and open the potential for significant infrastructure and growth over the next decade.

Marginal cost of production

During my debates with supply-side oil economists and engineers, I often hear, "Look at how expensive production is from Canadian oil sands. Prices will stay high", along with other marginal cost arguments to justify that crude oil prices cannot go down.

Remember prices are set by both supply *and demand*. Not just by supply or marginal cost pressure. If a product is too expensive to produce, it may simply not sell as consumers switch to cheaper alternatives to satisfy their needs.

Look at the 1970s, when crude oil was priced out of the power generation stack. If a cheaper and reliable alternative emerges, crude oil may be priced out of the transportation sector too.

The monopoly of crude oil over the transportation fuels sector has been in place ever since the application of the combustion engine to transportation in the early 1900s. This is increasingly being challenged by electric cars, compressed natural gas vehicles, ethanol or biodiesel cars, and solar power. Yes, they are a small minority for now, but the dynamics are changing quickly.

The complacent assumption that crude oil has no competition can be a lethal miscalculation in the long run.

The "unconventional" resources

My view is very simple: "everything that goes in your tank is conventional".

Yet, the industry tends to differentiate between "conventional" and "unconventional" resources, where "unconventional" refers to methods that are not "conventional" in our current technology and engineering statu quo.

Some people argue that unconventional oil "doesn't count", which I find childish at best. Assuming that principle, no oil production is valid unless it's onshore surface drilling.

Furthermore, the distinction is not binary. There are many degrees of "unconventional". Over the years, the technologies and techniques have improved steadily and are now major reliable contributors to global supply.

Yet, new technologies have often faced technical and environmental challenges during their early days. Look at offshore drilling, for example, with a plague of high profile accidents making it truly unpopular. But accidents become lessons. And the lessons have become new regulations and better practices, helping reduce the probability and severity of accidents. Altogether, time and time again, the frontier has kept moving forward.

Onshore drilling, the "conventional" method, became a reliable source of crude oil production. It was only natural that the exploration and production expanded into shallow water, initially in lakes near existing production fields such as Texas, Louisiana, and Lake Maracaibo in Venezuela. Drilling in lakes proved relatively easy.

The next frontier was offshore drilling, in the ocean, subject to the waves, tides, and adverse weather. The efforts started gradually after World War II, and by the end of the 1960s shallow waters were becoming a significant source of oil.

The next frontier was then deep-water, with exploration efforts focused on the "Golden Triangle" of Brazil, West Africa, and the Gulf of Mexico. By 2009, shallow and deep-water production from the Gulf of Mexico was 30% of US domestic oil production, contributing to the first increase in US domestic oil production in two decades.[15]

And then was the ultra-deep-water. In Brazil, improved seismic techniques identified a supergiant field with an estimated 5 billion to 8 billion barrels of recoverable reserves. The biggest discovery since Kashagan in Kazakhstan in 2000, it is expected to produce 6 million barrels per day, twice the current output of Venezuela, by 2025.

But the opportunities were also inland, literally "mining oil". The large scale of the Canadian oil sands or the Orinoco Belt in Venezuela have been known for many decades. Developments in technology and techniques have helped increase production in Alberta, Canada. Conventional and unconventional output in Canada could reach almost 4 million barrels per day by 2020.

And the more recent one is tight oil, extracted from shale-like formations. Like oil sands, the vast resources were known of, and the development of shale gas via horizontal drilling and fracking has opened the potential for over 20 billion barrels in the United States alone, equivalent to adding half of Alaska, but without having to work in the Arctic north and without having to build a huge pipeline. Tight oil is already 3 million barrels per day today and expected to grow to 5 million barrels per day in the United States by 2020. The EIA estimates US technically recoverable resources of 345 billion barrels of world shale oil resources and 7,299 trillion cubic feet of world shale gas resources.[16]

And do not forget natural gas liquids, still the biggest source of nonconventional oil. *Condensates* are captured from gas when it comes out of the well. *Natural gas liquids* are separated out when the gas is processed for injection into a pipeline. Both are similar to high-quality light oils.

Discoveries vs. additions: "can we rely on finding new oil fields?"

Contrary to what many people think, most of the increase in supply comes from additions to existing reserves. Not from new discoveries.

When a field is first discovered, very little is known about it, and initial estimates are limited and generally conservative. The more the wells are drilled, and with better knowledge, proven reserves are very often increased.

The difference in the balance between discoveries and revisions and additions is dramatic. According to one study by the United States Geological Survey, 86% of oil reserves in the United States are the result not of what is estimated at the time of discovery but of the revisions and additions that come with further development.[17]

Let's look at discoveries. According to the IEA, Goldman Sachs, and Cambridge Energy Research Associates (CERA), an average of 3 billion bbl of oil was discovered each year between 2003 and 2005. This compares to 8 billion bbl per year from 2006 to 2009. Most of the discoveries over the last five years have been made in the deep offshore, with Brazil dominating on size, followed by the Gulf of Mexico, and Ghana. Onshore discoveries of large size have been rare and in general limited to Iraq (Kurdistan) and Uganda, although oil shales and field redevelopments in Iraq have provided very material additions to the pipeline of onshore oil projects.

Now let's look at the additions. For some reason, the analysis of resource additions tends to focus only on conventional oil "as we knew it in the late 1990s". Why? Not clear. But by that measure, why don't we disregard any oil that is not onshore Saudi Arabia or why not disregard any oil that is not American Petroleum Institute (API) perfect? Furthermore, very much in line with most peak oil theories, the pessimistic analysis completely forgets nonconventional and liquids. By only including the addition of shale oil resources and heavy oil in Venezuela and Iran the reserve replacement is well above 120%.[18] And not to mention the giant discoveries in West Africa, which have added to the base of low sulphur crude.

Ignoring nonconventional, pre-salt, and heavy oil today is equivalent to ignoring deep water in the 1970s, or oil sands in the 1980s.

The excess capacity at high complexity refineries of 8 million barrels per day provides plenty of processing capacity and at a cheap cost. Drivers and motorists do not make any distinction between conventional and unconventional. They only care about what goes in the tank!

It is also worth noting the trend of promised volumes has dramatically increased over the past five years to c.95% from historically c.75%.[19] This proves that the "below to above ground" analysis of many peak oil defenders is not linear and that industry technology and delivery have greatly improved.

Sorry, no peak oil

> *We were wrong on peak oil. There's enough to fry us all. A boom in oil production has made a mockery of our predictions.*
>
> George Monbiot[20]

Peak oil is a myth

Over the years I have had many debates, including on television and in written media, with unconditional "peak oil supporters".

In 2012, during the Oil & Money Conference, Maria van der Hoeven, president of the EIA, alongside a panel of experts, said "This is the 33rd Oil & Money Conference. In 1979 in the first page of the *Herald Tribune* run the headline where President Carter said oil production had peaked, and the press said OPEC production would collapse to 15 million barrels per day in 2010. But here we are, global production is at record 87 million barrels per day, and OPEC produces 30 million barrels per day".

Arguments like "population and demand will continue to grow", "rising standards in emerging markets", or "every barrel of oil that we consume is gone forever" are undeniably true, but the conclusions often implied from them such as, "we are running out of oil", or "prices must continue to go up" are undeniably not true.

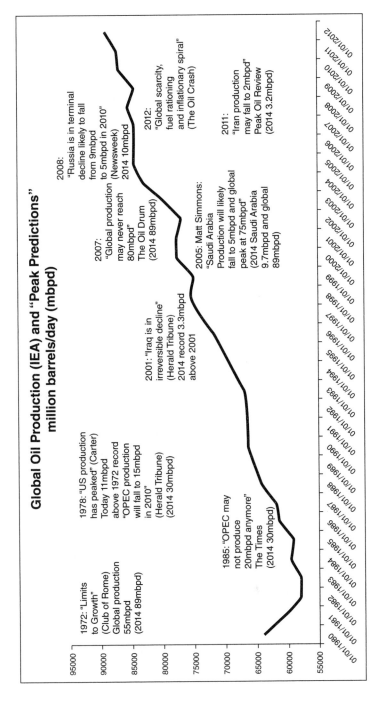

Global oil production and "peak predictions" (million barrels per day (mbpd))

And beyond our discussions, the peak oil theory is being disproved by the market itself both on the supply and demand sides of the equation. Supply is larger and more diversified than ever. Demand is growing at a slower pace with efficiency, technology, and less energy-intensive economic growth eroding peak demand. Supply has over and over responded to incremental demand. Just like demand has responded to incremental supply.

The core of the problem is an over-simplistic and static analysis, a dangerous mix of "realities and myths", that misses the true complex dynamics of the energy markets and reaches the wrong conclusions.

Yet, despite the vast resources and dynamic defence mechanisms of the market, there seems to be an unconscious bias in our human brains that supports the notion of peak oil.

But the last barrel of oil will not be worth millions. It will be worth zero.

And by the time that decline is a real issue, substitution will be more than evident.

"The Stone Age did not end because of a shortage of stones".[21] It ended because humanity moved into the Bronze Age. And the Bronze Age did not finish because of a shortage of bronze either. It ended because we moved into the Iron Age. And so on and so forth, the world has continued to evolve thanks to new technologies.

And the "oil age" will be no different. The end of the oil age will not happen because we ran out of oil. And it will not be a sudden or terrible shock that will bring economic hardship to people. The end of the oil era will be gradual, cyclical, and will open a new and more prosperous era for humans.

And it may be closer than many people think.

The spirit of peak oil

Peak oil theory is not that exciting in itself. The theory tries to estimate the point in time when production will peak, never to rise again, and puts energy to blame for almost any crisis and economic downturn. Many smart men have predicted the peak and failed. Many more will also try.

In addition to the numerous "fatalist" and "gloomy" conclusions that peak oil supporters derive from their analyses, perhaps one of the most relevant is "oil prices will continue to rise forever". Not true.

As I set out to "debunk" the peak oil theory and its faulty conclusions, I have chosen the format of the main "realities and myths" used by peak oil defenders, which show the dangerous mix of misinformation and shortcomings in their thought processes to reach the wrong conclusions.

No better place to start than taking a look the historical context of the theory and its evolution.

1. The historical perspective of peak oil

The combined threat of demographics and scarcity of resources is nothing new, as famously described by Thomas Malthus in the nineteenth century.

Another century later, in 1956, M. King Hubbert introduced the "theory of peak oil", which predicted that US oil production would peak in the early 1970s and decline thereafter, never to rise again.

The analysis was based on the then prevailing "limits of exploitability, technology, and market pressures".

But reality has turned out to be quite different from what Malthus and Hubbert predicted.

Not only has global production risen, and US oil production almost back above the 1970s record, but it is expected to continue to rise . . . and adjust as needed to address structural needs.[22]

Looking back, with the benefit of hindsight, it is easy to see why and where peak oil has gone wrong. The analysis missed the potential for new discoveries, new additions, and new technologies opening up known large unconventional resources, as well as the potential for conservation, substitution, and demand destruction, entirely missing key fundamental dynamics of the market, where "demand creates supply", just like "supply supports demand".

Looking ahead, the exact same forces will continue to push the boundaries of peak oil forward, just like they have done in the past.

The "known unknowns" (such as new discoveries, additions, efficiency, and demand destruction) and the "unknown unknowns" (such as new technologies, geopolitical conflicts, and natural disasters), while impossible to predict, cannot be ignored.

2. The peak oil mindset

In the summer of 2008, during an Energy Conference in London I asked my audience "Who thinks oil will be above $300/bbl in 10 years' time?" Crude oil was making fresh new highs around $140/bbl and, not surprisingly, more than half of the audience raised their hand.

"And between $200/bbl and $300/bbl?" I asked. And quite a few more people followed.

And repeated the process with lower and lower ranges until I finally asked: "Anyone below $50/bbl?". . . And the audience laughed!

I did not have a firm target price in my head, but I was very aware of the strain high commodity prices were putting on the global economy. In addition to $140/bbl oil, natural gas and coal were also making historical highs around $15/MMbtu and $130/Mt (metric ton), respectively.

My colleague and good friend Francisco Blanch, head of commodities research at Merrill Lynch, was paying close attention to the percentage share of energy to the overall nominal GDP in US dollars. In simple terms, the model showed that the global economy had limits. If energy as a share of the economy became too large or too small, the global economy would collapse, and determined a "sustainable" share of energy between 3% and 10%.

In 1998, energy became just 3% of the overall economy.[23] The Asian crisis had sent oil prices towards $10/bbl and coal and natural gas prices were very depressed too. Oil-producing nations such as Russia were under severe pressure and eventually "cracked", resulting in the Russian moratorium. The energy producer industry was breaking down. Such low prices were unsustainable.

In the 1970s, energy surpassed 10% of the overall economy.[24] The oil shocks had quadrupled oil prices. The "energy bill" was too large, and consuming countries around the world suffered from inflation and weak growth through the 1980s. The energy consumer industry was breaking down. Such high prices were unsustainable.

But there we were, in 2008, with a share of energy around 12% surpassing the levels of the oil shocks of the 1970s. The situation looked unsustainable, yet, at that time, many reputable analysts were calling for "$200/bbl". They, like many others, were caught up by the momentum of the strong demand from emerging markets. It was easy to lose perspective of the impact that energy markets had on the overall economy. But the model challenged the view. If oil prices rose towards $200/bbl, and natural gas and coal also continued their trend, the situation would "make the 1970s look like a walk in the park", as Francisco used to say. Yes, it was impossible to predict the *exact* top of the market, but we knew the dynamics were unsustainable.

The model had many other valuable insights. For example, it was able to identify the channel of adjustments required in order for the world's economy to sustain $200/bbl without falling apart (that is, remain at 10% of nominal GDP in US dollars).[25] One path was via sharp dollar devaluation. Another path was a larger global GDP. And another path was inflation. All perfectly plausible, but any of those would take years. There and then, in the short run, something had to give. Either prices went down, or the economy would "crack". Or both!

The dynamics described above should not be confused with the "peak oil" view that the economy collapses as demand grows. The dynamic is a simple price–response situation, as in any other cost in an input–output world. When costs rise beyond reasonable, the economy responds by slowing down. It has nothing to do with depletion. At that time inventories were at the top end of the five-year average. Supply growth exceeded demand. The distorting factor? A $581 billion stimulus plan from China and growth in money supply of 13% per annum driving currencies, and the US dollar in particular, much lower.[26]

So, when I raised my hand, supporting $50/bbl within 10 years, many people thought I was joking.

"That's impossible", someone said. In November 2014, with oil falling to four-year lows, this opinion would have been very different.

I was not surprised by the audience's reaction. At that time, $50/bbl seemed extremely low. Demand growth from emerging markets seemed unstoppable. Several theories had emerged that supported the bull case for demand and prices. Just a few years earlier, in 2001, Jim O'Neill, the then head of research at Goldman Sachs, had coined the term "BRIC" (in reference to Brazil, Russia, India, and China) in a report called "Building Better Economic BRICs" and looked at the new dynamics of the world by 2050. And a few years after that, my friend Jeff Currie published "The Revenge of the Old Economy", which identified the bottlenecks on the supply side of commodity markets. And, of course, peak oil was peaking. All these reports reinforced the view that super-cyclical demand *and* supply forces were converging.

But the reaction also made me realize, in puzzlement, how short term our human memory can be. Just nine years before, in 1999, oil had reached $10/bbl. Just five years before, in 2003, we were comfortably trading at \$30/bbl. And in 2005, half of the world was outraged when a Goldman Sachs analyst raised the possibility of a \$105/bbl "super-spike".[27] Yet, in 2008, \$140/bbl seemed a "stepping stone" towards \$200/bbl, and the majority of the audience saw \$300/bbl as the most likely scenario for oil prices in 10 years' time.[28] Amazing.

But within just few months, by September 2008, Lehman Brothers collapsed. Global excess of credit, which had been wrongly perceived as "sustainable growth", was suddenly evident in all corners of the world. The term "total debt" (public and private) became fashionable.

That is when many analysts woke up to the fact that global GDP demand and growth had been built on an enormous bubble of debt.

And when the credit bubble burst, the "unthinkable" happened. The demand shock arrived and prices collapsed towards \$30/bbl within a few months. They did not stay there for long, as OPEC cut production aggressively and tightened the market, but showed that in the markets, just like the movies, "reality always beats fiction".

3. Will global population, economic growth, oil demand, and oil prices rise "forever"?

While most of the peak oil arguments are based on "supply-side" issues, another key pillar of the theory is based on demand.

It is an undeniable truth that the global population is growing, and there is an implicit assumption that energy demand will grow with it.

Yet, the energy intensity of growth and efficiency are also at play, and are key in debunking the peak oil myth.

The argument goes like this: "The United States consumes almost 25 barrels per capita per year. China does not reach 5 barrels per capita per year. If China develops and consumes as much as the United States, we will have a supply shock".

But this argument fails to recognize that peak oil *demand* is very real. Despite the growth in population, wealth, and economic output, the global oil usage per person per year has remained boringly stable since 1985 due to the impact of efficiency and technology. While industrialization reaches its maximum level of needed capacity, oil consumption declines.

The United States, the Euro-zone, and Japan are already past peak oil demand. In absolute terms, they consume less today that they did before. The peak in oil consumption in these regions happened in 2005.

The compounded result of slower growth rates in population, changes in the demographic structure, and changes in energy consumption per capita are likely to result in continued growth in absolute levels of demand, but growing at a slower and slower pace.

However, predicting global population growth, economic activity, and energy consumption are extremely difficult challenges, and are very sensitive to key variables such as fertility and mortality.

Yet, it is precisely because of the optimistic assumptions about demand that the world tends to develop protective cushions of excess capacity, both as a combination of centralized government planning as well as reacting to the super-cyclical market forces.

Converting those into price forecasts is even harder, as demand interacts with the supply. And, as we look at the future, the range of possible prices seems much wider than ever before. Even industry experts are diverging dramatically about the path and direction of prices.

4. Depletion vs. replacement: "Are decline rates accelerating?"

Another typical argument is "every barrel of oil that is extracted and consumed means one less barrel in reserves, so we must be running out of oil, right?"

Well, to start, it is worth clarifying that "peak oil" is often confused with oil "depletion". Peak oil is the point of maximum production, while depletion refers to a period of falling reserves and supply.

Depletion of fields is a reality, a fact. Every barrel of oil that is extracted and consumed means one less barrel available for future consumption. There is no "recycling" of fossil fuels. Once consumed, they are "gone".

Declines in production are normal and to be expected. As of today, 60% of world oil production declines between 1.5% to 2.5% annually,[29] far more stable and lower than the 5% to 6% decrease that some peak oil defenders argue, thanks to enhanced recovery and advanced technology across horizontal drilling or deep-water.

But the fact that oil fields face depletion and decline rates does not imply a fatalist view of the world.

Replacement of reserves and production levels is not easy. It requires investment, and has often been slowed down by environmental and geopolitical issues. Yet, on average, the oil industry has invested around $750 billion a year, which has led to new discoveries and +100% reserve replacement.[30]

5. Will oil production fall abruptly and unexpectedly?
No. The main issue of production is not *geology*, as the late Christophe de Margerie (ex CEO of Total, one of the greats of the industry) or Rex Tillerson (CEO of Exxon) say over and over again. The main issue is geopolitical. The world could produce 90–92 million barrels per day today, if it wanted.

Exxon, which is well known for being prudent and conservative, sees steady growth between 2010 and 2040 in global oil and gas supply: +5.3% pa (unconventional), +4.8% pa (heavy/oil sands), +3.5% pa (LNG), +2.8% pa (deep-water), and +0.3% pa (conventional). No sign of peaking in any of them.[31]

According to Goldman Sachs research, there are more than 125 projects in OPEC alone that will be adding between

3.8 and 6 barrels per day [32] to supply in the short term that are just waiting to go on execution pipeline after receiving final investment decision (FID). The constraint is not projects, but project execution and human resources (engineers and capex) to develop them.

The global stated recoverable oil reserves, including conventional and unconventional sources, total 1.65 trillion barrels, or 54 years of supply.[33] Those 54 years improve notably when we include efficiency and technological revolutions like . . . shale oil!

6. EROEI: Does it take more and more energy to produce energy?

> So long as oil is used as a source of energy, when the energy cost of recovering a barrel of oil becomes greater than the energy content of the oil, production will cease no matter what the monetary price may be.
>
> M. KING HUBBERT[34]

The energy return on energy invested (EROEI) is commonly used as the ratio of the amount of usable energy acquired from a particular energy resource, to the amount of energy expended to obtain that energy resource. The EROEI ratio has no units. It represents "energy divided by energy".

Unconventional and new technologies fall towards the bottom end of the spectrum, which is used by many peak oil defenders as a problem.

However, they miss the key consideration that EROEI needs to be attached to profitability. A ratio of energy to energy without any economics is not enough.

Furthermore, EROEI is a dynamic ratio. Not static. Shell's analysis of oil sands production shows that energy used per unit produced falls dramatically over time across virtually all industry projects. The EROEI theory takes an individual projection (and this is typical for peak oil), leaves the negative elements untouched and stable (as if technology and resource development do not improve) and then expands it to the entire base. This, obviously, leads to a massive generalization and a leap of faith that can be easily denied just by looking at 20-F filings, that is detailed analyses per project, which are available to all shareholders in strategy presentations and fact books, where the undeniable fact that the oil sector's electricity and gas consumption has been falling while productivity, particularly in nonconventionals, has soared.

Since 1978 peak oil defenders have incorrectly estimated the decline in both production and reserves almost every year. Using EROEI is a very common excuse, and turning the debate to its alleged unsustainability is an incorrect justification.

7. "Are reserves being overestimated by the producers?"

In his famous book, *Twilight in the Desert: The Coming Saudi Oil Shock and the World Economy* (2005), Matthew Simmons, an investment banker, wrote that Saudi Arabia was running out of oil, and that no one would be prepared to deal with the impact. A highly controversial argument that gained a lot of supporters during the bull market, and almost 10 years after, the market remains very well supplied and Saudi Arabian production well above 2005 levels.

Some analysts say that OPEC-stated reserves skyrocketed from 878 billion barrels to 1.2 trillion barrels throughout the 1980s and 1990s, without any new significant discoveries being made. Is this correct? No. Analysts forget the additions from heavy crude that become commercial as extraction techniques and costs improve. This explains the additions of Iran and Venezuela perfectly, and the fact that international companies are interested in developing reserves in these countries proves the hydrocarbons are there.

But it is true that there is little incentive for producers such as Saudi Arabia to aggressively pursue exploration at this point in time. There is plenty to support demand growth. Production is at record levels. Some producing countries, such as Russia, Kuwait, United Arab Emirates, and Saudi Arabia, have combined short-term spare production capacity of 3.5 barrels per day to help them mitigate the impact of potential supply disruptions.

Other producing countries that produce at full capacity, such as Brazil and the United States, are expected to grow their output by 8% pa from current levels, with a potential acceleration from US shale oil.

As Christophe de Margerie, ex-CEO of Total, said in the Oil & Money Conference in 2012, "We have all the oil and gas we need. Apologies to those who want us to be running out".

No peak gas either

Jumpin' Jack Flash, it's a gas, gas, gas

Mick Jagger/Keith Richards

As I commented before, in 1991 when I joined the oil industry, a friend asked me "Why are you doing this? There are barely 40 years of reserves left". He obviously was wrong. A few years later, when I joined a gas transportation company, I was not surprised to hear him say "Why are you doing this? With renewables there is no future for gas. Everything will be powered by solar and wind by 2015".

At that time, natural gas was largely viewed as a byproduct of oil extraction. Whenever possible, it would be consumed locally or transported via pipeline, but often the associated gas was simply burnt (flared) without any environmental consideration. It was more convenient to burn it than do anything productive with it. That's how bad it was.

But the LNG revolution made it easily transportable and quickly monetizable, and although it required large capital expenditure and knowhow, it opened markets for gas that would otherwise be stranded.

Today, natural gas is at the epicentre of the energy markets, clean and abundant, well positioned to expand on power generation and break into transportation fuels, challenging the monopoly of crude oil and OPEC.

Gas formulas: "Water at Coca-Cola prices"

New pipelines and LNG infrastructure projects are very capital-intensive businesses.

Consumers and producers had a "mutual interest" to build and develop the necessary infrastructure and in most cases would join forces and shared the risks by sharing the ownership of assets and financial risks though long-term commitments of often 20 or 30 years.

Long-term "take or pay" agreements ensured the gas would change hands, but at what price?

Fixing the price for 20 or 30 years was too risky. What if prices collapsed? And what if prices exploded? The party who had bought or sold at a fixed price would have a large financial loss or gain.

The solution required a "floating pricing" mechanism to ensure that contracts would be in line with the then prevailing market conditions.

But the problem was that there was no available benchmark for spot LNG cargoes. There were reliable reference prices for deliveries into Henry Hub (HH) in North America or the National Balancing Point (NBP) in the UK, but these prices reflected domestic supply and demand conditions in the US and UK, respectively, not Japan or Germany. And the difference could be very significant.

The solution was to create a "gas formula" that would link the price of natural gas to alternative substitute fuels.

Japan adopted formulas based on the Japanese Crude Cocktail (JCC), which once upon a time, before the oil weapon was unleashed in 1973 and 1979, competed with natural gas as feedstock for power generation.[35]

Europe adopted formulas based on crude oil, products, coal, inflation, and any other relevant factors. To protect both buyers and sellers against extreme divergences, the gas formulas often incorporated an "S curve" mechanism, a cap and a floor, so that the realized prices would stay within a reasonable and agreed upon range.

The formulas were then "calibrated" via coefficients. For the sake of argument, a simple formula where LNG = 0.1 × JCC meant that if the Japanese crude cocktail was $30/bbl, then LNG would be $3/MMBtu. The calibration was such that the prices on "day one" would be in line with the then prevailing market conditions.

For example, using the above formula if JCC prices increased towards $100/bbl, then the price of LNG would be $10/MMBtu, irrespective of where HH or NBP were trading.

Over the years, the gas formulas have been increasingly using other gas benchmarks, such as HH or NBP, looking to reduce the basis between LNG and crude oil, refined products, and coal. But these formulas are not perfect either. The way to minimize the basis risk was to create a proper benchmark for imported gas prices.

In practical terms, the gas formulas meant that the buyers were receiving physical natural gas but paying a price linked to oil. This created a significant risk that not many consumers were aware of, that is they were effectively paying for gas at crude oil prices.

Finally an Asian benchmark

In February 2009, Platts launched the JKM (Japan Korea Marker), an index based on daily assessments of LNG cargoes into Japan and Korea, the largest LNG importers in the world.[36]

The JKM benchmark is an important development for the LNG market, increasing the transparency and liquidity and reducing the basis risks, as Asia already contributes 55% of the LNG world trade.[37]

Let's buy Africa!

Large consumers like the UK or the US have benefited from large domestic resources and production. China is also one of the largest producers of most commodities, but unfortunately is an even larger consumer, making it very dependent on imports. For Japan it is even worse, as its domestic production is virtually non-existent.

Both Japan and China have taken an interesting approach towards energy security. Both have been aggressive in the acquisition of natural resources assets. The rationale is a combination of factors.

First, economics. Buying natural resources at the right time of the cycle can be an extremely rewarding business. Producers tend to suffer from the triple whammy of lower prices, lower volumes, and expensive financing. A great combination for anyone with cash and hungry for resources.

Second, financial risk management. Buying these resources reduces the exposure towards higher commodity prices. The profit on these reserves helps offset the losses. As a country, it may become a "zero sum game" controlled by the government, which can help subsidize consumers through other indirect ways.

Third, physical risk management. By controlling those assets, it can also control the off-take of the physical flows. They help "vertically integrate" the exposure, from the production to other added value processes such as refining of oil or metals.

But these investments are subject to local laws, local taxes, and the risk of expropriation and nationalization. No wonder China and Japan have a strong preference for countries like

Australia. But the value and their cash is more needed in other remote and perhaps riskier countries. Look at Myanmar for example. And neither China nor Japan are "shy" to expand to their reach to new markets across Africa or Asia.

In addition to the size, most of the reserves in sub-Saharan Africa are accessible to international investors, in contrast with some other regions of the world. While oil reserves are diversified across the continent, proved gas reserves are still largely dominated by Nigeria, although potential future gas-producing provinces are being discovered elsewhere as the emergence of export and local markets for gas in Africa should provide incentives for gas exploration and increase further proved African gas reserves in coming years.

The growth of proved oil and gas reserves in sub-Saharan Africa in the past 30 years has resulted in the growing importance of Africa as a major world hydrocarbon producer. Africa has consistently gained market share of the world hydrocarbon supply.

Currently 25% of US oil imports and 30% of Chinese oil imports are sourced from Africa, and those proportions are expected to increase in the future. More than $120 billion have been earmarked for investments in resources in the African continent in the past years.

These investments are increasing the cultural exchange, with the Chinese and Japanese becoming more integrated within the host countries. Who knows, Africa in 50 years' time may look a lot like Brazil today, a wonderful mix of races and cultures.

NOTES

1. Chris Rochelle (16 April 2014). *Methane Hydrate: Dirty Fuel or Energy Saviour?* http://www.bbc.co.uk/news/business-27021610

2. *BP Statistical Review of World Energy – June 2013.* http://www
.bp.com/content/dam/bp/pdf/statistical-review/statistical
_review_of_world_energy_2013.pdf

3. http://www.eia.gov/petroleum/data.cfm#crude

4. Ibid.

5. Bureau of the Fiscal Service. http://www.fiscal.treasury.gov/fsreports
/rpt/goldRpt/current_report.htm

6. Economic Research. Federal Reserve Bank of St. Louis. http:
//research.stlouisfed.org/fred2/series/GFDEBTN/

7. Bureau of the Fiscal Service (2014). *Status Report of U.S. Treasury-
Owned Gold.* US Department of the Treasury, 30 April.

8. US Energy Information Administration. *Technically Recoverable
Shale Oil and Shale Gas Resources.* http://www.eia.gov/analysis
/studies/worldshalegas/

9. Organization of the Petroleum Exporting Countries. *Brief History.*
http://www.opec.org/opec_web/en/about_us/24.htm

10. Organization of the Petroleum Exporting Countries. *Our Mission.*
http://www.opec.org/opec_web/en/about_us/23.htm

11. Francisco Parra (2005). *Oil Politics: A Modern History of Petroleum.* London: I.B. Tauris.

12. Luis de Sousa (2011). OPEC quotas and crude oil production. *The
Oil Drum,* 31 January.

13. Daniel Lacalle (2012). Peak oil: realities, myths and risk. *Cotizalia,*
12 November.

14. Adam Williams, Eric Martin, and Nacha Cattan (2013) *Mexico Passes
Oil Bill Seen Luring $20 billion a Year.* http://www.bloomberg
.com/news/2013-12-12/mexico-lower-house-passes-oil-overhaul
-to-break-state-monopoly.html

15. US Energy Information Administration. http://www.eia.gov/dnav
/pet/pet_crd_crpdn_adc_mbblpd_a.htm

16. US Energy Information Administration. *Technically Recoverable
Shale Oil and Shale Gas Resources.* http://www.eia.gov/analysis
/studies/worldshalegas/

17. United States Geological Survey (October 2000). *Reserve Growth
Effects on Estimates of Oil and Natural Gas Resources.*

18. *BP Statistical Review of World Energy – June 2013.* http://www
.bp.com/content/dam/bp/pdf/statistical-review/statistical
_review_of_world_energy_2013.pdf

19. Goldman Sachs (2007). *360 Projects to Change the World*. http: //www.docstoc.com/docs/119164686/Goldman-Sachs ---360-projects-to-change-the-world

20. George Monbiot (2012). We were wrong on peak oil. There's enough to fry us all. *The Guardian*, 2 July.

21. Richard Sears (April 2010). *Planning for the End of Oil*. http: //www.ted.com/talks/richard_sears_planning_for_the_end_of _oil/transcript?language=en

22. US Energy Information Administration (2014). *Annual Energy Outlook 2014*. http://www.eia.gov/forecasts/aeo/

23. International Monetary Fund. *International Capital markets Developments, Prospects, and Key Policy Issues*. http://books.google.es /books/about/International_Capital_Markets_Developmen .html?id=b0VqqA1ua8AC

24. This is the calculation of oil burden (oil imports in US dollars relative to GDP).

25. Estimating unchanged imports (consensus).

26. *The Economist* (12 November 2008). *The World in 2009. China's Stimulus Package*. http://www.economist.com/blogs /theworldin2009/2008/11/chinas_stimulus_package

27. *Geotimes* (8 April 2005). *Oil Prices Outlook High*. http://www .geotimes.org/apr05/WebExtra040805.html

28. Bloomberg and NARECO Advisors.

29. US Energy Information Administration. http://www.eia.gov/cfapps /ipdbproject/IEDIndex3.cfm?tid=5&pid=53&aid=1; *BP Statistical Review of World Energy – June 2013*. http://www.bp.com/content /dam/bp/pdf/statistical-review/statistical_review_of_world _energy_2013.pdf

30. *BP Statistical Review of World Energy – June 2013*. http://www .bp.com/content/dam/bp/pdf/statistical-review/statistical _review_of_world_energy_2013.pdf

31. ExxonMobil. *The Outlook for Energy: A View to 2040*. http: //corporate.exxonmobil.com/en/energy/energy-outlook

32. Goldman Sachs (2007). *360 Projects to Change the World*. http: //www.docstoc.com/docs/119164686/Goldman-Sachs ---360-projects-to-change-the-world

33. US Energy Information Administration. http://www.eia.gov/countries /index.cfm?view=reserves

34. David S. Ginley and David Cahen (2012). *Fundamentals of Materials for Energy and Environmental Sustainability.* New York: Cambridge University Press.

35. US Energy Information Administration. *International Natural Gas Pricing – A Challenge to Economic Modelling.* http://www.eia .gov/naturalgas/workshop/pdf/Session1_Jensen.pdf

36. Platts (2014). *JKM (Japan Korea Marker) Gas Price Assessment.* http://www.platts.com/price-assessments/natural-gas/jkm -japan-korea-marker

37. US Energy Information Administration. *Developing a Natural Gas Trading Hub in Asia.* http://carrepair-manualpdf.rhcloud.com /tag/developing-a-natural-gas-trading-hub-iea-international-

CHAPTER SIX

FLATTENER #3 – HORIZONTAL DRILLING AND FRACKING

First you have to learn the rules of the game. And then you have to play better than anyone else.

Albert Einstein

Never bet against an engineer

If you give enough time and money to an engineer, he will find a solution.

Technology in energy exploration and production has consistently pushed the boundaries of what we thought was possible, both in terms of volume and price. For example, what was once considered "science fiction", such as extracting crude oil from depths of five thousand feet or more, or from shale formations, is today a reality.

There is a long history of "game changers", all the way from offshore drilling, to deep-water, to ultra-deep-water, to "mining" Canadian oil sands, or more recently horizontal drilling and hydraulic fractioning, all of which have consistently pushed the boundaries of peak oil further and further into the future.

Yet, despite how impactful new technology has been in the past, it amazes me how we tend to disregard the potential and impact of *future* technologies. "Seeing is believing" or "a bird in hand is worth more than two in the bush" seem very entrenched in human nature.

And so, today, we remain very sceptical of our ability to develop "large known reserves" such as methane hydrates in Japan. Our perspective is probably not much different from what we thought about shale formations just 10 years ago or offshore ultra-deep 30 years ago. Well, just like in the past, the volumes and economic incentives are there. Engineers are investing money and time, and, who knows, perhaps solutions may not be as far away as we think.

New technologies are resulting in larger and more diversified energy reserves around the world, which in time will become production. In addition to the large and proven shale gas and tight oil reserves in North America, the potential for application in the rest of the world is huge. China, for example, has vast reserves, domestic and cleaner than coal. Despite the less favourable geology and other considerations, these will surely be developed over time, perhaps sooner than many expect.

Technology increases volume

History tends to repeat itself. Cycles of tightness are followed by cycles of excess. But these cycles often experience more "super-cyclical" behaviour, or quantum leaps, thanks to the development of "game changers".

In the 1970s–80s, the development of the North Sea was a major engineering feat. In his book, *North Sea Innovations and Economics*, Ron Goodfellow explains that "through the latter half of the 1970s and into the 1980s the scale and problems of North Sea development drilling were crucial in the evolution and adoption of new technologies. This was the era when the major North Sea fields were being brought on stream with multiple platforms, often with two drilling rigs on each. The level of drilling activity was sufficient to encourage the development of new technologies which can now be identified with the North Sea".[1] It was precisely the challenge that encouraged engineers to come up with efficient and competitive solutions that are now used in hundreds of ultra-deep-water rigs all over the world, safely.

Thanks to the ingenuity of these engineers, production at deep and ultra-deep waters is perfectly viable technologically, commercially, and environmentally. Imagine how different the world would be if those efforts and developments had been banned or abandoned because of technical difficulties.

In the 1990s, the development of ultra-deep water, such as Brazil and Mexico, once again pushed the boundaries of what was thought technically and economically possible.

In the early 2000s, horizontal drilling and hydraulic fracturing opened a vast amount of resources that had been known for a long time, but were thought to be both technically and commercially unfeasible. This new technology is having a major impact, and it has become the largest growing source of crude oil via the so-called "tight oil" from shale formations.

Yet, even today many remain sceptical. Some think that fracking and shale are "just" a North American phenomenon. Yes, there are some constraints such as geology, water resources, environmental concerns, and property rights, but the proven reserves outside North America, and China in particular, are simply enormous and will be developed over time.

The scepticism and environmental concerns are common in almost every new technology. Remember the early developments of the offshore production, plagued with large-scale environmental disasters. Time after time, the industry has managed to find solutions to the challenges. And the incentives for China are there. Time will tell how quickly they develop them.

Technology reduces costs

New technologies are often dismissed when extrapolating today's cost structure, thus overestimating marginal costs, but engineers have found new processes and techniques to improve and reduce costs across every part of the process.

The result is invariably higher volumes at cheaper prices than anticipated.

And do not forget about the potential savings from the optimization of existing techniques. The more wells you dig, the better you get at it. Problems become the need for solutions. Mistakes become lessons learnt. And so we keep producing more, cheaper, and safer.

Despite cost inflation in the service industry, finding and lifting costs are more than adequate. US on-shore stands at $34/bbl and off-shore at $52/bbl, Africa at $45/bbl, and the Middle East at $17/bbl.[2]

Innovation vs. imitation

I remember when I bought my first MacBook laptop, one of the things that impressed me the most was its magnetic plug. How many times had I tripped over a cable when my computer was charging, and dropped it. Well, it turned out that now when I tripped over, the magnetic plug would come off, thus protecting the computer. "Genius!" I thought. But it was only a few years later, as I was reading a book about Steve Jobs, that I learnt that he had actually "stolen" the idea from deep-fry cookers, which had been using them for decades. Yes, the consequences of tripping over the deep-fry cooker with boiling oil could be devastating. The deep-fry engineers got on the case, and came up with the idea of using magnetic plugs. A fantastic invention that was used within a narrow "niche" for decades, before it was applied to the computer industry. Beyond the obvious considerations of intellectual property, Steve Jobs had a relentless ambition to learn from his own industry and from other industries. "Artists copy. Geniuses steal", as he was famously quoted.

The same dynamics of "innovation and imitation" apply to oil and gas engineering too. Look for example at horizontal drilling and fracking. They were initially developed to extract natural gas from shale formations, but engineers quickly realized that a similar technique could also be utilized in the extraction of crude oil. And look at the growth in light tight oil across North America.

Technology has been a key driver of exploration and production. Think of the developments in exploration. Since the early days of a pretty much "blind lottery" of prospecting, to today, where Brazilian engineers devised a way to "look through" a mile-thick layer of salt to find a supergiant field with estimated 5 billion to 8 billion barrels of recoverable reserves.[3]

Technology has also been a key driver of refining. Consider the simple distillation units, and how they have evolved over time with the addition of low pressure "vacuum" distillation, and adding both thermal and catalytic processes that allow us to convert the "raw" and often heavy and sulphurous crude oil into the clean refined products that we consume every day.

But technology also impacts demand. "Volume creates volume", and new processes and techniques respond and take advantage of developments on the supply side. Look for example at electric cars where technology is addressing the many challenges to develop more powerful cars with greater autonomy and smaller batteries.

The "frontiers" of the industry often looked insurmountable, but more often than not the combination of time, money, and human ingenuity managed to conquer them. Offshore drilling, ultra-deep-water, horizontal drilling, and hydraulic fracturing ("fracking") are game changers for both the natural gas and oil markets, but over the past century the limits have been pushed, facilitating incremental demand growth.

"Fracking" and horizontal drilling

Hydraulic fracturing consists of the injection of large amounts of water at high pressure, combined with sand and small amounts of chemicals, which break up the underground rock and create exit pathways to the well, from otherwise trapped natural gas and oil.

The production of shale gas started quietly in the early 2000s, but by the end of the decade to the surprise of many, it was becoming a noticeable source of production and more than off-setting the declines in conventional natural gas. In 2000 shale was just 1% of US natural gas production and by 2012 it was 37%.

Furthermore, shale gas was proving to be even cheaper than conventional natural gas.

As a result of the shale revolution, North America's natural gas base is now estimated at over 100 years of consumption, and has reversed the situation from shortage into a substantial surplus.

Europe, despite having over 90 years of demand covered by domestic reserves, with the biggest potential in Poland, France, the UK, and Spain,[4] is lagging in the development of the reserves.

Indeed, despite the economic success story of shale gas in North America, the rest of the world seems to be lagging behind. Part of the reason is the lack of political support, influenced by a dangerous mix of myths and realities which I now set out to clarify.

Myths and realities of shale gas and tight oil

> *Progress is the product of human agency. Things get better because we make them better.*
>
> Susan Rice

> *Don't fear change, change fear.*

What environmental impact?

Hydraulic fracturing is a proven and safe technology.

However, public opinion has been influenced by a range of alarmist and unfounded reports. There is even a documentary *Gasland* and a movie *Promised Land,* which were immediately refuted by the industry, scientists, and the US Department of Energy as inaccurate.

It is ironic that all these alarmist reports, such as the Cornell study, add as disclosure "we could not confirm accurately any of these claims".[5]

Yet, public opinion seems to hold a "guilty until proven innocent".

During the following sections, I will review and debate some of the main arguments used against shale gas. And no better place to start than water.

What contamination of drinking water aquifers?

According to the US Department of Energy, over the past 60 years, more than one million wells have been "fracked" in the United States.[6] Not even once has a state or local department found evidence of water pollution of aquifers, and five lawsuits have been dropped recently in the United States due to lack of evidence.[7]

Critics argue that fracking may damage drinking water aquifers, but fracking takes place a mile or more below drinking water aquifers and is separated from them by thick layers of impermeable rock. As Robert W. Chase put it: "Some mistakenly say the practice can pollute water tables which lie just a few hundred feet or less below the surface. Fracking is done well below 7,000 feet, and solid rock separates the oil and gas deposits from shallow groundwater aquifers. This rock buffer makes contamination from fracking virtually impossible".[8]

In addition, wells are built with at least four layers of steel casing and concrete and are cemented in place, creating a solid divider between gas production and any fresh-water aquifers. The industry is currently using more than 5000 tons of steel and cement to protect the groundwater.[9]

Fracking can be done with water or other liquids. The general trend in the industry is to disclose the liquids and chemicals, with average 90% water, 9.5% sand, and the remaining 0.5% a mixture of chemicals.[10] Of these chemicals, the majority (hydrochloric acid, ethanol, methanol, ethylene, and sodium hydroxide) can be recovered in the extraction process. The water is often treated, which reduces the need for chemicals and therefore minimizes any risk of contamination even further.

Energy Secretary Steven Chu recently asserted: "We believe it's possible to extract shale gas in a way that protects the water that protects people's health. We can do this safely".[11]

It is important to understand correctly what is in fracking fluids and why concerns are overstated[12] as well as how industry develops nontoxic fracking fluids.[13]

What flow back?

There are also environmental concerns around the water that "comes back" to the surface.

The industry actively manages the flow back via any of the following three alternatives: reinject it into deep disposal wells; water treatment facilities; or recycle back into operations.[14]

In traditional oil and gas states, the wastewater has often been reinjected. But in some places, such as some parts of Pennsylvania, the geology does not lend itself to reinjection, so water is either put through local treatment facilities or trucked out of state for reinjection in more suitable fields.

Aboveground water management is being developed along with production, and following the completion of new large-scale water treatment facilities, the industry is now recycling 70% to 80% of the flow back.[15]

There is also intensive focus on innovation, such as developing new methods to reduce the amount of water going in and to treat the water coming out, and the drilling of more wells from a single "pad" to reduce the footprint.

How about water scarcity?

The CEO of Nestlé said "the world will run out of drinking water before it runs out of oil".[16] Indeed, for large countries like China, India, and Pakistan, the issue of "water scarcity" may be around the corner. However, similar to oil, there is no scarcity of water on a global scale. There is an issue of uneven distribution of the water resources. Some areas have excess water, and other areas have shortages. To address this issue, during the 1930s the United States made large investments with water networks between Colorado and California.[17] A similar investment process needs to take place in China, between the north and south.

The water industry requires large investments in infrastructure. But the problem is that the price of water is too low, which prevents the necessary investment and maintenance. To prove the point, look at water leakage. London is thought to have more than 50% losses in the network due to old water infrastructures and an estimated 646 million litres lost a day from water leakage.[18] A third of London's water infrastructure is 150 years old. There is technology, such as membranes, that could be used to address this issue, but current prices are not high enough to incentivize the right behaviour or investment in infrastructure. Government debt and fiscal pressures are adding to the problem.

Nevertheless, as demand for water exposes the bottlenecks in the water infrastructure, countries will have to allocate and prioritize its usage between household, industry, and agriculture.

According to a report by the UK's Tyndall Centre for Climate Change, fracking operations carried out on a six-well pad would require 54,000–174,000 cubic metres of water.[19] This presents the problem of water shortage in Europe, particularly parts of Central Europe. Production may cost more than $2/MMBtu, and given the enormous cost of water in Europe, represents nearly 60% of the cost of drilling.[20] However, the use of water is shrinking fast and fracking uses less every year, as well as improving its recycling processes.

Interestingly, water required to frack all US wells is 0.1% of the total[21] and falling, while 4% of water consumption globally is used as a cooling agent in power generation.[22]

What induced seismic activity?

In 2012, the US National Research Council issued a study on seismic activity and concluded that "even those man-made tremors large enough to be an issue are very rare. In more than 90 years of monitoring, human activity has been shown to trigger only 154 quakes, most of them moderate or small, and only 60 of them in the United States. That's compared to a global average of about 14,450 earthquakes of magnitude 4.0 or greater every year ... Only two worldwide instances of shaking, a 2.8 magnitude tremor in Oklahoma and a 2.3 magnitude shaking in England, can be attributed to hydraulic fracturing".[23]

The report was chaired by Murray Hitzman, a professor of economic geology at the Colorado School of Mines, who concluded that "There's a whole bunch of wells that have been drilled, let's say for waste water and the number of events have been pretty small. Is it a huge problem? The report says basically no".[24]

Furthermore, quoting Robert W. Chase's excellent "Five Myths about 'Fracking'": "William Leith, senior science adviser for earthquake and geologic hazards at the U.S. Geological Survey, told National Public Radio recently: 'Fracking itself does not put enough energy into the ground to trigger an earthquake. That's really not something that we should be concerned about'".[25]

Oil and gas waste water disposal wells, on the other hand, do have a history of causing tremors, most recently in Youngstown, Ohio. However, by reducing the volume of water injected and the depth of wastewater injection wells, and avoiding earthquake-prone areas, the risk of inducing tremors, however small, can be reduced.[26]

What methane migration?

A more recent concern is the possible "migration" of natural gas towards the surface of water wells. This is a controversial subject.

Methane has been found in water wells in gas-producing regions but there is no agreement on how this can happen. Some cases of methane contamination in water wells have been tied to shallow layers of methane, not the mile-deep deposits of shale gas where fracking takes place. In other cases, water wells may have been dug through layers of naturally occurring methane without being adequately sealed. It is difficult to know for certain because of a lack of baseline data, i.e., measurements of a water well's methane content before a shale gas well is drilled in the neighbourhood.

Gas developers are now routinely taking such measurements before drilling begins in order to establish whether methane is pre-existing in water aquifers.

A new question concerns whether there are significant "fugitive emissions" and if these emissions should be captured. The main component of natural gas is methane, a gas associated with global warming when released into the atmosphere, but reduced emission completion (REC) technologies can now capture the emerging gas at the wellhead and are increasingly being used.[27]

Are horizontal drilling and fracking commercially viable?

Some anti-fracking groups say that shale gas and oil are uneconomical. I shed a tear at their concerns about other people's money.

Shale gas is a sector where private investors and entrepreneurs risk their own money. Tens of billions of dollars are put to work in shale gas, with no subsidies, no government funding, financed with private capital, and very little debt. According to research by UBS and Goldman Sachs, the average return on invested capital (ROIC) of the shale gas sector since 2010 has never been worse than 5% . . . with gas prices falling 21% in 2010 alone![28] Compare that to any utility in Europe, or any renewables company ex-subsidies, or coal companies.

The EIA estimates tight oil in the United States has estimated reserves of 24 billion barrels,[29] which given the current state of the technology with hydraulic fracking techniques and recycled water, are economically viable at $60/bbl.

Chesapeake estimates that in order to achieve 10%[30] rates of return, it will require oil prices of between $30/bbl and $50/bbl, depending on the basins. If we assume $100/bbl, each well repays its total investment cost in eight months. Three times faster than a conventional oil well.

Are governments supportive of fracking?

Governments around the world have taken dramatically different positions with respect to fracking.

US politicians have strongly supported the development of fracking. The United States recognizes the multiplier effect through the creation of jobs and cheaper electricity and industrial fuels. According to CERA, shale gas has created 2.1 million jobs, $75 billion in tax revenues, $283 billion in GDP, and raised household income by $1200 per year.[31]

Ironically, the defenders of subsidized energies and intervention in energy price mechanisms forget the effect of shale gas on energy bills and are suddenly worried about investment returns.

The development of US shale gas and tight oil is widely recognized as a major competitive advantage against Europe, Japan, and China. A competitive advantage that may last for a long time, with deep and possible irreversible repercussions.

Europe is estimated to have 156 tcm (trillion cubic metres) of shale gas reserves.[32] That means over 90 years of demand covered.

However, in Europe, the development of shale gas has been highly politicized. Similar to nuclear power, politicians across key countries have taken the "not in my backyard" approach to shale gas.

"Moratoriums have been imposed in France (July 2011), Bulgaria (January 2012) and Romania (May 2012), whilst the Netherlands has put shale gas drilling on hold for a further year as an investigation is carried out into the environmental risks."[33]

It is ironic that Europe wants energy independence, cheap and environmentally friendly energy, and should be looking to develop its natural resources efficiently in a clean and competitive manner. Instead, politicians and lobbyists across Europe are looking to ban shale and continue to favour heavily subsidized technologies.

The economic impact of high energy costs is a disaster for Europe. Energy costs paid by businesses and consumers are the highest among the OECD countries, limiting its ability to compete.

Across the OECD countries, Europe is incurring 100% of the burden of carbon dioxide through the European Carbon Scheme, and 70% of energy subsidies. Europe could save 900 billion euros (equivalent to almost all the government debt of Spain) and achieve its objective of reducing carbon dioxide emissions by 80% by 2050 if, in addition to further renewable energy, the continent developed its shale gas reserves according to the "Making the Green Journey Work" sector study.[34]

Ironically, the conventional gas industry in Europe has joined coal and solar lobbies against shale gas. None of them are interested in cheap gas prices, because they have seen – with horror – how gas prices in the United States have plummeted due to the shale gas revolution, and therefore obliterated the use of coal for power generation and the grants of succulent subsidies as abundant energy reduced power prices.

And the potential for shale in Europe is significant. In Poland, for example, Wood MacKenzie estimated 48 trillion cubic feet of unconventional gas[35] (tight and shale) which, if confirmed, would mean an increase in European gas reserves of 47%.[36] Poland is currently very dependent on Russian gas and imports more than 75% (11.6 bcm/year).[37] The development of unconventional gas reserves could enhance both the energy security and economic situation. Furthermore, Poland can become a net exporter as European countries take advantage of the geographical proximity and lack of geopolitical risk. No surprise that many of the oil and gas majors such as Total, Chevron, ExxonMobil, Marathon, Talisman, and Conoco, and independent exploration companies are already expanding in Poland as the government has awarded over 85 exploration licenses.

According to the EIA, Ukraine is thought to have the third largest shale gas reserves in Europe, at 42 trillion cubic feet.[38] Chevron has been actively prospecting in Zamosc. Most of the projects are still in the exploration phase and are far away from development but the potential could be phenomenal.

The last time I met with the management of Statoil and Chesapeake in March 2014 they were confident of the geology, but not optimistic about political support. Both are analysing more than 15 new areas in Germany, France, and the North Sea, among others.

How about shale gas and tight oil in China?

I visited Shanghai for the first time in the early 2000s. I had been to Beijing several times before, and was expecting Shanghai to be a very large city, but what I saw left me speechless. From the top of my hotel in the Pudong area, I could see literally hundreds and hundreds of modern skyscrapers expanding in all directions. It made Manhattan look like a small town.

I was even more shocked when my Chinese colleague told me: "Did you know that 10 years ago this whole area was a rice field?". It was very hard to believe. "If someone had told me 10 years ago that Pudong would look like this today, I would have laughed and said they were crazy". It was the first time I realized how powerful centralized planning could be. Once the Chinese set their mind to do something, they do it. It became crystal clear to me then.

And then my Chinese colleague told me: "Do you see those fields over there, in the far distance?". I nodded. "Well, the government is planning to develop it in a similar way to Pudong". Shanghai was to become the largest harbour in the world, ahead of Hong Kong and Singapore. The urbanization of China and the migration of the people to cities like Shanghai was simply scary. But I believed him.

So when the National Development and Reform Commission of China (NDRC)[39] unveiled what looked like ambitious strategic plans to explore and develop China's huge shale resources, I believed them.

And China has the largest shale gas reserves in the world, at 25 trillion cubic feet.[40]

And yes, China is determined to develop them. They face significant challenges such as deep gas deposits with complex geology, lack of domestic technology for horizontal multi-stage hydraulic fracturing, high human population density, significant capital investment and longer lead time to commercial production, which may result in slower capital recovery; while government incentives are not yet in place, and given reserves are in central and west China, far from demand, more pipeline capacity and coverage is needed.

But all these barriers can be surmounted with the right amount of capital, incentives, help of international oil companies and, of course, time.

It is too early to call the end of coal in China, but certainly domestic shale gas is a major development that will have a dramatic impact across all those industries and subsidies.

The State Owned Enterprises (SOE) such as PetroChina, Sinopec, CNOOC, and other smaller players, such as Yanchang Petroleum, have already discovered shale gas and have agreements for cooperation with large and experienced companies such as Shell, Statoil, ConocoPhillips, BP, Chevron, and ExxonMobil.

Interestingly, China is pushing ahead with its support for natural gas vehicles. A sign, perhaps, of the commitment and expectations of its natural gas supply.

What about the EROEI of shale gas?

The IEA puts it simply: "As long as consumers are willing to pay for it and resources are there, consuming some energy to produce energy is fine".[41]

"A hydraulic fracking published paper shows the energy return on investment (aka EROI) with a total input energy compared with the energy in natural gas expected to be made available to end users is similar to or better than coal".[42]

Shale gas is a game changer. A powerful flattening force and a relevant factor in the energy security of supply battle, allowing traditional importers to develop their own resources.

NOTES

1. Ron Goodfellow, (1993). *North Sea Innovations and Economics*. London: Institution of Civil Engineers.
2. US Energy Information Administration. http://www.eia.gov/dnav /pet/pet_crd_crpdn_adc_mbbl_a.htm
3. US Energy Information Administration. http://www.eia.gov/today inenergy/detail.cfm?id=13771
4. http://www.centrica.com/files/pdf/making_the_green_journey _work.pdf
5. http://www.eeb.cornell.edu/howarth/web/Marcellus.html
6. DoE, CERA
7. Robert W. Chase (2012). Five myths about "fracking". *Akron Beacon Journal*, 26 January. http://www.ohio.com/editorial/robert-w -chase-five-myths-about-fracking-1.257129

8. Ibid.
9. *Fracking Fluids.* http://www.energyfromshale.org/hydraulic -fracturing-fluid
10. Ibid.
11. http://blog.cleveland.com/pdextra/2012/01/energy_secretary _steven_chu_sp.html
12. *Fracking Fluids.* http://www.energyfromshale.org/hydraulic -fracturing-fluid
13. http://www.coloradoan.com/viewart/20130204/NEWS11 /302040011/Energy-industry-develops-nontoxic-fracking-fluids
14. Pam Boschee (2014). Produced and flowback water recycling and reuse: Economics, limitations, and technology. *Oil and Gas Facilities*, February.
15. David Wethe and Peter Ward (26 November 2013). *Fracking Bonanza Eludes Wastewater Recycling Investors.* http://www .bloomberg.com/news/2013-11-26/fracking-bonanza-eludes -wastewater-recycling-investors.html
16. Peter Brabeck-Letmanthe (2010). *World Water Day: Why Business Needs to Worry.* BBC News Business, 22 March.
17. Historic American Engineering Record. *Colorado River Aqueduct From Colorado River to Lake Mathews.* San Bernardino County California. HAER No. CA-226.
18. Thames Water. *Reducing Leakage.* http://www.thameswater.co.uk /cr/Preciousresource/Reducingleakage/index.html
19. Ruth Wood et al. (2011). *Shale Gas: A Provisional Assessment of Climate Change and Environmental Impacts.* Tyndall Center for Climate Change Research, University of Manchester, January.
20. Consensus estimates from Bloomberg.
21. http://theenergycollective.com/jessejenkins/205481/friday -energy-facts-how-much-water-does-fracking-shale-gas-consume
22. Evangelos Tzimas (2011). *Sustainable or Not? Impacts and Uncertainties of Low-Carbon Energy Technologies on Water.* Washington, DC.
23. Seth Borenstein (15 June 2012). *Don't Worry Much about Quakes and Fracking.* http://finance.yahoo.com/news/report-dont-worry -much-quakes-fracking-170610770.html
24. Ibid.
25. Robert W. Chase (2012). Five myths about "fracking". *Akron Beacon Journal*, 26 January. http://www.ohio.com/editorial /robert-w-chase-five-myths-about-fracking-1.257129
26. Ibid.

27. Chesapeake CEO.
28. Goldman Sachs UBS.
29. US Energy Information Administration.
30. Consensus estimates from Bloomberg.
31. http://www.businessweek.com/news/2012-10-23/fracking -will-support-1-dot-7-million-jobs-study-shows
32. US Energy Information Administration.
33. Carol Reyes Avila (21 August 2013). *The Shale Revolution and Emerging Markets.* http://blogs.law.harvard.edu/carolblenda/2013 /08/21/78/
34. *Making the Green Journey Work. Optimised pathways to reach 2050 abatement targets with lower costs and improved feasibility.* http://www.centrica.com/files/pdf/making_the_green_journey _work.pdf
35. http://www.felj.org/sites/default/files/docs/elj321/18_145_shale _gas_in_poland.pdf
36. US Energy Information Administration.
37. US Energy Information Administration.
38. US Energy Information Administration.
39. http://en.ndrc.gov.cn/
40. China resources ministry, May 2012.
41. US Energy Information Administration.
42. M.L. Aucott and J.M. Melillo (2013). A preliminary energy return on investment analysis of natural gas from the Marcellus Shale. *Journal of Industrial Ecology*, 17, 668–679.

CHAPTER SEVEN

FLATTENER #4 –
THE ENERGY BROADBAND

Buying a lettuce gives me the right, but not the obligation, to make myself a salad.

Professor Graham Davies

The energy world is responding to the price signals and incentives, the game changers – shale gas and tight oil – and the ongoing pressures from geopolitics and other market forces, creating what I call the "energy broadband".

The energy broadband is a large network of oil and gas storage, pipelines, LNG liquefaction and regasification plants, shipping, and logistical infrastructure that is literally "wiring" the energy world, just like fibre optics and cable wired the oceans and continents during the internet revolution.

But, as was the case with the dotcom bubble, overly optimistic demand expectations can result in overvaluations and overcapacity, so that when the bubble bursts, excess capacity means cheaper prices to consumers, and flattens the world in the process.

The energy broadband is being developed fast and across multiple dimensions.

The network of assets gives optionality (the right, but not the obligation) to all its users. It gives choice. It flattens the world.

Pipelines open new markets

During my trips to the Middle East and North Africa, I visited pipeline facilities that were closely guarded by military troops. From Northern Iraq, to Libya, to Egypt, everyone understood the importance of a well-protected network.

"It is a very well-paid job", a friend of mine told me as we saw the tanks and army personnel protecting the infrastructure in the Sinai peninsula. "The pipelines are guarded 24/7 by the best of the best. Nothing can go wrong".

Yes, these pipelines are simply too important to go wrong, which is precisely the reason why the system tends to build overcapacity and alternative routes. Both are flatteners.

And pipelines are important because they connect markets.

I also remember those western classic movies that tell the story of how the US railway system was built, and the change that the "iron horse" brought to the country. Indeed, the railway boom that took place from the 1830s to the 1870s in North America was perhaps one of the most important developments that allowed the expansion of the then "emerging market" of the United States of America. Railroads opened up remote areas, drastically cut the cost of freight and passenger travel, and stimulated new industries such as steel and telegraphy. Yet another case where "volume creates volume".

Similarly, in the oil and gas market, the development of pipelines helped connect producers, with refiners, and consumers. As of today, according to data from the Central Intelligence Agency, there are over 2.5 million miles[1] of oil and gas lines across the United States, enough to circle the Earth 100 times, making North America the most developed network of oil and gas pipelines in the world. Other countries and regions are aggressively building their networks too, connecting producing and importing hubs across key consuming and producing regions such as Russia and China.

For natural gas, the large majority of the global trade is already via pipeline. Most of Russia's gas exported to the European markets and China is via pipeline. As of today, LNG is still a small part of the global gas trade.

For crude oil, the share of seaborne oil is larger, with the Middle East exporting the large majority of its crude via oil tankers.

Pipelines are very capital- and time-intensive investments

However, pipelines are very expensive and can take many years to be completed. Look at Nord Stream, for example, it cost $7.4 billion for 1224 kilometres and an estimated six years to complete.[2]

Both cost and time are barriers of entry to the construction. Furthermore, despite the economic incentives, many pipelines are delayed because of environmental issues. Look at Keystone XL for example.[3]

But, once built, a pipeline is the cheapest way to transport gas. Variable costs due to, for example, compression are minor, relative to the cost of shipping gas that is. Using Nord Stream as an example, again, it is a saving of €60 million compared to other means of gas transport.

And once there is overcapacity, the competition can be fierce. So pipelines, like many other energy assets, tend to be built on long-term supply contracts that secure the off-take and financing.

It is interesting to note that the industry is also "reversing" the flow of existing pipelines to adapt to the changing dynamics.

Although it is not as easy as it sounds, reversing the direction of a pipeline is significantly cheaper and faster than building new pipelines. In the case of Cushing, for example, some pipelines were originally built to source imported crude into the ports of Texas to feed refineries inland, but with the development of incremental capacity in Canada and domestic tight shale oil, there was less need for imports and instead the refineries in the South have a strong preference for more reliable and cheaper feedstock.

The network of pipelines is also increasingly interconnected through trading hubs, which facilitate the redistribution of gas and reduce bottlenecks.

The Eurasian continental network

Russia is one of the top oil and gas producers and exporters in the world. Its commodity exports represent about half of the Russian government's revenue, by far its largest source.

Historically Russia has relied on Europe as its primary customer, but its strategic focus has shifted towards the East over the past few years and it is already a notable trading partner. In the mid-2000s Asia represented just 4% of Russia's energy exports. Today it is more than 17%, with a target of 30% within the next two years.

To achieve this expansion, Russia has aggressively invested in both railways and pipelines to the Pacific coast and the Chinese border. The greater growth has been via pipelines, following the completion of the Eastern Siberia-Pacific Ocean pipeline. Combined, the new projects increased Russia's export capacity to Asia from 0.5 to 2.1 million barrels per day.[4]

Russia understands the importance of being a "first mover" and developing infrastructure and strategic relationships with the Asian buyers. As it expands and diversifies its client base, Russia may also deter the entry of competitors.

But China is also expanding its options with oil, pipeline gas, and LNG from a wide range of sources. China is also importing crude oil from Kazakhstan, with a target of 1.5 million barrels per day from the massive Kashagan Field.[5] It also imports half of its natural gas needs from Turkmenistan,[6] and has also agreed to import up to 10 billion cubic metres of natural gas from Uzbekistan.[7] All these imports add to the increase in domestic production, as China is developing the Xinjiang region into a resource base for newly industrializing provinces in the Chinese interior.

LNG and the globalization of natural gas

Under standard temperature and pressure conditions, methane is in its gaseous state. But when compressed and frozen to −260°F it becomes a liquid with a volume of just 1/600 of what it occupies in its gaseous state, which allows it to be transported using appropriate equipment for very long distances.

LNG liquefaction, shipping, and regasification plants are extremely expensive, complex, and time-intensive.

Why would anyone build spare liquefaction capacity without a guaranteed off-take? Historically, this is precisely the reason why producers entered into long-term contracts of 30 years, on a "take or pay" basis (if the gas buyers no longer wanted the gas, they would still have to pay for it). So, the liquefaction and regasification capacity were largely matched, with limited amounts of spare capacity in the system.

But the shale gas revolution in North America changed this dynamic. Following the energy shortages of the 1970s, the United States developed regasification plants to import gas from different parts of the world, including the Middle East.

As a real option, LNG regasification capacity provides the right, but not the obligation, to buy LNG from the international markets, regasify it, and sell it in the domestic markets. But, if domestic prices are lower than international prices, the consumers can resell the LNG cargoes, let the regasification plant go idle, and buy the gas domestically. This process has effectively freed up LNG cargoes, which have been snapped up by Asia.

Furthermore, producers around the world are responding to the incentives of high prices and optimistic demand expectations.

Look at Australia, which, as discussed, are investing over $500 billion[8] in new LNG liquefaction capacity, as they look to develop and export the large natural gas reserves, taking advantage of its geographical proximity to the North East Asian markets. And Australia is not alone. There are many large expansion plans all over the world looking to export to Asia via LNG.

The expansions are based on what is generally perceived as "Asia has unlimited demand for natural gas, and at unlimited price". Neither is true.

Investing without the security of demand or the security of fixed prices can be lethal, especially when consumers are also investing and creating overcapacity at their end.

From regional to global

Historically, natural gas prices have been regional, dominated by three largely independent consuming regions: Asia, Europe, and North America.

Despite being exactly the same molecules, the price of natural gas at the Henry Hub (HH) in the United States moved totally independently from prices at the National Balancing Point (NBP) in the UK, or imported gas in the Japan Korea Marker (JKM).

Many investors have tried to "arbitrage" the differential in prices, but with very little success. I remember in 2012, when HH was trading at $2/MMBtu and NBP at the equivalent of $8/MMBtu. Those who bought HH and sold NBP expecting the differential to narrow ended up losing money, as the differential continued to widen.

There are many reasons why prices have remained dislocated, from legal and regulatory restrictions in North America all the way to logistical constraints, but LNG is the "glue" that will eventually bring these markets together.

LNG super-cycle

The global LNG market is responding to the price incentives created by Fukushima, shale gas, and the geopolitical tensions between Russia and Ukraine.

There is a good degree of visibility on the capacity additions and start of operations.

By 2017, the global LNG market will experience a wave of new export capacity equivalent to 32% of currently traded LNG volumes. The increased volumes will have to be absorbed by the market, possibly by displacing other alternative fuels, and creating some deflationary pressures across energy markets.

By 2020, the global LNG market is likely to see a second wave of export capacity. Some of the projects might be at risk if prices were to correct sharply, but the commitments to Yamal LNG in Russia and the contract and regulatory progress made by the Lake Charles liquefaction project in Louisiana support the view of additional supply to the market.

The winners and losers of the big asset write-off

Altogether, the incremental competition across domestic production, pipeline gas, LNG gas, and storage, has the potential to tilt the balance of power towards the consumers into a "buyers' market".

As discussed, the large capex acts as a barrier to entry. But once built, plants act as a barrier to exit. And given the nature of the cost structure, liquefaction plants will continue to operate as long as they can cover their variable marginal cost of production, potentially resulting in very low LNG prices.

Once again, the biggest winners of the overcapacity will be the consumers, who will have access to abundant and cheap energy.

Solid methane

In addition to liquid and gas, methane can also be exported indirectly in the form of goods and services.

Petrochemicals and fertilizers, both very natural gas intensive, are good examples where the shale gas revolution has resulted in "re-shoring" these industries back to the United States.

Electricity prices are a key driver of industrial activity and competitiveness across countries. Once again, the United States has enjoyed the benefits of cheaper and abundant natural gas through lower bills for consumers and industrial users.

In the United States, the "energy disinflation" is a strong stimulus for the economy, and has been a key contributor to the recovery and outperformance of the US economy.

Japan, in stark contrast to the United States, following Fukushima, suffered a "double whammy" via lower supplies of nuclear power generation and higher LNG prices, both deteriorating the industrial competitiveness of the country.

Storage bottlenecks and commodity islands

A man is only as faithful as his options.

Chris Rock

There's not much compensation, When everything's been stained, some have sentimental value that cannot be erased, Go store it in a cool dry place.

Traveling Wilburys

Storage capacity is another key component of the energy broadband.

Unlike other asset classes, we cannot "print" commodities, and therefore the role of storage and inventories is critical to help balance the market in the short run.

During periods when consumption is greater than production, the market will draw from the inventories. In an extreme situation when the market runs out of inventory, prices and volatility will increase, incentivizing demand destruction and substitution.

On the other hand, during periods when production is greater than consumption, the excess supply will be accumulated as inventory, subject to storage capacity constraints. In an extreme situation when the market runs out of storage capacity, prices will collapse and volatility will increase, incentivizing supply destruction and substitution demand.

It is during these times, when there is too much of any commodity, that owning storage capacity can be very lucrative. The owner of the storage can buy at a steep discount, store it, and sell it at a future date via futures at a guaranteed return, capturing the contango.

As such, storage capacity can be viewed as a real option, where the buyer has the right, but not the obligation, to store a given commodity. The "premium" of storage is the cost to buy or rent the land and deposits. The "strike price" at which the option is exercised are the variable costs, including financing and insurance. The return depends on the ability to lock-in returns through what is known as a "cash and carry" trade.

In 2013, the supply of oil *into* Cushing (the delivery point for West Texas Intermediate (WTI) crude oil) that was coming from Canada substantially exceeded the local demand from refineries. Cushing had limited pipeline capacity to transport the crude oil to other regions further south. And as a result, the excess crude oil had to be stored. As the market approached full storage, extreme discounts were reached.[9] Those players with available storage capacity could buy WTI crude oil for immediate delivery and sell at a steep discount for a guaranteed steep return. Storage owners were making a fortune.

But the market defends itself. The large demand for storage resulted in a major wave of investment in new storage and

Cushing capacity grew significantly. Furthermore, new pipeline capacity was built to send crude out of Cushing to other locations. So at one point, once the market was in overcapacity, the income from storage collapsed.

Looking forward, as the domestic production in North America continues to grow and the restrictions to export crude oil remain in place, the risk of full storage across Cushing and the Gulf will be a reality. It is quite likely that the super contango and super-economic returns for storage owners will return, in yet another wave of the boom and bust cycle.

The high watermark and volatility dampeners

The 1973 oil crisis came as a surprise, and proved very costly.

The second oil shock in 1979 was somewhat expected, but even then it was very costly.

These crises were much larger than anyone had anticipated or was prepared for, but they set up a new "watermark" for potential disruptions.

Consumers defended themselves and took aggressive steps to protect against similar *extreme* circumstances. Aggressive exploration, diversification of supply, strategic petroleum reserves, new and alternative fuels, conservation and efficiency policies, and even biofuels, all looking to protect against new extreme events.

What the high watermark means is that the world can cope much better with *normal* shocks, as it is better prepared for *extreme* shocks. Just like the protective walls at nuclear plants will be at least twice as high as prior to Fukushima, it will take a much larger tsunami to pass above them.

The high watermark is a very "deflationary" force that also dampens volatility as it reduces the risk and magnitude of potential price spikes.

Global strategic petroleum reserves

One of the "first lines of defence" that consumers built in the 1970s was strategic reserves. And "the bigger the consumer, the bigger the reserves", and so the Strategic Petroleum Reserve (SPR) was born, which holds up to 90 days of demand in storage.

Over the past 15 years, the US SPR has completed three emergency releases. The most recent one during the Arab Spring in 2011.

But looking forward, given the growth in domestic production and the lower need of imports, it is possible that the United States may not need to hold such a large strategic reserve in the future. And if it does, as the imports effectively converge towards zero as the United States becomes energy independent, they will effectively protect against a very long period of time.

It will be interesting to see if the United States looks to reduce the size of the stockpile.

Shipping, floating pipelines and storage

> *How do you become a millionaire? You start as a billionaire and then you buy an airline.*
>
> Richard Branson

The boom and bust of shipping

The reason I have identified shipping as a key flattener is because of its potential to create bottlenecks in the energy broadband.

Economic history shows us that industries that have suffered long periods of overcapacity and low returns tend to be among the most explosive when things turn around. They are the perfect candidates for a surprise, as was the case in the super-cycle of dry freight.

The market differentiates between different types of ships depending on the type of commodities they can carry, and the size of the ship. "Dry freight" refers to shipping bulk commodities, such as coal, iron ore, and grain. The main benchmark is the Baltic Dry Index (BDI). "Wet freight" refers to tankers that carry mainly crude oil and clean products. LNG carriers are specially designed to transport liquefied natural gas.

The BDI, after averaging the 1000 value for over 20 years, showed there was little incentive to investment in new dry bulk shipping capacity. But by 2003, relentless growth in demand from China and emerging markets forced prices to spike above 6000[10] in order to destroy enough demand and balance the market. The very high prices provided the signal and incentives to build new supply, which did not take long to respond, and after an extremely volatile 18-month period, new shipping capacity started to hit the market.

During the winter of 2006 I had the opportunity to visit Stavanger, in Norway, as part of a detailed visit to the main deep-water oil fields and their service industry. Towards the end of the trip, I had the pleasure to meet in person the owner of one of the largest shipyards in the world. It was a freezing day, at least for me. I was wearing so many layers of clothes I felt like an onion (while, of course, he was wearing a T-shirt). The head engineer showed us the impressive facilities and praised the benefits of technology and their top personnel. But when I asked about Korea, the smiles on their faces suddenly turned to frowns. I could feel that the previous 20 years of depressed prices and overcapacity had left some painful scars that were very fresh in their memories. Competition from other shipyards and the flattening force of overcapacity were very real and could send vessel prices much lower and tighten financing conditions, within the blink of an eye. They had seen it before. But at that time the order book was as busy as ever. Day-rates continued to make new highs, although within extreme volatility, like only freight and power traders know. The stage was set for another big move.

And so, by 2007 the market had absorbed all the new capacity and prices spiked towards new historically high prices of

12,000,[11] twice the previous peak and 12 times the average price. The supply response was phenomenal. And then Lehman Brothers happened. As is often the case, the wave of new supply came at the worst time, when demand had completely dried up. Prices collapsed.

At the end of 2013, the BDI was back towards a 1000 average.[12] A full circle. In 2014 the index continued its way down to fresh lows as weak global trade growth and capacity surplus continued.

Shipping rates have the potential to be extremely volatile, which is the reason why the norm for the market is oversupply.

Debottlenecking and super-backwardation

The way down can potentially be as volatile as the way up.

One of the main questions is "How long will it take for new capacity to hit the market?"

The answer for each commodity is different.

Back in 2003, our initial estimation for dry freight to respond was 18 months – so relatively fast. For other commodities the time lag of the supply response could be much longer. For example, new oil refineries could take between two and three years, new copper mines could take three to five years, and new crude oil from brownfields might take seven to ten years or more.

One other main debate was about the "new long-term equilibrium price".

The argument was that the BDI would find equilibrium at a "new normal" level, which would reflect the higher cost of the raw materials and other aspects of inflation. Just thinking about the idea that the BDI could return to the 1000 level, where it had spent 20 years, gave goose bumps to the ship-owners.

But similar to a spring that is compressed, the greater the price incentive, the greater the supply response.

Add leverage to the mix, and then the downward spiral can be as scary as on the way up.

And so, as of writing, the BDI has indeed reverted to those terrifying levels, highlighting once more the sheer deflationary power of overcapacity.

NOTES

1. CIA Central Intelligence Agency. *The World Factbook.* https://www.cia.gov/library/publications/the-world-factbook/geos/us.html

2. *Secure Energy for Europe: The Nord Stream Pipeline Project.* http://www.nord-stream.com/

3. *Keystone XL Pipeline.* http://keystone-xl.com/

4. US Energy Information Administration. http://www.eia.gov/countries/cab.cfm?fips=ch

5. *China Buys into Giant Kazakh Oilfield for $5 bln.* http://www.reuters.com/article/2013/09/07/oil-kashagan-china-idUSL5N0H302E20130907

6. *BP Statistical Review of World Energy – June 2013.* http://www.bp.com/content/dam/bp/pdf/statistical-review/statistical_review_of_world_energy_2013.pdf

7. CNPC.

8. Goldman Sachs. *360 Projects to Change the World.* http://www.docstoc.com/docs/119164686/Goldman-Sachs---360-projects-to-change-the-world

9. Bloomberg and NARECO analysis.

10. http://www.bloomberg.com/quote/BDIY:IND

11. Ibid.

12. Ibid.

CHAPTER EIGHT

FLATTENER #5 – OVERCAPACITY

With my sunglasses on I'm Jack Nicholson; without them, I'm fat and 60.

Jack Nicholson

Crude oil in its raw form, as it appears in nature, is not very useful.

Refineries play a key role and convert *useless* crude oil into *useful* refined products such as gasoline, diesel, and jet fuel. Refineries buy crude oil, process it, and sell a basket of refined products to capture the "refinery margin".

The most complex refineries have the ability and flexibility to optimize the output and today we can generate greater volumes of cleaner products than we did before.

But neither the refiners nor the consumers have benefited in economic terms. Due to the structural overcapacity of the industry, it has been the producers and the governments of the consumer nations who have, for the most part, captured the economic returns.

And the refiners have no one to blame but themselves.

Déjà-Vu

In 1995, the oil company I was working for decided to expand its refining operations. At that time, global overcapacity exceeded 7 million barrels per day,[1] but our senior management had a "long-term view" of the sector. I visited several refineries across Europe looking for suitable assets to buy, and we even considered building a new one in China (until we saw the requirements of the Chinese government, including the minimum number of workers, minimum output, suppliers to be approved, just to name a few). In the end, we didn't buy or build any new refineries, but all the estimates from research houses, brokers, consultants, and industry experts estimated that the overcapacity in refining would be fully absorbed by demand before 2000.

In 2013, during a visit to some of the key oil-producing and refinery assets across Latin America, I gazed through some research notes and found an interesting sentence. "Global refining overcapacity stands around 7 million barrels per day. However, we estimate that this will be fully absorbed by demand growth by 2020". I put the iPod on and listened to "Déjà vu" by Crosby, Stills, Nash & Young.

In addition to suffering from long periods of overcapacity, refiners have also suffered the squeeze between producers (who limit production) and consumers (who set the price they are able and willing to pay).

The "revenge of the old economy" was particularly acute in refining. The surge in demand from emerging markets surpassed the most optimistic forecasts, and refining bottlenecks played a key role in the run up towards $140+/bbl in 2008.

For the first time in decades, refining was in charge and OPEC was on the back foot.

Unfortunately for the refiners the party did not last long, and new refining and upgrading capacity responded quickly to the incentives of high refinery margins.

Since then, refining has become a tail of two regions, with North American refiners enjoying the benefits of cheap domestic landlocked crude oil, while the European and Asian refiners are suffering more than ever from overcapacity and the squeeze between producers and consumers.

Diplomatic demand outlook

The rolling optimistic mindset of the industry, by which "demand will absorb the overcapacity within x years in the near future" is perhaps partially to blame, but there are other flatteners and deflationary forces that have played an important part too.

Historically, some of the largest refineries in the world were located within the producing countries themselves, who would then export the refined products to the consumers.

Consumers, on the other hand, have their own incentives to build capacity at home, partially as a way to protect themselves against the risk of supply shocks.

Whatever the rationale, the fact is the growth in capacity across both producers and consumers has contributed to the rolling structural overcapacity.

Saudi Arabia heavy sour crude oil

Saudi Arabia produces "heavy sour" crude oil. The term "heavy" means that distillation would yield larger quantities of residual fuel oil and "sour" means it contains sulphur, which if not removed could create acid rain. WTI and Brent are "light sweet" crudes, yielding larger quantities of cleaner products, such as gasoline, diesel, and kerosene.[2]

During the 1980s and 1990s, crude oil prices were anchored around $20/bbl, subject to the cyclical ups and downs, and the supply and demand shocks of 1991 and 1998, but were overall quite stable, helped by Saudi Arabia and OPEC.

But in 2002 crude oil prices started to move up, slowly but steadily. By 2006, the price was $60/bbl, and the super-cycle was evident in other commodities. There was no shortage of physical crude oil, but the spare refining capacity was tightening up, while politicians were blaming the apparent disconnect between prices and supply and demand on the speculators.

I was on the trading floor in London when the news came out. "Saudi is cutting production by 500,000 barrels per day". The news came as a shock to many people. While production cuts to support the price were nothing new, this cut was happening in a rising market. What was going on? Saudi's oil minister Al-Naimi had openly said that crude oil prices were too high, and disconnected from the supply and demand reality. Wouldn't a cut send prices even higher?

OPEC had lost control of the market.

For the first time in decades, the refiners were in control.

Saudi's heavy sour crude oil was closer to fuel oil than to WTI or Brent. And for months, the inventory of fuel oil had been increasing. The fuel oil forward curve was by then in super-contango, reflecting the glut in the physical markets. The world needed more clean products, not more fuel oil.

But the refineries at that time were not ready to convert the large amount of Saudi crude into clean products without creating a large residual amount of fuel oil that no one wanted.

As a result, Saudi was forced to cut the production of its heavy sour crude to try to stabilize the price of the fuel oil market, and with it the price of the sour heavy crude. Yes, Saudi Arabia was acting in its own self-interest. Anyone surprised?

Saudi's cuts managed to stabilize the fuel oil market, but tightened the market of light clean products even further, and the light sweet crudes started an unstoppable run towards $140/bbl. Producers were enjoying the ride, particularly the high-cost producers such as the Canadian oil sands.

And the refiners were having the time of their lives. While WTI was trading at \$140/bbl, the prices of the middle distillates such as jet fuel were trading above \$200/bbl.[3]

These refineries were buying sour heavy crude at a steep discount, turning it into light clean products and were making a fortune.

And then Lehman Brothers happened.

The super-economic returns had already triggered a wave of investing in new refinery capacity, particularly "upgrading capacity", which has dramatically reduced the spread between light and heavy crudes. Refining is a very capital-intensive business. New assets are expensive to build, but once they are built, their average life is around 30 years.

Not good news for the refiners, who in addition to the structural overcapacity, have historically been squeezed between the oligopolistic producers and the price-sensitive consumers.

Location, location, location

The location of refineries has turned out to be a major driver in the profitability of refiners.

In North America, the surge in domestic production, combined with the regulatory restrictions to export crude oil, have dramatically widened refinery margins and enhanced profitability. The bottlenecks in Cushing we discussed in the previous chapter, allowed refiners in the region to buy crude oil at much discounted levels, which they could convert into higher valued refined products. North American refiners are enjoying a period of bonanza, but at the expense of the North American producers and consumers.[4]

In Europe and Asia, on the other hand, refiners are struggling. The price of Brent and other relevant crude oils has remained at a high premium, as the overcapacity in the sector has led to extreme competition and lower margins. Outside of

North America, the producers continue to enjoy a period of bonanza, much at the expense of the refiners and consumers.[5]

Pro-cyclical behaviour

The overcapacity is also a result of the pro-cyclical nature of the energy industry, which is particularly evident in the refining and power generation sectors. The structural optimism of demand growth has resulted in structural overcapacity and, alongside, declining profitability. "The industry always invests in the incorrect belief that no one else is going to do what they are doing", a seasoned colleague once told me. How true.

NOTES

1. Consensus estimate of global productive capacity versus demand.
2. *Crude Oil Grades and Types*. http://www.intertek.com/petroleum /crude-oil-types/
3. *Oil Prices, Industry News and Analysis*. http://www.platts.com /commodity/oil
4. Ben Lefebvre (2014). Shale-oil boom spurs refining binge. *Wall Street Journal*, 2 March. http://online.wsj.com/news/articles/SB10 001424052702303874504579376962979450296
5. Claira Lloyd (21 February 2014). *European Refining to Remain Uncompetitive*. http://www.energyglobal.com/news/processing /articles/European_refining_remain_uncompetitive178.aspx #.U4MEbfmSx8E

CHAPTER NINE

FLATTENER #6 – GLOBALIZATION, INDUSTRIALIZATION, AND URBANIZATION

Arguing against globalization is like arguing against the laws of gravity.

Kofi Annan

I remember my first trip to China as if it was yesterday. I was in my early twenties, living and working in London at the time, and starting to travel for business on a regular basis. It was easy to fall into the routine of the flight, work a bit, watch a movie, have a glass of wine, and sleep as much as possible, but this trip was special. I remember thinking to myself "in 10 hours I will be the first member in my family to ever set foot in China". I had a sense of pride and responsibility, and kept thinking about my parents, their parents, and their parents' parents, and how proud they were that I was able to see parts of the world that they would probably never see with their own eyes.

Ten hours on a plane can be a long time, but for me, that day, it was not enough. As we cruised, I kept reminding myself that the same journey would have taken me ten days by train and several weeks by boat. I thought of Marco Polo, on his horse, and about his trips to China in the thirteenth century. The adventure of visiting remote cultures, the extraordinary physical effort subject to the inclemency of the weather, and the dangers of the unknown. But there I was, comfortably sitting on a warm plane, watching the freezing Russian steppes underneath, just a few hours away from Beijing's airport where a car would be waiting to take me to a luxury hotel downtown. It was easy to lose perspective of how air transportation had "shrunk" the world. In my firm, flying in the "red eye" overnight flight from London to Beijing, New York, or Johannesburg, and back the night after was pretty common. That's globalization for you.

But this time I forced myself to make it different. I wanted to make sure I kept the perspective of what was happening. I spent a good part of the trip reading about China and peeping through the window, mesmerized by the vastness of the plains and mountain chains as we flew across Eastern Europe, Russia, Kazakhstan, Mongolia, and finally China. The "world is almost empty" I remember thinking to myself. With the exception of a few scattered cities along the way, the landscape was largely bare. "Who knows how much oil, gas, and coal is waiting for us below those fields", I thought. The world just felt small as we spent our lives going from crowded "point A" to crowded "point B" without the full appreciation of the dimensions, but the world was not that small nor full after all.

So, there I was, caught between the perspective of a small and crowded world and the perspective of a large and empty world, thanks to air travel and globalization.

And then we landed. I was in China. Finally. But the excitement quickly gave way to the crude reality. The strong smell and pollution hit me first. Then, the thousands and thousands of bicycles, buses and cars stuck in endless heavy traffic as far as my eyes could see in all directions. Not the idyllic postcard I was hoping to describe to my grandfather over the phone.

The empty world I saw from the plane seemed very distant now. Beijing had about 15 million inhabitants by then, and reached 21 million by 2014 according to UN data.[1]

In March 2014, the Chinese government announced its intention move 100 million[2] people from the rural areas to cities within the next seven years. Currently, about 54% of China lives in cities, compared with 80% in developed countries and roughly 60% in other developing countries with similar per capita income levels as China. The "National New-type Urbanization Plan" aims to bring China closer to 60% by 2020[3] through the massive build-out of transport networks, urban infrastructure, and residential real estate under the government promise of make China's urbanization more "human-centred and environmentally friendly".

These trends of globalization, industrialization, and urbanization point towards ever-increasing demand from China, and supply is expected and set to respond to the expectations of demand growth. But there is room for disappointment.

Testing the hypothesis of "Ever-Increasing" demand

There seems to be an unconscious bias in our brains that points towards "ever-increasing population", "ever-increasing energy demand", and "ever-increasing pollution", with fatalistic conclusions to the world. None of which is necessarily true.

Let's start with the main demographic trends.

Demographic trend #1. The global population is growing, but at a slower pace

According to the United Nations, by 1900, the world population was around 1.7 billion people. Before then, population growth had been slow. The age structure of the population was broadly constant, and very few people lived beyond age 65.[4]

During the first half of the twentieth century, rising life expectancy boosted population growth. By 1950, the population of the world was 2.56 billion.[5] But during the second half of the twentieth century fertility rates declined dramatically, by almost one-half, causing population growth to slow down and the share of the elderly to increase.

By 2013, the world population had surpassed 7 billion people, and is expected to grow towards 9 billion by 2050 and towards 11 billion by 2100.[6] These are just predictions, they do show that the population is growing but at a slower rate of growth, from current 1.25% pa towards 0.25% pa.

Furthermore, over the next 50 years, the population of some countries/regions is expected to decline by as much as 30% in Central and Eastern Europe, 22% in Italy, and 14% in Japan.

On average, the world population is therefore expected to continue to grow, but at a slower pace.

Demographic trend #2. The age structure is changing

Another major development in global demographics is that the age structure, the "population pyramid", is changing.

On average, the global population is getting older. The share of elderly people is increasing, although this changes markedly across different regions.

This trend is important as it is expected to pose challenges to the global economy in the form of slower economic growth, and difficulties in funding pension and health care systems.

And it also poses the question of how it will impact energy consumption as different age groups and regions have obvious different consumption patterns.

Population growth vs. economic growth vs. energy demand growth

Economic growth is closely related to demographics, but the relationship between the rates of population growth and economic growth has been the subject of debate for centuries.

In 1798, Thomas Malthus, in his *Essay on the Principle of Population*, argued that "the rate of population growth was held in equilibrium by the pace of economic growth."[7] Yet, today's dynamics seem to be the exact reverse. As economic prosperity has risen around the world, fertility rates have fallen, life expectancy has increased, resulting in slower population growth and aging.

Beyond past trends, the key question becomes "how energy intensive will economic growth be in the future?" The recent trends indicate that, on average, economic growth is becoming less energy intensive. Although, yet again, the energy intensity shows significant divergences across regions, as developing economies are more energy and commodity intensive than the developed world.

As the developed markets become less energy intensive, their share of global demand will continue to decrease. For example, as of today, North Americans are just 5% of the world's population but consume 24% of the world's energy.[8] Clearly unsustainable.

In terms of economic growth, the International Monetary Fund (IMF) estimates the world's real GDP will rise by an average of 411% (that is, 3.6% pa) from 2010 to 2040, with a polarized regional pattern, with 4.7% pa outside the OECD, and 2.1% within the OECD.[9]

In terms of energy demand growth, the IEA estimates that world energy consumption will grow by 56% (that is 1.1% pa) between the same period 2010 and 2040, also with a polarized regional pattern, with 90% growth outside of the OECD and 17% increase within the OECD. By 2040, China's energy consumption will be twice the United States and four times that of India.[10]

At this stage it is important to differentiate the source of energy demand. And we tend to differentiate between two major categories. On the one hand, power generation and industrial demand. And on the other hand, transportation demand. These sectors are today very fragmented, but will become more equalized and interrelated in a flatter energy world. We will discuss these very important trends extensively throughout this chapter and the rest of the book.

Comparing the estimates from the UN for population growth, the IMF for economic growth, and the IEA for demand growth, it seems as if a global population growth of 0.7% pa may be able to generate economic growth in real GDP terms of 3.6% pa, while increasing energy consumption by 1.5% pa.[11]

These trends are consistent with the work from Laherrere, who claims that world oil consumption and production per capita peaked in 1979.[12]

The "Diplomatic" demand clause

As discussed, official demand estimates tend to be "diplomatic".

For example, the IEA demand forecasts are based on GDP estimates of the countries themselves, which tend to have a bias towards being "too optimistic" in their economic growth. Which country would "shoot itself" in the foot with overly negative outlooks that may impact consumption and investment?

Anyone involved in forecasting knows how difficult it is to predict so far in the future. The longer term the prediction, the greater the room for error. Small changes in key variables can have a compounding effect. Predicting global population growth, economic activity, and energy consumption is an extremely difficult challenge, and very sensitive to key variables such as fertility and mortality.

Forecasts are necessary, but we need to be realistic about their limitations. That's why I am not looking to forecast future prices, but rather focus on the forces at play, the likely direction of the impact, and the interrelationship between them through "virtuous", "vicious", and "mean reverting" processes.

NOTES

1. Central Intelligence Agency (2014). *The World Factbook. Major Urban Areas – Population.* https://www.cia.gov/library/publications/the-world-factbook/geos/us.html

2. Li Keqiang (5 March 2014). *Report on the Work of the Government.* Delivered at the Second Session of the Twelfth National People's Congress Speech. http://online.wsj.com/public/resources/documents/2014GovtWorkReport_Eng.pdf

3. Zhu Ningzhu (16 March 2014). *China Unveils Landmark Urbanization Plan.* http://news.xinhuanet.com/english/china/2014-03/16/c_133190495.htm

4. *Graphical View at Evolution of Population by Continent.* http://www.geohive.com/earth/his_history1.aspx

5. Ibid.

6. http://www.un.org/esa/population/publications/longrange2/WorldPop2300final.pdf

7. T.R. Malthus (1798). *An Essay on the Principle of Population.* London: Oxford World's Classics.

8. US Energy Information Administration. http://www.eia.gov/countries/data.cfm

9. IMF *World Economic Growth Report.*

10. International Energy Agency (2012). *Key World Energy Statistics 2010.* http://www.worldenergyoutlook.org/media/weo2010.pdf

11. International Energy Agency (2012). *Key World Energy Statistics 2010.* http://www.worldenergyoutlook.org/media/weo2010.pdf

12. Jean Laherrere (2014). The End of the Peak Oil Myth. http://aspofrance.viabloga.com/files/JL_MITParis2014long.pdf

CHAPTER TEN

FLATTENER #7 – DEMAND DESTRUCTION

There can be economy only where there is efficiency.

Benjamin Disraeli

I grew up in the 1970s. I was too young to remember the first oil shock, but I can recall with great nostalgia those cold winters sitting next to the wood fires. And that, despite our complaints, my parents would only set the electric heating on at night. Electricity prices had skyrocketed, but the main reason why the house felt so cold was the very poor insulation. The windows seemed to whistle when the wind was blowing hard. No matter how high we set the thermostat, the house always seemed to be freezing. Plus the wood fires were more fun.

Today, energy efficiency and conservation are more relevant than ever. Buildings and residential are the largest energy consumers, with nearly 35% share of global energy consumption and much stricter regulation for energy savings is in place today.

Clearly, the path taken in terms of energy efficiency will be critical to the future of power consumption worldwide.

More with less

Efficiency is about doing "more with less". It is about being smarter about how the resources are produced, refined, transported, and consumed.

As discussed, game changers tend to result in "quantum leaps", where technology opens new frontiers and unlocks potential that was known to exist, but was not commercially viable. Game changers are a line in the sand, a "before and after".

On the other hand, efficiency is about "small steps", where technology, experience, and better practices allow us to do more with less.

Efficiency of *demand*, known as *energy conservation*, is perhaps the best known and most obvious one.

Efficiency of *supply*, also known as the *learning curve*, has also had a relentless contribution across all energy sectors, from exploration, production, refining, distribution, and consumption.

Efficiency tends to be dismissed as "too small" and is often missed by the naked eye, but its effect adds up and compounds exponentially.

The demand and supply *learning curves* have been important contributors to demand destruction.

Yes, they are difficult to model, but they simply cannot be ignored.

Therefore, ignoring the impact of efficiency gains (as is often the case with industry forecasts) has a pessimistic bias by construction, which adds to other similar biases such as ignoring the potential of game changers.

How can we try to estimate what the demand will be in 50 or 100 years without careful consideration of efficiency? Impossible. Yet, most analysts and forecasts do. And, given the negative bias, this is yet another reason why demand expectations tend to be overestimated.

Compounded efficiency adds up and has the potential to help win the battle and dramatically impact long-term balances.

Today 1 in 10 barrels of oil produced globally go to US gasoline engines. However, gasoline consumption peaked in the US at c9.3m b/d in 2007, according to UBS.

If the average US car goes from 24mpg to 34mpg then that would cut global oil demand by 3.65 million barrels/day, or around 4%. Indeed, over the long run, the impact of efficiency can be comparable to, if not greater than, any game changer.

The "Invisible Hand" of efficiency

The "invisible hand" of the market (as described by Adam Smith in his book, *The Wealth of Nations*[1]) creates the signals and incentives for efficiency gains, without the intervention of governments or regulation. Demand destruction driven by pure market forces.

The "Visible Hand" of efficiency

The "visible hand" of governments provides incentives and mandates for efficiency gains, by monetizing or imposing efficiency gains through the use of "carrots" and "sticks". Government intervention has been a positive relentless force for energy consumers looking to reduce foreign dependence, conserve resources, and protect the environment.

As we look back in history, efficiency has played a key role.

As we look forward, it is sensible to believe that it will continue to be the case.

NOTE

1. Adam Smith (1776). *An Inquiry into the Nature and Causes of the Wealth of Nations*. London: Methuen.

CHAPTER ELEVEN

FLATTENER #8 – DEMAND DISPLACEMENT

The future is already here. It's just not widely distributed yet.

William Gibson

The battle for transportation demand

As of today, crude oil and OPEC are undisputed leaders in the transportation industry, and very few people believe their monopolies and domination are at risk.

The threat of "outsiders" such as natural gas vehicles, electric cars, hybrids, and fuel cell cars is largely dismissed as "too small", or "there is no viable alternative", or "will take a long time", or simply "it will never happen".

But complacency is dangerous.

And the threat of these "outsiders" is real, and represents an uprising against the monopoly of crude oil and OPEC.

The battleground is transportation.

The timing is now.

I am not saying that crude oil will disappear from the transportation sector. We will certainly continue to drive cars on gasoline and diesel for the foreseeable future.

What I am saying is that the monopoly is at risk, and that it does not take that much displacement to generate a change in prices.

A sustained scenario of "ever-increasing demand", "ever-decreasing supply", and "no competition" is "wishful thinking", and in my view, OPEC is faced with increased competition and will meet difficult choices.

During a road show through the Middle East in the summer of 2013, I had the opportunity to meet a series of senior executives and ultra-high-net-worth individuals. I was presenting some of the early ideas from this book. The discussions were very engaged and, to my great surprise, few people viewed shale gas and tight oil as a threat. Most of them were focused on ambitious expansion plans based on the "status quo" of high oil prices and ever-increasing demand.

But whether you are Nokia, Blackberry, crude oil, or OPEC, complacency can be costly and a lack of awareness of the dangers will make you more vulnerable to the risk of lower volumes at possibly lower prices.

What the production engineers missed

For most production engineers, crude oil prices are all about marginal costs and supply. Demand is taken for granted. The threat of substitution is dismissed as negligible.

But dismissing demand and focusing on the supply side only misses the key dynamics of prices.

First, that prices are set by both supply *and* demand. Yes, marginal cost pressure is important and supports prices over the long run, but if demand is lower than supply, those high marginal cost producers will eventually be taken out of the market.

Second, they assume consumers have no alternatives. That is, they *must* consume crude oil. Here again, refined products have had virtually no competition in transportation demand for decades, but things are changing. Consumers have a choice. And if prices are too high, they will switch and displace demand. Consumers can and will switch away from crude oil into cheaper, greener, and more secure alternatives. It is just a matter of time.

Third, there is a perception that oil producers are in control and can "defend" the price forever. As if lower prices did not hurt them. But this is very far from the truth. Producing countries have become used to high oil prices, which in some cases are used to fund unsustainable and/or lavish programmes.

Look at Venezuela, for example, which runs large subsidies and social programmes backed by oil revenues relying on ever increasing oil prices.[1] A bit like the rogue traders at Barings, Société Générale, or UBS, who were hiding losses and doubling up their bets, hoping for the market to "let them out".[2] But in the case of Venezuela, which has already mortgaged a large portion of its future revenues and massively underinvested in infrastructure, not even high oil prices are likely to save the country. Let alone a collapse in prices.

Or look at much of the Middle East. While the situation is quite different from Venezuela, most countries also run large subsidies and massive social programmes, which are taking an increasingly large share of their revenues. They too are vulnerable to lower prices and volumes through a "double whammy" effect.

As crude oil prices decline, producers are forced to sell greater volumes to maintain their revenues measured in US dollars unchanged. That is, in order to generate $100 million per year, they only need to sell 1 million bbl at $100/bbl, but if prices decline to $50/bbl they need to sell 2 million bbl to generate the same amount of revenue. This process means that the lower prices go, the more volume these countries are forced to sell, which in turn pushes prices lower.

Or take 1986, when Saudi Arabia had been defending the price of crude oil, effectively acting as a "swing producer". Saudi was confident that it could control the market, but the impact of the global recession, demand destruction from power generation, conservation measures in transportation, and new production from the North Sea, meant that the world needed less and less Saudi crude, which saw its production decline from over 10 million bpd to just 2.2 million bpd, and a dramatic reduction in market share. At one point, "enough was enough" and Saudi folded, bringing its large volumes onto the market and effectively pushing prices even lower.

The "Challengers"

Gasoline, diesel, and jet fuel have had little competition from other fuels, but the increased availability of cheap natural gas, electricity, and other alternative fuels is a greater challenge than many give credit for.

Biofuels

In the 1970s, following the oil embargo and high oil prices, consumers around the world focused on alternative sources of domestic fuels.

"Why not feed our cars with corn?" they thought, as the industry enjoyed the strong support of the visible hand of governments and regulation, both through "carrots" like tax rebates, as well as "sticks" such as mandates.

As of today, biofuels currently account for about 3% of the global transportation demand and according to the IEA biofuels could provide 27% of total transport fuel by 2050.

Ethanol is the main biofuel used in transportation. Despite having 32% lower energy content than gasoline, its high octane results in increased engine efficiency and performance.

In the United States, ethanol is mostly produced from corn. Under current US federal regulations, ethanol blends of up to 10% (E10) may be sold for use in all gasoline-powered vehicles, which currently account for about 4% of the US road transportation demand.

In Brazil, ethanol is mostly produced from sugar cane. As of today, over 25% of its road transport fuel runs on biofuels. Flexible fuel vehicles are designed to run on gasoline or a blend of up to 85% ethanol. Currently, Brazil has the highest fleet of flexible-fuel vehicles, where flexible-fuel cars reached a record 94% of total car sales in 2009.

Biodiesel is mostly produced from vegetable oils to fuel diesel engines, and can be used in conventional engines with little or no modification.

Bio jet fuel was approved for commercial use in aviation in July 2011, and provides a cleaner fuel thereby reducing the carbon footprint in the growing air travel sector.

Natural gas
Another challenger fuel is natural gas.

Compressed natural gas (CNG) vehicles are the most common type of natural gas vehicle (NGV), and carry the gas in a pressurized tanks, which enhance both the range and the security. CNG vehicles have been used for public transportation for decades worldwide.

Liquefied natural gas (LNG) vehicles carry the gas in cryogenic tanks in liquid form, which reduce the volume of the gas even further, but require greater upfront and running costs and infrastructure.

According to the US Department of Energy, currently about 12–15% of public transit buses in the United States run on either CNG or LNG. And the number is growing, with nearly one in five buses on order today slated to run on natural gas, largely thanks to environmental considerations.

Bi-fuel engines

In the Latin America region almost 90% of NGVs have bi-fuel engines, allowing these vehicles to run on either gasoline or CNG.

Similarly, in Pakistan, almost every vehicle converted or manufactured for alternative fuel retains the capability to run on ordinary gasoline.

Coal to liquids (CTL) and gas to liquids (GTL)

Converting coal to a liquid (CTL) fuel, also known as coal liquefaction, allows coal to be utilized as an alternative to crude oil, able to produce a range of refined products for transportation and other uses.

South Africa has been producing coal-derived fuels since 1955 and has the only commercial CTL industry in operation today, where CTL fuels are used in cars and other vehicles, and even commercial jets. Currently around 30% of the country's gasoline and diesel needs are produced from indigenous coal.

There are other countries around the world, like China, that rely heavily on oil imports and that have large domestic reserves of coal where CTL could grow. The process is very energy intensive and the economics depend on the access to coal but it can reduce the dependency on crude oil imports.

Technological developments will continue to play a key part, especially in a world where coal may be displaced from the power generation sector and larger amounts of crude coal may be available at cheaper prices, and used for environmentally-friendly solutions such as CTL.

Similarly, gas to liquids (GTL) is a refinery process that allows the conversion of natural gas into gasoline or diesel fuel.

Electric vehicles (EVs) and hybrids (HEVs)

There are three main types of electric vehicle. Those that are directly powered from an external power station; those that are powered by stored electricity originally from an external power source; and those that are powered by an on-board electrical generator.

A hybrid electric vehicle (HEV) combines gasoline and electricity.

Market penetration and EV sales vary significantly among countries. Overall, the market share of EVs and HEVs is 3% of the registered passenger cars globally, but it is growing rapidly, particularly in the cities and led by Japan, the United States, and China.

Air transportation

The aviation industry consumes around 1.5 billion barrels of jet fuel annually. Modern aircraft achieve fuel efficiencies of 3.5 litres per 100 passenger km.

Alternative fuels, particularly sustainable biofuels, have been identified as excellent candidates for helping reduce the carbon footprint of the air industry. Biofuels derived from bio-mass such as algae, jatropha, and camelina have been shown to reduce the carbon footprint of aviation fuel by up to 80% over their full lifecycle.

Sea transportation

The battle for sea transportation is less critical for crude oil, since fuel oil has historically been treated as a residual product.

But due to increasing environmental concerns, low sulphur fuel oil is being enforced sometime in 2015, which can have a significant impact on pricing and may accelerate the use of LNG as a cleaner option for fuel.

The end of crude oil's monopoly in transportation

In my view, the end of the monopoly of crude oil in transportation fuels is not a matter of "if", but "when".

While there is significant inertia in the system to continue to use conventional gasoline and diesel cars, the barriers to entry and exit are being lowered and there are strong incentives in place for a more diverse mix of technologies.

Below are some key considerations that will determine the penetration and speed of the conversion of alternative fuels in transportation, perhaps the greatest battle of all, as far as crude oil is concerned.

#1 Upfront cost

NGVs, EVs, and HEVs are currently more expensive to buy than traditional internal combustion engines (ICE) models, but the price is narrowing due to improvements in technology, economies of scale, aggressive incentives, and tax breaks and rebates.

#2 Running cost

Against the higher upfront cost, alternative fuels in general, and NGVs in particular, are enjoying lower fuel costs taking advantage of low domestic natural gas and electricity prices. Industry studies show that over the long run, all else being equal, the total cost of ownership (upfront plus running cost) is cheaper for NGVs, EVs, and HEVs, than for ICEs.

#3 Range and convenience

ICEs enjoy greater ranges than alternative fuels, but here again technology continues to make progress and the gap is narrowing. The Tesla EVs are now able to do over 200 miles using lithium-ion batteries. NGVs' charging times and range are highly competitive as well.

Interestingly, the assumption is that EVs will be charged mostly at night, when electricity demand is in the "valley" (minimum consumption) level and the price is cheaper. The success of the industry, with say 1 or 2 million cars charging at night, is likely to change the power generation pattern significantly. Yes, another flattener at play!

The "Chicken and Egg" of Refuelling Stations

> Think about it. Go back 20 or 30 years ago. Diesel wasn't very ubiquitous in this country. Forty percent of our gas stations today nationally have diesel in them. If 40 percent of them had a compressed natural gas station, think of the impact that would have in our foreign currency deficits, our trade deficits. The impact it would have on our environment.
>
> DANIEL AKERSON, CHAIRMAN & CEO, GENERAL MOTORS

The lack of fuelling stations has historically hampered NGVs in what seems like a "chicken and egg problem". That is, there are not enough NGVs in circulation to support a full range of stations. And there are not enough stations because people do not buy NGVs. But the number of NGV refuelling stations is growing slowly and steadily and with government support and economic incentives, we may well see a typical "tipping point" situation when we reach enough stations and NGVs for the system to break into a "viral growth" mode for passenger transportation.

Also remember that the largest consumers, such as FedEx and TNT, have their own refuelling stations to support their own fleets, and given long haul trucks which drive very long distances and consume much more fuel than passenger vehicles, the benefits of using cheaper fuels like natural gas are much higher.

Re-fuelling at home

"My home is heated with natural gas. Can I tap into my home system to fuel my vehicle?" The answer is yes. Homeowners with an existing natural gas supply line may be able to purchase a home refuelling system designed to fill their vehicle overnight. Gas from the same supply line that feeds their house is compressed and stored on-board the vehicle by a "vehicle fuelling appliance".

Some of these devices are about the size of an outdoor house air-conditioning unit and the unit is installed outdoors, usually adjacent to your garage. There also is a unit called the Phill that is smaller and can be installed in the garage. The larger (outdoor) vehicle refuelling appliances compress and dispense about 0.9 gasoline-gallon-equivalent per hour. The Phill compresses and dispenses about 0.4 gasoline-gallon-equivalent per hour. For more details, see http://www.impco.ws.

The caveat here is the "oil tax weapon" in the hands of governments, which I will discuss in detail in a later chapter, by which governments are currently hooked to the income they earn in oil taxes and may look to maintain such revenue by taxing other sources of fuel, including your power and natural gas at home. This is a key risk and development to watch.

#4 Performance

There is a myth that alternative fuel vehicles have lower performance than traditional ICEs, but this is not necessarily true, particularly for NGVs. Many of the top sports and high performance car manufacturers have developed or are in the process of developing models that do not compromise on the performance when using an alternative fuel.

#5 Environment and subsidies

If you're a business that needs to transport goods, I'm challenging you to replace your old fleet with a clean energy fleet that's not only good for your bottom

line, but good for our economy, good for our country
and good for our planet.

PRESIDENT BARACK OBAMA

The war on pollution and climate change is also taking
place in the transportation sector. Governments are aggressively
supporting more environmentally friendly alternatives, with an
aspirational goal of "zero emissions" transportation alternatives
such as FCVs.

#6 Safety

There is a myth that NGVs are more dangerous than ICEs, that
is, the tanks of compressed gas can explode. But this is not true,
as supported by extensive industry analysis. Yet, there is much
more work to be done across all the alternative fuels when it
comes down to better scores in crash tests, particularly FCVs.

#7 Security of supply

In the United States, the shale gas revolution has made NGVs
ever more appealing as a way to reduce the dependency on
Middle Eastern oil. And it could be natural gas vehicles or electric cars. The potential displacement across the barrel is huge,
as I will discuss in detail in the following.

The new frontier: hydrogen fuel

During the 2013 Motor Show in Tokyo, Toyota shocked the
transportation world with the announcement of the commercial
launch of a Fuel Cell Vehicle ("FCV").

FCVs are powered by fuel cells, which generate electricity
from hydrogen. They are not only environmentally friendly but
also highly energy-efficient according to Toyota, who by 2015 is
looking to start with a small quantity of costly (between $50,000

and $100,000) to be sold mostly in California, where Toyota says a small chain of hydrogen filling stations will satisfy demand for the fuel.

Historically, the main obstacles to their commercialization have been their size, complexity, and high cost. Another obstacle to practical use of fuel cells (which Toyota says it's solved) has been low temperature, which causes water vapour to freeze, thereby inhibiting the flow of hydrogen.

There are reasons to take Toyota seriously. At the end of the day, they have built a successful track record as a "first mover". During the 1980s they launched the Lexus luxury cars. During the 1990s they launched the Prius, the petrol-electric hybrid. Both initiatives were received with great scepticism and have been major successes. It is particularly noteworthy that despite their lead and dominant position in the hybrid, Toyota is betting for the FCV. They do not only have a high level of conviction, but they also have a strong portfolio of technologies. Whoever wins, they will be there.

"Who killed the electric car?"

The development of alternative fuels and electric in transportation has been delayed relative to their potential . . . But they were not "killed" by the oil companies or energy lobbies. Here is a list of the "murder suspects" that have delayed the pace of development:

#1 Government bail-outs and subsidies

It is ironic (if not cynical) how the governments that on paper were supporting the electrification of transport were the ones who agreed to bail-out the conventional car industry with billions in public funds.

During 2008–2010, the aids given by the EU and US to buy a new car (and reduce the brutal inventory of unsold combustion engine vehicles) exceeded by six to one the amount devoted to electric car developments.

So, as consumers absorbed the large inventory of conventional gasoline and diesel cars in the system through an accelerated fleet renewal, they significantly reduced and delayed the adoption of electric cars for years. Anecdotally, 2010 was the year of highest sales of SUVs since 2006, largely thanks to the incentives and subsidies.

So much for a push towards alternative fuels.

#2 The tax cash cow

Yes, consumer governments are addicted to oil taxes. Based on a report by Ernst and Young on oil and gas tax, the EU collects €250 billion in taxes from petrol and diesel, with taxes on petrol that range between 40% and 65%.

Most people know the price of gasoline in $/litre. Most people also follow the price of crude oil in $/bbl. But very few people think about the price of crude oil in $/litre, which makes it notably cheaper than water.

Are consumer governments able and willing to "kill the goose laying the golden eggs?" Clearly, given the tight finances and high level of direct taxes, many countries will have a serious problem trying to make up such potential loss of tax revenue.

Are consumer governments able to charge similar levels of taxes for alternative fuels such as natural gas and electricity as they do for gasoline and diesel? Well, both natural gas and electricity are available to many households which allows them in principle to "plug and recharge their cars" at home. Any increase in the gas or electric bill would have an impact across the board, not just transport. If the consumer governments transferred the gasoline/diesel tax to electricity, the favourable economics of switching to electric vehicles would be slashed to be virtually non-existent.

#3 The wrong model for the industry?

With the electric car, where the most important obstacles are the upfront cost and the battery life, the industry has made the mistake of replicating exactly the model of the traditional car, where the buyer takes all the technology, battery and maintenance risk for no discernible cost benefit.

Perhaps the electric car industry should learn from its own successes. In the early days, the power generation industry suffered from large inefficiencies and high costs due to the large investments required by the business, the duplication and triplication of efforts around the distribution with several companies laying wires down the same alley, building capacity, and competing head to head to supply the same customer. Prices to the customer would end up higher, not lower. By contrast, because of the efficiency of its investment, a natural monopoly state public utility commission would determine the "fairness" of its rates. The "regulatory bargain" imposed a fundamental responsibility on the natural monopolist – the utility had the obligation to "serve" – to deliver electricity to virtually everyone in its territory and provide acceptable, reliable service at reasonable cost. Otherwise, it would lose its license to operate.

According to UBS, penetration of Electric-Hybrid Vehicles is high in Norway 6.1%, Netherlands 5.6% vs 1.3% for the US, 0.6% for Japan, and just 0.2% for the UK & Germany or 0.1% for China.

If EV and NGVs take just 5% of the US and UK fleet, global oil demand could fall c1%.

The battle for electricity and industrial demand

> *The great menace to the life of an industry is industrial self-complacency.*
>
> Joyce Carol Oates

The case for ever-increasing power generation capacity

Power generation is a long-term and extremely capital-intensive industry, where plants can operate for 60 years or more.

The infrastructure is not just about the power plants. The system requires transmission lines, substations, distribution lines, poles, and wires all the way to the final consumer.

The challenge is how to meet the incremental demand in the most efficient way, since electricity can be generated from many sources, including natural gas, coal, oil, uranium, water, wind, and the sun.

The choice of the fuel mix requires a balanced approach based on diversification, security of supply, economics, and environmental considerations.

As of today, the United States, Europe, and Japan share a similar energy mix, with a somewhat diversified basket dominated by coal, natural gas, nuclear, and renewables.

In the United States, coal represents about 45%; natural gas is second with 23%, but rising; nuclear 20%; hydropower 7%; wind 2%; and oil is currently less than 1%.

In Europe, nuclear, coal, and natural gas represent about 25% each with hydro about 15% and wind and oil close to 3% each.

In Japan, nuclear, coal, and natural gas are close to 27% each. Somewhat surprisingly, crude oil is still 8% while hydro is another 8%, with negligible solar and wind.[3]

The situation is markedly different in emerging markets. China produces 80% of its electricity from coal and 16% from hydro. India produces 69% from coal and 13% from hydro.

Future fuel mix

In the United States, natural gas "ticks all the boxes", as it is available domestically in large volumes and with a much lower carbon footprint than coal.

Coal is clearly abundant and cheap, but its environmental footprint is likely to keep it on the back foot and result in steady loss of market share. It will continue to play a key part, but more from necessity than choice.

In the United States, the Obama administration said it would continue to support nuclear power, and would incorporate lessons learned from accidents into the regulations.

It is the same with France and China. Germany and Italy have a moratorium on new nuclear power, but ironically import nuclear electricity from France. Another example of "yes, but not in my backyard" approach.

And Germany's reaction to Fukushima was dramatic. Three days after the accident, German Chancellor Angela Merkel ordered the closing of seven nuclear power plants, and withdrew her support for life extension for existing plants. "We all want to exit nuclear power as soon as possible and make the switch to supplying via renewable energy",[4] she said. Several weeks later it was official, and the government announced the closing of all the German nuclear plants by 2022.

Alternative and renewable sources of power such as solar, wind, and biomass have strong political support across the world and are already having a dramatic impact in the power generation market.

The most important impact is that of adding a completely new source to the energy mix creating a structural overcapacity in Europe, for example, which has been a major cause for the collapse of wholesale power prices. Global solar power capacity rose by a record 37 GW in 2013[5] as Asian countries installed a number of projects, according to the European Photovoltaic Industry Association. Cumulative installations reached 136.7 GW from about 101 GW in the previous year even as European markets slowed down due to subsidy cuts.

However, the unintended consequence includes a massive increase in tariff costs for consumers due to the upfront excessively generous subsidies, which have overburdened the consumer tariff without benefiting from the subsequent massive reduction in solar and wind unit costs. This situation needs to be changed.

The energy domino

Don't wanna discuss it, Think it's time for a
change, You may get disgusted, start thinkin' that
I'm strange.

Van Morrison

In 2010, one of the largest conventional utilities in Germany presented its view of the power market. It argued that solar and wind would have very little impact on power prices and the market by showing that investors didn't understand the tightness of the market using "peak capacity".

By 2013, German wholesale power prices were at almost half the levels of 2009 and more than 10 billion dollars of write-downs had been accounted for in the traditional utilities' balance sheets.

At the same time, solar manufacturers were also closing production capacity because demand expectations had been simply too optimistic, contributing to the collapse in the cost of solar panels, which has fallen by 75% since the early 2000s.

Demand displacement is the direct result of optionality. All else being equal, consumers will buy the cheapest alternative.

Look at "flexi-engines" in Brazil, for example, designed to run on any proportion of ethanol and gasoline. The consumer has a very simple decision to make at the pump station: buy the cheaper fuel. The engine will do the rest, adjusting as necessary. In this particular example, ethanol and gasoline will displace or substitute each other, thus bringing the market a natural equilibrium. If gasoline is too expensive, people will consume more ethanol, which will tighten the market, and increase prices towards a level of gasoline.

Consumers have more choices and room for permanent substitution than ever. This dynamic acts as a strong rebalancing and flattening force, as demand is created and destroyed in response to prices and volumes.

The substitution has a domino effect, where displacement and cheapening of one energy source will cascade down to the next one, thus resulting in deflationary pressures across the complex.

Natural gas displaces coal in power generation

Combined cycle coal–gas plants can burn either coal or natural gas, somewhat similar to the flexi-fuel engine, but applied to the power generation sector.

As a result, the utilities will switch the demand in favour of the cheapest alternative, with the additional consideration of the cost of carbon permits, if any. As a rule of thumb, natural gas emits approximately one-third of carbon dioxide per unit of power when compared to coal.[6] This makes natural gas a preferred alternative to coal.

In 2012, following the collapse in natural gas prices due to shale gas, large volumes of cheap natural gas became available. The price incentive was so large that utilities started to run their gas-fired production as baseload, instead of reserving for peak demand as was normally the case.

Demand displacement could be viewed as temporary, where a reversal in prices might bring coal demand back, as happened between ethanol and gasoline, but there is a case for permanent demand displacement too. New plants are favouring gas-fired units to replace older, less efficient facilities. In some cases, the closures are being forced by the regulator, showing that both the visible hand of the market and the invisible hand of the regulation are at work displacing coal in favour of gas.

In 2013, the consumption of US natural gas for power generation purposes increased by 34% from the year before, and given the demand of electricity remained largely unchanged, as a zero sum game, the increase in natural gas was pretty much entirely at the expense of demand displacement from coal.[7]

The imbalance in the supply and demand of coal resulted in a large increase in coal inventories and a reduction in prices, which forced high-cost producers to shut down operations.

But the collapse in US coal prices made it very competitive in Europe.

European gas prices were supported by Fukushima and high demand for LNG, which meant that European coal prices, combined with the low cost of carbon permits in Europe[8] and reduced penalties for burning coal, kept profit margins at coal-fired power plants healthy while slashing profit margins for gas-fired plants. Anecdotally, the increase in coal burning pushed German carbon emissions up in 2012–13,[9] the opposite of what was supposed to happen.

The displacement of European gas by coal was exactly the opposite of what was happening across the Atlantic, where natural gas was displacing coal. And the lower demand for natural gas in Europe meant lower competition for Japanese gas via LNG, which therefore kept global natural gas prices lower than they would have otherwise been. The "energy domino" in full force, advancing like water through canals, filling the demand with the lowest possible cost across the flexibility in the system.

US natural gas displaces diesel in transportation

In 2009 Warren Buffett acquired the US railway system, which happens to be the second largest consumer of diesel in North America, only behind the US military.[10]

Well, it turns out that those trains could run on liquefied natural gas instead of diesel, a safe and proven technology. Think about the savings for the company.

And think about the amount of diesel that is suddenly available for others to consume, within the United States or abroad. Any barrel of diesel not consumed by the trains is one barrel of diesel available for incremental demand.

In addition to trains, the competition for crude oil in the transportation fuels sector is increasing. Natural gas vehicles, electric cars, hybrids, coal to liquids, gas to liquids, biofuels, fuel cells – the list of new technologies is long. It is not clear who will win, but it is clear that crude oil no longer has the monopoly it once enjoyed.

The energy domino and potential for demand displacement of crude oil products in the transportation sector can have enormous implications for prices.

Solar displaces crude oil for power generation in Saudi Arabia

Saudi Arabia is one of the few countries in the world that continues to produce electricity from crude oil, and the extraordinary demand growth relative to production means that it is tightening the exportable balance.

As discussed earlier, the cost of solar PV panels has come off as a result of technology, input costs, and overcapacity, which is creating a large incentive for countries like Saudi, who recently announced it would invest $109 billion in solar power.

The amount of crude oil no longer needed for power generation will be released for refining into crude oil products, thus easing the balance and increasing spare exportable capacity.

Renewables displace natural gas from peak power demand

Negative German power prices are a clear reflection of the new dynamics and displacement of natural gas, and even coal, as peak and baseload demand.

And such low prices have an impact as excess power can be transferred across national borders and thus displace more expensive power generation. Germany has been actively exporting to Denmark, where wind generation is approximately 30% of overall production.[11]

Clearly as more markets take on a greater proportion of renewables, the ability to "dump" power across borders becomes less (as they will have their own renewables), and hence grid stability becomes a greater issue.

The storage of power is incentivized, a new frontier for the power market.

The "visible hand" of environmental regulation displaces coal

The forced displacement of coal in environmentally conscious countries means there is more coal available for those looking to "grow at any environmental cost", as has been the case for China and India, but that may push the boundaries to the new emerging economies who are also becoming more environmentally focused. In India, newly elected President Modi has introduced an ambitious energy plan looking to place solar in every single home by 2016.

The "visible hand" of politics displaces nuclear

Nuclear power suffered a massive political backlash in Japan and Germany, with temporary shutdowns and more long-term implications. In this case, the destruction of nuclear supply has been a powerful inflationary force which will likely result in a large supply response as LNG capacity is built. So, for now there are short-term bullish prices, but there is the potential for extremely negative energy prices across the board in the long term, especially as alternatives are built just as nuclear output resumes, which will probably leave large investments and large excess capacity globally.

The transmission to equity valuations

In 2012, the displacement of coal via natural gas, and the resulting decrease in volumes, prices, and outlook, had a direct impact on the valuation of coal producers.

The shares of some of the biggest coal producers in the United States have dropped dramatically in the past three years, creating the effect of "cheap becomes cheaper".

And so, the domino continues, through multiple channels, creating disinflation across the board.

Producing countries that rely on high prices for their budgets are possibly the ones who will lose the most from a widespread energy domino.

Notes

1. Osmel Manzano and Jose Sebastian Scrofina. *Resource Revenue Management in Venezuela: A Consumption-Based Poverty Reduction Strategy.* http://www.revenuewatch.org/sites/default/files/Venezuela_Final.pdf
2. Deborah Ball, Paul Sonne and Carrick Mollenkamp (2011). UBS: Rogue trader hit firm. *Wall Street Journal*, 16 September. http://online.wsj.com/news/articles/SB1000142405311190406060457 6571931690088522?mg=reno64-wsj&url=http%3A%2F%2Fonline .wsj.com%2Farticle%2FSB1000142405311190406060457657 1931690088522.html
3. *BP Statistical Review of World Energy – June 2013.* http://www .bp.com/content/dam/bp/pdf/statistical-review/statistical_review _of_world_energy_2013.pdf
4. *Merkel Signals Faster Exit From Nuclear Power.* http://online.wsj .com/news/articles/SB1000142405274870381820457620060301 79424162
5. Marc Roca (11 February 2013). *Global Solar Capacity Tops 100 Gigawatts on Asian Markets.* http://www.bloomberg.com /news/2013-02-11/global-solar-capacity-tops-100-gigawatts-on -asian-markets.html
6. US Energy Information Administration. http://www.eia.gov /environment/emissions/co2_vol_mass.cfm
7. US Energy Information Administration. http://www.eia.gov /forecasts/aeo/MT_naturalgas.cfm
8. Carbon Trade Exchange.
9. Robert Wilson (20 January 2014). *Why Germany's Nuclear Phase Out is Leading to More Coal Burning.* http://theenergycollective

.com/robertwilson190/328841/why-germanys-nuclear-phase
-out-leading-more-coal-burning

10. BNSF Railway Company (6 March 2013). *BNSF to Test Liquefied Natural Gas in Road Locomotives.* http://www.bnsf.com/employees /communications/bnsf-news/2013/march/2013-03-06-a.html

11. Marc Roca and Wael Mahdi (11 May 2012). *Saudi Arabia Plans $109 Billion Boost for Solar Power.* http://www.bloomberg.com /news/2012-05-10/saudi-arabia-plans-109-billion-boost-for-solar -power.html

CHAPTER TWELVE

FLATTENER #9 – REGULATION AND GOVERNMENT INTERVENTION

Policies that aim to thwart market forces rarely work, and usually fall victim to the law of unintended consequences

Lawrence Summers

One of the penalties for refusing to participate in politics is that you end up being governed by your inferiors

Plato

Competition is an unsound economic regulator

Samuel Insull

The role of the government

During a recent interview on television, following the launch of my book, *Journey to Economic Freedom: Why Debt Slaves You, and Austerity Frees You Up,*[1] I was being bombarded by questions on "the government is not doing enough", "they should be hiring more people to create jobs", as if it was the obligation and role of the government to hire people to reduce the unemployment. There was very little consideration to how the government would pay for them.

"The role of the government is to provide a supportive environment to stimulate the creation of jobs in the private sector. The role of the government is not to be the employer of last resort", I answered. I am a big believer in economic freedom, and support the austerity measures taken by the government, but do not agree with many other aspects, such as the increase in taxes or the heavy burdens to entrepreneurs.

As a liberal economist, I believe the government has an important role to play, but it must contribute and focus on the empowerment of private businesses to thrive, not the reckless misallocation of capital at the expense of ever-growing levels of debt.

Regulation vs. free markets

The virtuous mix of regulation and free markets

Regulation is vital for free markets. Regulation is not bad. It is not an obstacle.

When we use our cars, the rules and regulations of traffic support driving. Traffic lights, speed limits, road signals, and civic rules are there to ensure I can drive safely and efficiently. Without them, driving would be chaotic and dangerous.

There are many examples in economic and energy history where thoughtful and well-designed regulation has provided a successful framework for economic development. Look at the "grand bargain" and "natural monopoly" in the US power generation sector, for example.

The vicious mix of regulation and politics

The problem is not regulation in itself. The problem is when regulation is mixed up with political goals, with short-term horizons, with the view to suppress market forces, and with very poorly designed policies implemented. As former US Secretary of State Larry Summers famously said, "Policies that aim to thwart market forces rarely work, and usually fall victim to the law of unintended consequences".[2] Well, unfortunately, the history of the energy markets is full of them.

Look at the environmental regulation that was meant to diversify the fuel mix and reduce pollution via renewables, but has ended up with a much more unstable system with greater pollution as natural gas is displaced by coal.

Or look at the deregulation of power prices in California in the 1990s that was meant to reduce the cost of electricity, but ends up increasing the prices for consumers and sending the power generation sector to bankruptcy.

The issue of "freedom of choice" has been debated extensively. Should consumers decide by themselves, or should someone else (the government) decide on their behalf?

But the issue of freedom of choice is not always a binary process. In their excellent book called *Nudge*,[3] Richard Thaler and Cass Sunstein introduced the idea that we can maintain freedom of choice, but influence the decision-making process in order to achieve better decisions.

In their analysis they show that choice is never presented in a neutral way. The framing of the question tends to have implicit biases, which can be used to influence the decisions. Think for example of the same question under an "opt in" or "opt out". The status quo is generally preferred by many, and the results to exactly the same question can change by how we frame it and the choices we give.

The question becomes how and when to "nudge" in the right direction. There is plenty of application for the regulation of markets.

Carrot and stick

Government intervention takes places in multiple ways. The examples of the power generation sector discussed above are broadly based on strict rules and compliance. But, of course, as Plato said, "good people do not need laws to act responsibly, while bad people will find a way around the laws".

Incentives ("carrots") such as tax breaks can incentivize the right behaviour. For example, in the United States, many states offer financial incentives for switching to CNG or buying natural gas vehicles, mostly through tax credits.

Penalties ("sticks") are also a powerful way to ensure compliance and the desired behaviour. Look at the government mandates for biofuels or the European Emissions Trading Scheme.

Following the Macondo disaster, the Obama administration placed a moratorium on all drilling in the Gulf of Mexico.[4] The moratorium was eventually officially lifted, and regulation has not affected the industry.

Privatization and deregulation are not the same

Privatization is about changing ownership from the state to private owners.

Deregulation is about the reduction or elimination of government intervention, usually enacted to create more competition within the industry.

In the United States, deregulation gained momentum in the 1970s, and it was applied progressively across the transportation industry, energy, communications, and finance. As a result, the government stopped regulating everything from the cost of airline tickets, through the price controls on oil as gas, through the start of a multi-channel era in television, to brokerage fees.

The process of deregulation was generally accompanied by privatization. In 1990 UK Prime Minister Margaret Thatcher started a privatization programme[5] that spanned across industries, including the Central Electricity Generating Board (CEGB) that controlled the power generation and distribution sectors. The UK government broke the generating part of the CEGB into three private companies that would compete between themselves and against new independent generating in the wholesale market.

Independence of the regulator

The Central Bank is an *independent* body responsible for setting the monetary policy of a country. The US Federal Reserve, the European Central Bank, the Bank of England, and the People's Bank of China have the primary objective of financial stability and have extensive tools to directly and indirectly control interest rates and other key variables such as inflation and exchange rates. They control the monetary "accelerator and brake" of the economy.

The Treasury is a *government* body responsible for setting fiscal policy. The US Treasury and the Ministry of Finance have the primary objective of setting budgets and have extensive tools to set the level of taxes, government debt, and other key variables. They control the fiscal "accelerator and brake" of the economy.

But government has a political agenda, generally short term, driven by the primary goal of re-election. As such, it will try to use all tools possible to achieve re-election, which often comes at the expense of short-term and/or populist measures.

Similarly, in the energy markets, there is a combination of government and independent bodies.

The Department of Energy (DOE) is a government body. As such, it follows a political agenda. As of March 2014, the DOE has granted approval to seven terminals to export LNG to non-free trade agreement countries.[6] These approvals are gaining greater significance following the annexation of Crimea by Russia, as LNG exports from the United States are being seen as a geopolitical tool as the West aims to reduce its reliance on Russian natural gas. Prior debates were focused on the benefits and considerations for the US economy, but geopolitics is becoming a more relevant factor in the decision.

But the approvals from the DOE are not enough. The projects also require the approval of the Federal Energy Regulatory Commission (FERC), which is an *independent* body (similar to the US Federal Reserves for Monetary Policy). The FERC has approval over the site, construction and operation of a facility, including environmental impact assessments. The submission of the application and the approval process can be lengthy, and tends to cost tens of millions of dollars.[7]

These different layers of approvals can be a double-edged sword, as they have the potential to increase costs and delay approval times, but they also provide additional layers of professional analysis and expertise and a much longer perspective than politicians.

If we had to remove any layers of approvals, it should be the government and not the independent bodies.

The political cycle is too short

I have always thought that one of the big problems with the current system is that the political cycle is too short. Four years is a very short time, when looking at policy implementation cycles.

The first year in government is generally used to figure out where things stand. The last year is generally focused on re-election. That leaves just two years to try to get things done. In practice, even if the right decisions are put in place, the results may not show for many years. As a result, there is a strong bias towards "short-term patching".

What is the fastest way to generate artificial "economic activity"? Easy. Increase government debt and build infrastructure. A country like Spain has one of the best road infrastructures on the continent, with pharaonic bridges and tunnels. It is doubtful that those investments will ever be recovered, but time will tell. However, the markets put the "borrow and spend" cycle to an end and forced very controversial, but much needed, austerity measures.

The war on pollution and coal

The war on pollution

> *Smog is nature's red-light warning against inefficient and blind development.*
>
> Chinese Premier Li Keqiang[8]

In March 2014, the Chinese Premier Li Keqiang opened the annual meetings in front of 3000 delegates with a declaration of war: a "war against pollution".[9]

For decades China has favoured economic growth fuelled by "cheap and dirty" fuels, arguably ignoring the long-term implications to the health of its population. "We will resolutely declare war against pollution as we declared war against poverty".[10] The environmental "hidden cost" of burning coal was largely ignored, but has become a "visible cost" that, given the population pyramid of China and the one-child policy, may become a heavy burden for the years to come.

The battle against pollution in China looks to reform energy pricing to boost non-fossil fuel power generation and cutting capacity in the steel and cement sectors which are the sources of much air pollution. China's growth will become more "green". Greater focus on energy efficiency. Greater focus on clean technologies. China's lead will have a major influence on the world.

China is the largest polluter in the world, and by a long way, with almost 29% of total carbon dioxide emissions.

A significant part of the pollution comes from coal-fired plants and China is the largest coal consumer in the world.[11]

In a highly symbolic speech, like an alcoholic standing up in front of a crowd and admitting his addiction, Premier Li's "we will resolutely declare war against pollution as we declared war against poverty" is an important step forward, and a recognition of the obvious and tangible impact that the hazardous levels of pollution are having across China.

I remember how my regular trips to Beijing and Shanghai always started with a common feature. The strong smell of burning that hit me as soon as I landed and that would stay with me for the whole journey. And during the winter it was even worse. Once, in the middle of the day, it suddenly went dark. It felt like a total eclipse of smog. The driver turned the car lights on without blinking. It seemed normal. I checked the time, double-checked with my colleagues what was going on, and they said it was normal for Beijing in the winter. I was shocked. It was just unreal.

More recently, in Beijing, following protests from the foreign community who did not trust the official readings, the US embassy started to publish its own independent readings that confirmed consistently higher levels of pollution than the official ones. "In January 2014, Beijing made headlines when the pollution levels were so bad that they surpassed the top of the scale of the U.S. Environmental Protection Agency's Air Quality Index."[12] There is even an app, "China Air Index", that shows both readings. Check it out yourself.[13]

And all this leads to renewables.

The view that solar will suddenly grow exponentially is questionable particularly when US and European gas is still much cheaper than solar energy (photovoltaic) despite the cuts in the premiums seen in Germany, Spain, and other countries. To give you an idea, in Germany, the same government that takes action against nuclear plants has seen the brutal effect of solar energy on prices. Germany has accumulated 40% of global solar installations over the past two years and has seen the cost of subsidies reach to more than 56% of the retail price for the consumer.[14]

When solar and wind become competitive, substitution will come from natural demand, not policy.

It is worth continuing to invest in security and to investigate further about economically viable and safe energy, but the greatest risk we face now is to take populist measures that sink competitiveness, curtail security of supply, and make the system more expensive.

In energy, substitution can only come from competition. Either you compete or you disappear. Crude oil beat whale oil on price 120 years ago. The same happened with gas and coal. Anything else is dreaming.

The war on coal

Not all the coal that is dug warms the world.

Mary Harris Jones[15]

Coal is much easier and cheaper to transport and store than natural gas.

And there is certainly no current or future shortage of coal around the world.

Over the past few years, despite global GDP growth of 3% pa and 7% in China,[16] which consumes c.50% of all the coal in the world, supply–demand balance has remained more than ample, with inventories at 83% capacity, and a structural 20% oversupply.

Looking forward, Deutsche Bank and the IEA estimate that coal consumption will increase by 2.3% a year to 6.35 billion metric tons of coal equivalent in the five years to 2018, below the 2.6% growth predicted in 2012 for the period through 2017, and well below the estimates of 4% pa expected a few years before.[17] Crisis? Cycle? No, efficiency and substitution.

Technology vs. pollution

The "visible hand" of regulation via the Clean Air Acts has greatly contributed to the reduction of pollution by coal-fired plants.

Over the past few decades, particulate emissions have been almost eliminated, emissions of sulphur dioxide have been reduced by 99% and nitrogen oxides by 95%, but the amount of carbon dioxide responsible for the greenhouse effect is a more difficult and complex problem.[18]

On the power generation side, efforts continue to improve efficiency and reduce pollution and the latest generation of ultra-supercritical power plants emit 40% less carbon dioxide than plants built 20 years ago.[19]

As the price of coal collapses, I expect the market to defend itself and look for improvements in clean carbon technologies. One of them is Carbon Capture and Sequestration (CCS), designed to capture the carbon dioxide and bury it underground, as part of a closed circle, where carbon is mined from underground, burnt, captured, and buried, instead of being sent to the atmosphere.

As is often the case, these technologies exist, but are not viable at commercial cost and scale. But my fellow engineers are on the case, and there is certainly a strong incentive due to the low prices and sheer volumes.

Regulatory constraints to coal plants

In my view, real market substitution can be a much faster and more effective solution than trying to figure out complex mechanisms for trading permits, as Europe has tried and failed.

But government action is also evident. Most notably, China has recently introduced bans on new coal plants near Beijing, Shanghai, and Guangzhou, recognizing that coal-fired power plants are one of the major sources of severe air pollution problems in China, along with emissions from vehicles and industrial facilities.[20] As part of the effort, its National Development and Reform Commission (NDRC) is looking at a coal cap strategy to limit coal use, boost efficiencies, retire inefficient plants, and promote fuel-switching.

The Chinese strategy also looks to impose stricter emission targets and penalties for violations, while raising the amount of non-coal generation sources. The "12th Five Year Plan for Air Pollution Prevention and Control in Key Areas" includes coal cap pilots at key locations. Part of the strategy also calls for accelerating the retirement of inefficient power generation and other industrial facilities, particularly the coal-burning plants that produce a sizeable amount of air pollution.[21]

In addition to carbon emissions, China has a major problem with emissions of sulphur dioxide and nitrogen oxides (byproducts of coal burning), which cause acid rain, smog, and along with the fine particulate matter emitted, particularly PM2.5, are responsible for serious environmental degradation and health and breathing problems.[22]

Coal subsidies

Historically, the "visible hand" of government intervention in China had incentivized the wrong behaviour. Subsidized coal means consumers are being incentivized to consume and burn more coal.

> On January 2014 China announced a new plan to cut coal's share of energy use to 65.0% in 2014, down from 65.7% in 2013, in a bid to improve air quality in major cities.[23]

However, ironically, Chinese coal producers still receive large subsidies which are helping them stay in business, and despite sub-economical returns, they are not closing down due to support from the government. Overall Chinese production is still set to rise in 2014 and 2015, as rail expansions help reduce delivered costs to the consuming regions. In some regions, however, production could fall as a number of small producers are closing due to bankruptcy.[24]

The clean and dirty spreads

Coal-fired utilities buy coal and produce electricity. The profitability of their business is largely a function of the difference between the income they get from selling the electricity and the cost they pay for the fuel. This price differential between electricity and coal is often referred to as the "dark spread".

Similarly, natural-gas-fired utilities earn the difference between electricity and natural gas, or what is known as the "spark spread".

The introduction of carbon dioxide permits introduced a new additional cost and impacted the theoretical profitability of the utilities. The simple difference between electricity and coal referred to as the "dirty dark spread", with the additional cost of carbon dioxide permits, became the "clean dark spread".

Similarly, the market started to differentiate between "dirty spark spread" and "clean spark spread".[25]

The financial markets are a bit like playing LEGO, where the players can manage the risk on any of the parts separately or together.

Second order effects from cheap coal

Following the skyrocketing prices during the super-cyclical move up, the world has dramatically increased its production and logistical infrastructure.

The large investments have been completed and greater quantities of coal can be produced and transported with relative ease and cheap cost. Stocks are ample, and excess production capacity is likely to push coal closer to marginal cost of production, effectively displacing the high-cost producers. Although, as discussed, cheaper prices will make coal more competitive, and the overall process is not only deflationary for coal prices, but also for the rest of the energy complex.

On the negative side, ultra-cheap coal will make it more attractive for those emerging economies that are looking for "growth at all cost". As India and China become more environmentally conscious, other emerging markets may take the "pollution baton", with negative implications for health and pollution, as history is bound to repeat itself.

On the positive side, abundant and cheap coal creates a strong incentive to invest in clean coal technologies. The coal market will defend itself. The engineers are on the case and may be able to surprise us again, hopefully with dramatic improvements in efficiency and carbon capture, making coal a more environmental and viable alternative.

Overall, pollution considerations are likely to result in much lower demand growth than anticipated, particularly from China. Combined with the large growth in global production and logistical infrastructure, coal is set to be one of the major losers from a flatter energy world, and the impact will be highly deflationary across energy markets.

But some big opportunities will emerge, particularly around clean coal technologies.

The world of coal is flat

In the short to medium run, coal will remain the largest feedstock for power generation, more from necessity than by choice.

In the longer run, the future of coal will be increasingly polarized, as developed economies favour cleaner technologies, while emerging economies look for "growth at any cost".

Given the super-cyclical growth in production and logistical capacity and perhaps overly optimistic demand growth expectations, it is possible that coal prices will remain very depressed for a long time, forcing high-cost producers to cut production.

The possibility of ultra-cheap coal opens exciting opportunities ahead as the engineers set their minds to cleaner coal technologies.

Yes, you guessed it, another powerful flattener.

Renewable energy and the disinflation of power prices

No-one can embargo the sun from us.

Jimmy Carter

Central planning is as futile as trying to strap on wings and fly like a bird – and potentially as calamitous.

Don Boudreaux

Negative electricity prices

On 16 June 2013, the wholesale price of electricity in Germany fell to *minus* €100 per megawatt hour (MWh).[26] That is, generating companies were delivering electricity to consumers for free and paying a compensation to the grid to take its electricity.

It was a perfect storm. It was a Sunday, so demand was low. The light was bright. The wind was blowing. Nuclear and coal-fired power plants, designed to run baseload,[27] could not be shut down easily. The adjustment had to come from the gas-fired plants, triggered by the strong message of negative prices, which are part of the game to ensure that generators cut production to avoid the risk of overloading the grid.

From an environmental and consumer perspective, the growth of the renewables industry looks like a triumph. At the end of the day, renewables are cleaner technologies with zero carbon emissions that reduce the reliance on hydrocarbons. And, as per the observations in the German market, they also help reduce wholesale power prices.

But the question is, do the renewables pose some hidden costs and unintended long-term consequences?

From the perspective of the conventional utilities, the development of renewables has been an absolute disaster. Needless to say, periods of negative prices result in heavy losses for the utilities, unable to run a normal business where customers pay for services according to how much they consume.

Beyond the risk of occasional negative prices, renewables have changed the rules of the power generation game, which poses difficult questions to the future of the industry. As the supply of wind and solar power becomes unpredictable and intermittent, there is a risk that established utilities are being replaced by more intermittent, less reliable, and more expensive sources of energy, which have the potential to destabilize the grid and may lead to brownouts and blackouts.

The collapse in the valuation of European utilities

Since their peak in 2008, the top 20 energy utilities have lost more than 50% of their market value, wiping more than €500 billion in equity valuations.[28]

Their creditworthiness has also suffered. In 2008 the top 10 European utilities all had credit ratings of A or better. Now only five do.

And the outlook for valuations and credit is not encouraging. In the words of the CFO of RWE, the second-largest utility in Germany, "conventional power generation, quite frankly, as a business unit, is fighting for its economic survival".

But renewables are not to blame entirely for the drop in the market value and creditworthiness of the utilities.

During the 2000s, falling for the "diplomatic forecasts" of ever-increasing demand for electricity, European utilities grossly over-invested in generating capacity from fossil fuels, boosting it by 16% in Europe as a whole and by as much as 91% in Spain.

However, the demand did not grow as expected, and was hit further by the financial crisis, widening the imbalances. According to the IEA, total energy demand in Europe is set to *decline* by 2% between 2010 and 2015.

The growth of solar and wind was just "another nail in the utilities coffin" as they increased the overcapacity even further.

In Germany, renewables capacity is almost 50% of the total power-generating capacity. In Spain and Italy it is about 33%. Total capacity, including renewables, is significantly above peak demand in all three countries.

Lower wholesale prices have impacted profitability. According to the Bloomberg New Energy Finance (BNEF), 30%–40% of RWE's conventional power stations are losing money.[29]

Renewables have changed the rules of power generation

Back in the 1980s, when the market was regulated, and before the exponential growth of renewables in power generation, the electricity business was relatively simple.

The progressive deregulation of the sector introduced the "invisible hand" of market forces which incentivized generation according to the marginal cost of production, where nuclear and coal remained for the most part the main providers of baseload power.

In the 2000s, the growth of renewables changed the rules of the game in several ways.

Rule change #1 – Grid priority

Renewables were given "grid priority", meaning the grid must take their electricity first.

This was enforced by regulation to encourage the development of renewable energy in Europe. However, given the marginal cost of wind and solar power is zero, grids would take their power first anyway.

So, renewable energy is baseload, first in line to satisfy demand, irrespective of the level of demand or prices.

Rule change #2 – Intermittent baseload supply

Historically, baseload supply was steady and predictable.

The growth of solar and wind mean that baseload is now more weather dependent and therefore intermittent and unpredictable.

Furthermore, wind has the potential to add "wrong way" exposure as periods of high temperature, when the demand for cooling is high, tend to have little wind. Same when temperatures are low. Which means that wind power may not be there when we need it most, which can exacerbate the imbalances during peak periods.

Rule change #3 – Generous feed-in tariffs

A feed-in tariff (FIT) is a mechanism designed to incentivize investments in renewable technologies, by offering long-term contracts with cost-plus based compensation.[30] Subsidies throughout Europe, in particular, have been generous and aggressive.

Rule change #4 – FITs are disconnected from marginal costs

The FIT is typically adjusted to reflect the relative cost of each technology. For example, wind power, which has lower costs, is awarded a lower FIT per kWh than other more expensive technologies such as solar photovoltaics and tidal power.

But the FITs for each technology were relatively static and slow to react to changes in the industry and marginal costs of production. This had important implications for solar in particular.

Rule change #5 – Governments and consumers pay the subsidies

In Germany, subsidies for renewable energy are running at €16 billion a year (and rising) and the cumulative cost is estimated around €60 billion.[31]

But it is important to differentiate between redistributing wealth versus increasing debt.

Fossil fuel subsidies given by Iran, Saudi Arabia, Russia, and China, to name a few, are generated by the revenues that countries receive from energy sold or from a budget surplus. These subsidies are based on revenue redistribution.

On the other hand, renewable subsidies in Europe and the United States are granted by adding debt and deficit to the budgets of countries.

My personal view is that subsidies are not good and should be erased everywhere. All of them. The discussion that follows will address the unintended consequences and second- and third-order effects from subsidies and intervention.

Rule change #6 – Governments can change the rules anytime

Similar to Warren Buffett's "when investing, there are two basic rules. Rule number one: never lose money. Rule number 2: never forget rule number one", when dealing with governments and regulation there is an unwritten rule "never forget that governments can change the rules anytime, without warning, and without compensation".

Implications from the new rules

Implication #1 – Overcapacity in renewables

The FITs have generally been very generous. Rising energy prices during the mid-2000s accelerated the growth and support for renewables, as a source of energy security and environmentally friendly policies, but higher prices were also doing the work, by narrowing the cost gap between renewable and conventional energy.

In the case of solar, FITs failed to adjust quickly enough to reflect the rapidly falling costs across the industry, which resulted in very high expected rates of return guaranteed for periods of typically 10–20 years and supported the massive expansion in solar photovoltaic installations.[32]

Implication #2 – Greater risk of negative prices

Historically, baseload supply was predictable. Any supply shocks due to outages in generation or distribution were skewed towards *lower* supply and *higher* prices.

But under the new rules, baseload supply is intermittent and less predictable. Supply shocks, when baseload generation is much higher than anticipated, add a new dimension. As was the case on 16 June 2013 in Germany, periods of strong solar and wind generation may create supply shocks of greater supply and lower prices. And given power generation has no floor at zero, the probability of negative prices has notably increased.

Implication #3 – Gas-fired generation is being displaced

The traditional conventional gas- and coal-fired generation capacity is being forced to make the adjustments to the volatile and weather-dependent solar and wind.

The exponential growth in renewables is no longer negligible and gas-fired plants are being completely displaced and switched off, but may be needed during peak times or periods when the renewables are not producing.

Implication #4 – Coal-fired displacement adds costs and volatility

The increased capacity of wind and solar means that lowering the output or even switching off completely gas-fired generators may not be enough, and even some coal-fired ones may need to be turned down. This creates a problem and may be costly as scaling back coal-fired plants is harder. As a result, electricity prices become more volatile.

Implication #5 – Erosion of peak pricing (and profits)

Despite the low average utilization rates of solar power (load factors of 10–15% of installed capacity[33]), solar has significantly reduced peak pricing during the middle of the day, a period when traditionally utilities enjoyed strong margins.

In Germany, the premium of peak relative to baseload has fallen from €14 per MWh in 2008, to just €3 per MWh in 2013.[34] So not only have average wholesale electricity prices fallen by 50% since 2008, but the peak premium has also fallen.

Implication #6 – Lower wholesale prices

The large imbalance between supply and demand invariably resulted in lower prices. Electricity wholesale prices at peak hours in Germany fell from €80 MWh in 2008 to €38 MWh within five years.[35]

Implication #7 – "Utilities ain't treasuries no more"

The collapse in the market capitalization among European utilities was worse than the European bank shares lost in the same period.

These losses have important implications, and have impacted traditional core investors such as pension funds, who no longer view the sector as steady, reliable, and inflation-resistant that would help them balance their long-term liabilities.

Once upon a time utilities were viewed as the US Treasuries of the equity markets, but that's no longer the case. It turns out that renewables are not the only risky energy investment.

Implication #8 – High retail prices

The costs of FITs have been passed on to consumers in most cases, which has resulted in significant increases in retail electricity prices.

In Germany, retail prices stayed high, at €285 per MWh,[36] among the highest in the world, despite the collapse in wholesale prices.

Implication #9 – Sovereign risk

The global financial crisis of 2008 hit renewables hard.

Demand for electricity imploded. Alternative sources of energy became much cheaper, widening the gap to higher cost renewables. The crisis was centred on the banking sector, dramatically impacting the access to and cost of financing and refinancing across the full chain.

But the crisis also highlighted other hidden risks. The sovereign risk was implicit in these "guaranteed" investments. Look at the case of Spain, for example, which instituted extremely generous subsidies for renewables, eventually sending the pro-gramme wildly out of control, with far more capacity built than was initially targeted, costing the government much more than it ever intended. The financial burden was simply too much. In 2008 Spain substantially reduced its FITs, and did so again in 2010 amid fiscal austerity brought on by excessive govern-ment debt.[37]

Implication #10 – Diversification in power generation portfolio

In general, conventional utilities have been slow and reluctant when it comes down to investing and diversifying into renewables. In Germany, for example, utilities own only 7% of renewables capacity, as smaller and new players have been more aggressive adopters and developers of the new technologies.

Utilities have been more active in larger projects, such as offshore wind farms, but have been particularly slow in solar. At the end of the day, solar power generation is a very different game from what the large conventional utilities are used to. Conventional power plants tend to be large hubs of 1–1.5 GW of capacity from where they distribute power. Solar photovol-taic panels on the other hand tend to be arranged as nets with small capacity of just 0.01 GW. The size and the subsidies have made them very attractive to small and new players.

But in general utilities seem to be getting out of conven-tional power generation and into trading and added value services to clients. During 2013, three German firms, E.ON, RWE and EnBW, announced capacity cuts of over 15 GW, while EnBW predicts that its earnings from electricity generation will fall by 80% by 2020, offset by higher earnings from energy services and renewables.

Implication #11 – More brownouts and blackouts?

Conventional utilities in Europe are expected to take the role of generators of last resort. As a protective cushion to avoid brownouts and blackouts when solar and wind are not there.

So far, the conventional utilities have not failed. In fact, reliability indices show that the German grid remains as one of the highest scores in Europe. But as the price swings in Germany show, it is getting harder to maintain grid stability.

Utilities are not rewarded for offsetting the variable nature of wind and solar power. Instead, they are shifting out of electricity generation.

And the situation may get worse as Germany looks to achieve 35% share of renewables that government policy requires in 2020, let alone if they reach the national target of 80% in 2050.

Almost everyone acknowledges that as the share of renewable energy rises, regulation of the grid will have to change.

Implication #12 – Electricity storage as a real option

The storage of electricity is possible, but expensive, and could be a potential answer to the issue of intermittency from renewables.

As was the case with other forms of storage, the market will respond to the incentives, and there is no stronger incentive than buying electricity at negative prices to be sold later in the day at positive prices! Commercially, it is still far away, but yet again we expect to see "volumes attract volumes" and the learning curve and cost pressure will result in more efficient and cheaper storage capacity. The impact is of course a massive flattener in power prices.

In that sense, it is the "invisible hand" of the market that may incentivize the investment in storage, rather than the "visible hand" of regulation to try to make renewables cost competitive.

Under this storage scenario, baseload technologies (nuclear and coal) would benefit at the expense of gas, as storage provides the "flex" in the system previously provided by gas.

So, solar initially steals peak demand from gas, then at higher penetration rates it steals from baseload (nuclear and coal) requiring more gas capacity for flexibility, but then with storage, it benefits baseload at the expense of gas. Who would want to be a utility with this much uncertainty?

Implication #13 – Who will build the power infrastructure?

The current path is taking Europe towards a lower-carbon system with less reliable and more intermittent sources of base power, with more and smaller power suppliers, and more energy traded across borders. The traditional conventional gas- and coal-fired generation capacity is being forced to make adjustments to the volatile and weather dependent solar and wind, which is eroding profit margins, has dramatically impacted asset valuations, and eroded their creditworthiness – and they face a bleak outlook.

The role of utilities as investors is also being threatened. The sums required to upgrade the grid are huge, as much as €1 trillion in Europe by 2020. Companies worth €500 billion cannot finance anything like that amount. Instead, they are cutting capital spending. That of RWE (for example) has fallen from €6.4 billion to €5 billion since 2011, and most analysts expect it to fall to €2.6 billion by 2015. Of that, €1.6 billion will go on maintaining existing plants, leaving just €1 billion for development spending – half of present levels. In their current state, utilities cannot finance Europe's hoped-for clean-energy system.

And that has implications for the future. To make up for lack of investment by utilities, governments will have to persuade others to step in, such as pension funds or sovereign-wealth funds. But these entities have always invested in energy indirectly, by holding stakes in utilities, not directly. And for a reason: they dislike the political risks of owning projects in which governments play a role, either through planning or price setting. In some countries there are also laws against owning assets both upstream (generators) and down (distribution).

Furthermore, the fact that much of this generation is distributed (e.g. rooftop solar located at the point of use vs. large-scale centralized generation) has huge implications for the electricity grid. Fewer units will travel over an infrastructure that is traditionally remunerated on a per unit basis.

This scenario raises challenging questions about the future of Europe's electricity system.

Implication #14 – A full circle of regulation?

Over the past 30 years European governments have been trying to deregulate energy markets, privatizing state-owned companies and splitting electricity generation from transmission and distribution. The aims were to increase competition, boost efficiency, and cut prices.

Those goals are now harder to achieve. Renewable energy has grabbed a growing share of the market, pushed wholesale prices down, and succeeded in its goal of lowering the price of new technologies. But the subsidy cost also has been large, the environmental gains non-existent so far, and the damage done to today's utilities much greater than expected. Europe in general and Germany in particular see themselves as pioneers of low-carbon energy. If they are genuinely to be so, they will need to design a much better electricity system that rewards low-carbon energy without reducing reliability and imposing undue and unnecessary costs.

Ultimately, we believe that markets such as Germany must move to a "capacity payment" mechanism, whereby the owners of conventional plants are compensated (via consumer bills) simply for keeping this plant open and available (but not actually running), so that it is there when needed, that is in the winter.

This capacity payment model would essentially delink the results of these companies/assets from their operational characteristics.

Ultimately, this could see these conventional utilities reverting to rate of return, regulated asset-based companies, an ironically circular evolution back to the days of state-owned utilities prior to European market liberalization.

Moreover, the grid has to be maintained for use by centralized generation in the winter when solar is not running. Ironically this combined upward impact on electricity bills (of capacity payments for stranded generation and higher grid per-unit charges) is in our view only likely to make consumers more likely to put panels on their roofs in a desire for a greater degree of energy independence.

The big six British utilities, for example, have been sheltered by their long-term electricity-price agreement with the regulator, though their profit margins remain thin.

Are retail consumers better off?

Government intervention in renewables has resulted in significantly higher costs of energy for retail consumers (+70%) and overall has negatively impacted competitiveness.

Higher energy costs are the trade-off for cleaner fuels and energy independence with lower reliance on crude oil, coal, and gas, but governments need to realign the incentives to avoid excessive negative effect for retail consumers.

German wholesale power prices for industrial users *decreased* by 53% (all-time lows) from 2008 to 2012, while tariff retail prices to consumers *increased* by 25% during the same period.

In Spain the situation is very similar. Wholesale power prices decreased 12% while tariff retail prices increased by 70%.[38]

The reason for the increase in retail prices are the subsidies that are added to the tariffs. In Spain, renewable subsidies increased four-fold reaching €9 billion pa, equivalent to 39% of the overall costs of the system. And according to Forbes,[39] the size of the subsidies paid annually, which amounted to about $68 billion between 1998 and 2013, had increased by 800% between 2005 and 2013.

According to the FT, power prices paid by Germany's Mittelstand companies "have reached twice the level facing some of their US rivals, a study has shown, underlining the threat posed to the country's competitiveness by its shift to renewable energy". "A typical medium-sized German industrial company pays 9.14 euro cents per kilowatt hour compared with 4.82 cents/kWh in Texas, according to research carried out by Ecofys, a consultancy, and the Fraunhofer Institute for Systems and Innovation Research. The study, commissioned by the German government, is based on prices paid over the past two years".

In Spain, the regulator CNMC states that renewables have been the main cause of tariff hikes. They are 44% of the tariff's regulated part, which is 62% of the total. Renewable energy premiums rose +435% between 2006-2014.

Energy displacement can only happen if costs are low. If not, it's shooting ourselves in the foot.

Note: Worth reading Der Spiegel's Germany's Energy Poverty. High costs and errors of German transition to renewable energy   (http://www.spiegel.de/international/germany/high-costs-and-errors-of-german-transition-to-renewable-energy-a-920288.html

Are renewables more subsidized than fossil fuels?

In absolute terms, measured in total US dollars, fossil fuels are more subsidized than renewables. According to the EIA, in 2011, global subsidies for fossil fuels were $523 billion, almost six times higher than the $88 billion in global subsidies for renewable.[40]

But in relative terms, measured in cents per kWh, renewables are much more subsidized than nuclear or fossil fuels. According to the EIA, average global subsidies for nuclear were

c. 1.7/kWh, for fossil fuels c. 0.8/kWh, and for renewables (excluding hydro) c. 5.00/kWh!

In the United States, subsidies per unit of energy are significantly lower than in other parts of the world. Coal is the least subsidized source of electricity with c. 0.01/kWh. Nuclear and natural gas subsidies are c. 0.2/kWh. Renewables (excluding hydro) receive an average of c. 0.1/kWh, roughly five times more than nuclear or natural gas.[41]

In Europe, on the other hand, renewable subsidies are a disproportionate amount of the cost of energy. While Europe accounts for less than 20% of global energy consumption, it accounts for 75% of all global subsidies, making the cost of power to the consumer almost 35% higher in "green countries" than elsewhere in the OECD.[42]

And in energy equivalent terms, measured in cents per Btu, a study by the US Congressional Research Service in 2011 concluded that renewable energy subsidies per unit of energy in the United States were over 40 times greater than fossil fuel subsidies. "Renewables received a 77 percent share of total federal energy incentives in 2009, while fossil fuels received a 13 percent share but produced more than 7 times the energy due to higher load factors".[43]

The world of wind power is becoming flat

The answer, my friend, is blowing in the wind.

Bob Dylan

Don Quixote's windmills

As I was flying over the north of Spain, the endless lines of new massive windmills reminded me of a chapter of Cervantes' *Don Quixote* where the legendary deranged knight fought against the windmills believing they were giants. It was 2007.

Spain was booming. "We will surpass Germany in GDP per capita" said the Prime Minister, "the Spanish stallion is unstoppable" said one of the country's economists . . . and within that context of growth superpowers, electricity demand was forecasted to *conservatively* grow 2% pa through 2015.[44]

The Spanish economy was not unstoppable. After all, the growth had been fuelled by an enormous construction bubble which would eventually burst and send the country into a deep economic crisis and recession.

Despite the crisis, and the already evident overcapacity in power generation, from 2007 to 2012, Spain installed 21 gigawatts of additional renewable generation capacity, with the most generous subsidies across the OECD, at *only* €9 billion pa.[45]

And demand for power generation in Spain did not grow, to most people's disbelief it actually fell. By 2013, electricity consumption was back to the levels of 2005.

Somehow, despite the increased capacity and stagnant demand, retail prices had risen by 70% since 2008.[46] The answer: subsidies.

Wind power

Wind, with over 90% of the new renewable capacity, has been by far the biggest winner from the FITs.

However, the increase in demand and volume for wind is in stark contrast to the performance of the wind turbine companies, which have followed a similar fate to solar.

Based on overly optimistic demand expectations, the industry has found itself with excess productive capacity. Since 2006, the wind turbine industry has seen relentless cuts to its own estimates for orders and margins.

Hopes of "ever-increasing" demand artificially created by the debt and subsidies of the OECD countries did not materialize. Instead, the industry has found itself with overcapacity and cut-through competition. Remember that "imitation is simpler than innovation". It should therefore not be a surprise that the prices of turbines have been plummeting, margins have been falling, and with them the valuations and creditworthiness of the producers.

The marginal cost of production of wind turbines has also benefited from the "learning rates", although at a much smaller pace than solar. At the end of the day, a wind turbine is a mechanical item with efficiency gains coming from physical forces, whereas solar efficiency gains are more technological.

The story of overcapacity and marginal cost pressure is very familiar, and may force the sector to consolidation and shrink to grow capacity.

The main beneficiaries are the wind farm developers who can buy more, cheaper, and better quality turbines. Wind turbine costs represent approximately 70% of the total system costs.[47]

Wind competitiveness

Wind power suffers from intermittence and unreliability, but enjoys higher load factors than solar because wind can blow during the day and night.

Wind power is significantly cheaper than solar power, and in most countries wind delivers electricity at a far lower cost than the residential electricity price, and is approaching average wholesale electricity prices in a number of large markets, including Italy, Spain, the UK, and China, and has already attained and surpassed parity in Brazil.

The global installed capacity has grown from 74 GW in 2006 to 318 GW in 2013.[48] However, even using the expectations of the sector, which expects to multiply by three the number of global wind installations by 2020, turbine manufacturers would still have a 20% overcapacity.[49]

Wind power is already almost competitive versus natural gas-fired power across many regions. In Germany, with capacity factor of 21%, at $10/MMBtu. In Southern Europe, with capacity factor of 24%, at $9/MMBtu. And in the UK, US, and Australia, with capacity factor of 30%, at $7/MMBtu.[50] And, according to the EIA, further cost reductions and increases in efficiency could reduce the breakevens by 2020 by $1/MMBtu. Wind power will continue to grow, and the system will have to learn to cope with its challenges.

The world of solar power is far from flat

Losing everything, is like the sun going down on me

Elton John/Bernie Taupin

"No one can embargo the sun" famously said President Jimmy Carter in 1979. Pressured by the high oil prices, Carter had embraced a large development programme with the ambitious strategic goal of generating 20% of the US energy needs from solar by the year 2000.[51] At the end of the day, solar was clean, domestic, and would never run out. A perfect solution?

Well, 35 years later, solar photovoltaics (PV) represent a very small share of the world's total electricity, but, according to the EIA, are expected to grow towards 2% of global supply by 2035.

Germany and the European Union love affair with solar
The European Union currently accounts for over 75% of global solar PV capacity, led by Germany and China and is expected to grow capacity from 1% in 2010 to 5% by 2035, according to the EIA.

Since 2008, Germany has been installing 7.5 GW (the equivalent of seven and half nuclear power stations per year for the last three years).

In terms of peak capacity (which is different from actual production), Germany has 50% more solar capacity than natural gas, and is not far behind coal in terms of peak capacity.[52]

The large growth in capacity has been helped by the very generous tariffs which in some cases were not adjusted quickly enough to reflect the rapidly falling costs of solar PV, thus increasing the return on investment for solar. In some countries, governments responded quickly by reducing feed-in tariffs to levels that better reflected costs, but overall the combination of higher returns and low interest rate environments still supported the massive expansion in solar PV installations.

The actual production from solar is still much smaller than its capacity, but large enough to have profound implications on peak pricing.

The debacle of solar equities

Solar stocks were among the worst performers from 2010 to 2012, despite the Fukushima hype and extremely generous tariff support.

In yet another case of overly bullish "ever-increasing" demand from OECD and China, the production capacity for solar panels expanded very quickly, particularly in China, where the production capacity was looking to meet both domestic and export demand.

But manufacturing capacity has expanded much more quickly than actual demand, which has put pressure on margins in what has become a "buyers' market". By 2011, manufacturing capacity was 20 GW higher than production and two-thirds higher than the new capacity installed worldwide that year.[53]

Trade tensions have arisen between the United States, Europe and China, resulting in the imposition of import tariffs by the United States in 2012 on solar panels from China.[54] Several large companies have already gone bankrupt, such as Germany's Q-Cells (the largest solar cell manufacturer in Europe) in April 2012 and a wave of consolidation is underway.[55]

How quickly the balance is restored depends largely on the rate of growth of demand for solar PV. China represents a large potential market, but its demand for solar PV in the short term is uncertain.

What went wrong?

People tend to believe that tariffs that support volume growth and cut prices more rapidly will benefit the industry and valuations as a whole more, but will hurt higher cost participants sooner. Well, this is not necessarily the case. The reason is that the sector starts from overcapacity and excessive costs and even with costs falling 39%, and subsidies that guarantee on average €180/MWh, they still lose money.[56]

Developers in regional markets in some cases would prefer capacity caps with higher tariffs, thus enjoying the spoils of overcapacity-driven solar average selling price pressures from their suppliers.

The Asian manufacturers have shown zero discipline in capex or growth. They have responded to short-term price signals to further expand, which virtuously keeps driving down the cost.

At the heart of this we have an over-leveraged industry: 80–85% at project level is already unsustainable, but the companies are leveraged also at the holding level, making total gearing to the tune of 5–6x net debt to EBITDA.[57]

Overcapacity in all parts of the value chain, from wafers to polysilicon and development stands at more than 50–60% on average, and competitors (not just Chinese, Germans too) show low capital discipline and imperialistic market share aspirations.[58]

So at the minimum price signal (a tariff announcement, a government renewable plan confirmation), capacity would grow way above demand.

And despite the fall in costs, it is astonishing to see the companies unable to get their heads above water. Working capital requirements eat any equity internal rates of return and debt obliterates the profitability.

The Asian countries build more and more capacity, however, some parts of the production chain are much easier (from a technology and timing standpoint) and cheaper to add than others. To simplify, the lower is the value, the easier/cheaper it is to add capacity. As a result, the value chain today would look like an inverse pyramid with more capacity downstream than upstream.

If you wanted to be cynical, you could say that the Germans and Spaniards actually tricked the Chinese by sending positive price signals for a few years, enticing the Asians to build, build and build, and now that there is massive overcapacity, the cost of solar PV is moving close to grid parity.

With the limited ability of governments to keep these super-normal subsidies (85% of subsidies for solar are in Europe, mostly Germany), the industry is condemned to a massive restructuring.

Solar returns are collapsing because the key benefactor, government subsidies, altered basic economics. Subsidies created this industry and are now part of its demise. The subsidies caused artificial signals for demand that resulted in overcapacity of supply due to a combination of overbuilding and expansions. Is it temporary? Maybe, and if "temporary" means five years it will be death for many.

Solar energy is not a problem as a concept. Greed fuelled by government-led price signals, that fade as quickly as they come, added to unsustainable debt and undisciplined capital allocation are the problem.

Marginal cost of solar PV is getting cheaper

The cost of solar PV fell by 44% in just two years, from 2010 to 2012, due to the combination of overcapacity and lower input cost.[59]

In addition to overcapacity and cut-throat competition, the industry has benefited from a significant "learning curve" through research and development, as well as the reduction of key components such as purified silicon, which has suffered a sharp fall since 2008, and altogether have resulted in much lower marginal costs of production.

The installers of solar PV systems have benefited greatly from overcapacity in the solar panel manufacturing industry.

In fact, at current LNG prices, solar power is cheaper in many parts of Asia than electricity from LNG, meaning solar PV don't need subsidies to compete with fossil fuels.

The cost structure of solar will have a strong impact across the energy space, through the demand displacement, asset valuation, and in a world of deflating prices, oil and gas producers start to expect a world of deflating energy prices, they may be less inclined to sit on large reserves and may begin pumping faster.

Solar leasing and green bonds

The financing of solar projects, both residential and utility-scale, has been a positive contributor to the growth of the industry.

The most notable development here has been in the form of "solar leasing", whereby the rooftop panels are owned by a third party who effectively leases the rooftop from the home/factory/ office owner, the latter receiving payment normally through a reduction in electricity bills, paid for by the investor.

This provides the benefit of cheaper and cleaner solar electricity to the homeowner, while negating the need for the significant initial capital outlay.

The panel owner or lessee earns their return via incentive mechanisms such as the US Investment Tax Credit, and via the sale of electricity back to the local utility.

At the utility-scale level, the emergence of innovative financing vehicles such as "green bonds" is also facilitating deployment of the technology. Green bonds are essentially a pooled investment which invests in the debt of many different projects, potentially in different countries or jurisdictions, thereby reducing technology, political, regulatory and other risks via the portfolio effect. The long-dated nature of solar farms with their (relatively, depending on location) predictable revenue streams, low risk (no moving parts, low maintenance) and attractive returns relative to bond yields make them especially attractive to certain types of investor such as pension funds or insurance companies, as well as companies looking to boost their green credentials while earning an attractive return on capital.

Meanwhile, incentives continue to help flatten the energy world.

The overcapacity in manufacturing capacity, the technology learning curve, and the marginal costs have helped prices fall dramatically, but are still far from close to grid parity. Remember that as solar costs and wind costs fall and installations soar, oil and gas prices also become more competitive as supply is ample. The mother of all battles.

Biofuels and Food Inflation

Transforming food into fuels is a monstrosity.

Fidel Castro

Energy security in disguise

The biofuels industry was another government response to the need for energy security to reduce the dependence on Middle Eastern oil as, following the crisis of the 1970s, governments around the world took the desperate gamble of using what had traditionally been "food and feed" as "fuel".

The United States, the "Saudi Arabia of corn", decided to "feed" its vehicles with corn-based ethanol. Brazil, one of the largest producers of sugar in the world, had long decided to "feed" its vehicles with sugar-based ethanol. In all cases, the governments have played a key role in the development of the biofuels industry through a combination of incentives ("the carrot") as well as mandates ("the stick").

The "regulatory carrot"

Governments around the world actively incentivized biofuel infrastructure and consumption through a combination of tools.

In the United States, the government introduced ethanol tax credits of up to $1 per gallon for blending, and placed a tariff of 50 cents per gallon on imported ethanol. That is, not only was it incentivizing domestic production, it was also dis-incentivizing imports.

Furthermore, the US government incentivized infrastructure through a combination of loans and tax credits, and incentivized research and development through generous funding programmes.

The "regulatory stick"

However, governments have also imposed aggressive mandates and penalties to ensure their strategic goals were achieved.

In the United States, the Energy Policy Act put in place aggressive mandates for annual consumption that forced a geometrical growth of consumption irrespective of prices.[60] But, as is often the case, these "forced volumetric" targets tend to be very inflexible, and have had second order and unintended effects, as I will discuss shortly.

In China, the target is "10 percent biofuels mandate by 2020, as part of an overall 15 percent renewable target for 2020".[61]

In Europe, the Renewable Energy Directive (RED) specified a 10% renewable content by 2020 but has been scaled back to the 5–7.5% range in recent months.[62]

India is currently at 5% ethanol mandate, but is scheduled to move to 10% as soon as domestic production is in place, with a goal of 20% for all biofuels content by 2017.[63]

Renewable Identification Numbers (RINs)

RINs are a complex mechanism used by governments to ensure their biofuel volumetric mandates are implemented and biofuels are actually blended into motor fuel . . . "or else"!

RINs are issued at the point of biofuels production or import. They are some kind of "ethanol birth certificate" issued by the ethanol producer. When biofuels change ownership, the RINs are also transferred to the refiners and blenders, who are required to blend a portion of their supply with ethanol or biodiesel. In those years when ethanol or biodiesel industry-wide blending exceeds the mandated level, excess RINs are generated that can be used to offset blending shortfalls in future years. These excess RINs can be sold or purchased.[64]

In 2012, the United States suffered its worst drought in 50 years. The devastating dryness had a brutal impact on corn yields and production. Prices rallied above $8/bushel, almost triple than three years earlier. The mandates had to be fulfilled, and most of the demand destruction came from the feed sector.

As a result of the lower production and the need to fulfil the mandates, over 40% of the corn produced in the United States was used for ethanol.[65] It was undeniable that the rigidity of the system had an impact on prices. Yet, many politicians were quick to blame the "speculators" for higher agricultural and food prices. How cynical.

The "ethanol blend wall"

Under current US federal regulations, all gasoline-powered vehicles must be able to accommodate ethanol blends of up to 10% (E10). There is another fuel with higher ethanol blend of 70–85% (E85) but it can only be used in vehicles that have been specifically designed to accommodate such higher ethanol content.[66]

The aggressive volumetric growth targets for biofuel blend were based on the assumption of growing gasoline demand. But once again reality is turning out to be quite different from what the politicians and regulators had anticipated. With nearly all fuel ethanol sold as blend for E10, and demand for gasoline not growing as anticipated, the mandated production volumes for ethanol are too large to be absorbed by the gasoline market, creating a saturation commonly referred to as the "blend wall", which poses a severe problem for ethanol producers.

Once again, regulation seems to be leading to overcapacity. Yes, another flattener.

Food inflation and inequality

Food inflation was the expected collateral damage for using "food and feed" as "fuel". Governments around the world, faced with the trade-off between energy security and food inflation, chose energy security. And they did it with their eyes wide open.

However, food inflation was a big issue, particularly for poor people and poor countries.

The policies were disguised as "domestic" but had a global impact. Yes, higher corn prices in North America, historically the largest exporter of grain in the world, mean higher global corn prices. Anyone surprised?

And the impact of higher food prices would be felt the most by poorer countries. Yes, while food may be a small portion of the inflation basket for the average North American citizen, it is a large portion for the average Indian, Chinese, and Indonesian.

No wonder biofuels remain highly controversial.

Shortages and physical hoarding as flatteners

Agricultural commodities have the most volatile supply of all commodities. Drought, floods, and freezing temperatures can have a dramatic effect on the harvest.

And lower supply, combined with low price elasticity of demand, results in sharply higher and volatile prices, as the market is forced to destroy demand and incentivize substitution.

Faced by inflation and possible shortages, producing countries have not been shy in imposing export quotas and restrictions. The list is long. In 2007 "Argentina put quantitative limits on wheat exports and raised export taxes on wheat, corn, soybeans, and soybean products. Ukraine, Serbia and India banned wheat exports. Russia and Kazakhstan raised export taxes on wheat. Kazakhstan banned exports of oilseeds and vegetable oils. Malaysia imposed export taxes on palm oil. India, traditionally an important rice exporter, placed an absolute restriction on all exports of non-basmati rice. Other countries panicked and bought rice and wheat at peak prices, just as a precaution".[67] And the list continues.

But, as is always the case, the market defends itself. Consumer governments such as China respond to the risk of food shortages in an even more aggressive way than to the risk of energy shortages.

The response and the defence mechanisms to these crises are, that's right, powerful flatteners.

Energy efficiency of biofuels

As a chemical engineer, you would probably scratch your head when you see that it takes approximately the same amount of energy to convert corn into ethanol as what we get out when we burn that ethanol. That is, from an energy perspective, the process of converting corn into ethanol is "energy neutral".

In the case of sugar-based ethanol the process is energy positive, which makes more sense than corn. That is, from an

energy perspective, it makes sense to transform sugar into ethanol and burn it in the car.

However, the rationale for the conversion is not necessarily
energy efficiency. The rationale for the conversion is about
economics and fuel independence.

From an energy-independence perspective, biofuel policies
are viewed as "domestic fuels", yet, as discussed above, the
impact can be global and will hurt poorer countries the most.

From an economics perspective, I remember during a conference where the CEO of a large agricultural multinational said
"the proof that food is too cheap is that we are using it to feed
our cars". Well, I don't necessarily agree with the statement due
to the impact of government mandates (which oblige that food
goes in the car) but he had a good point. People will blend
cheaper inputs to produce a more expensive product, without
any consideration to energy efficiency.

Meat prices: "corn with legs"

I remember the super-cycle price action in 2007 and how
energy and agricultural prices were moving up in tandem, with
the renewed fundamental linkage and increased correlation of
the biofuels channel.

But "chicken, pork, or beef are nothing more than corn with
legs". As a rule of thumb on the desk, we assumed that for
poultry, it took 2 pounds of corn to create 1 pound of meat.
For pork, the relationship increased to 4 to 1, and for beef it
was almost 8 to 1.[68] That is, the impact of high grain prices
would be reflected into higher meat prices. It was just a matter
of time.

But the meat producers were often unable to pass the
increasing costs to the consumers. The margins were eroded,
and many producers were being forced to liquidate their inventories and in some cases were taken out of business. Eventually,
the consolidation in the industry and higher feed costs did

respond, and today's higher meat prices reflect the accumulated pressure of higher feed and competition.

Another important implication of the trends in protein consumption is across emerging markets. According to the Food and Agriculture Organization (FAO), per-capita consumption of macronutrients (that is, energy, protein, and fats) is just 50–70% of that in developed countries.[69] There is a strong positive relationship between the level of income and the consumption of animal protein, with the consumption of meat, milk and eggs increasing at the expense of staple foods.

The super-cycle of farmland and agricultural logistical infrastructure

Farmland as a real option provides a right, but not an obligation, to the farmer, where the intrinsic value is given by the net profit value of estimated cash flows based on crop prices, yields, production costs, and other considerations. No surprise farmland has expanded in response to higher agricultural prices.

In particular, Brazil has emerged as a major agricultural powerhouse during the past few years. A net importer of agricultural products in the 1970s, the country now ranks among the world's five largest agricultural producers and exporters. Current cropland is 31% of land area, including corn, soybean, coffee, and sugar. Agribusiness accounts for nearly 38% of the country's exports.[70]

The increase in production had to be met with an increase in export capacity. In Brazil, the expansion of ports has allowed it to become the largest exporter of corn, overtaking the United States. In April 2013, Bloomberg reported a 20-mile-long line of trucks waiting to offload the record harvest of soybeans while more than 200 vessels waited to dock and load the cargoes. On average, the ships waited 39 days, at an estimated cost of US$30,000 per day.[71] Currently, Brazil sits in the bottom third in the global rankings for competitiveness in road, rail, and port infrastructure. But the incentives are there.

The new frontier is Sub-Saharan Africa, where the focus is on productivity. "In 2009, G8 countries committed $20 billion (including $3.5 billion from the United States) to support sustainable agricultural development in the world's poorest regions, including Sub-Saharan Africa".[72] Fertilizers help increase yields and prevent plagues. Currently China, India, the United States, and the EU countries account for more than two-thirds (65%) of the world's fertilizer consumption in agriculture.[73]

Genetically modified crops

Technology is playing an important role in agriculture through genetically modified (GM) crops, which are altered in the lab to tolerate herbicides better, fight off pests, and produce higher yields.

GM crops are widely used worldwide. In the United States, approximately 95% of soybeans and 75% of corn are GM. In Argentina, more than 95% of soybeans are GM. In Brazil, 50% of soybeans are GM.[74]

GM crops are a game changer. In India, insect-resistant cotton has led to yield increases on average more than 50%.[75]

Like all technologies, there is a learning curve and some downside risks. In the United States, engineers had found a GM corn that would fight off a feared plague of moth, but turned out to produce a pollen that could possibly kill larvae of the monarch butterfly!

A flatter agricultural world

In the longer run, the biofuel super-cycle may be good news for emerging markets via the food channel as well as the export trade.

Over the past few years, the prices of grains have reached multi-year highs due to a combination of biofuel demand as well as acute drought in North America and other parts of the world.

The high grains prices have incentivized the expansion of planted land and the development of new infrastructure. Brazil, for example, has significantly expanded its ports and shipping capacity, and is set to overtake the United States as the largest exporter for corn in the world.

These supply-side developments, like the dotcom bubble, combined with a slowdown in demand for biofuels from the transportation sector, may bring much lower grain and food prices in the future. A food flattener in full force.

Good news for the food consumers. Good news for poor countries.

NOTES

1. Daniel Lacalle (2013). *Viaje a la Libertad Economica*. Deusto.
2. Lawrence Summers (16 February 2014). *America Risks becoming a Downton Abbey Economy*. http://www.ft.com/intl/cms/s/2/8751 55ce-8f25-11e3-be85-00144feab7de.html#axzz32xxVuATv
3. Richard H. Thaler and Cass R. Sunstein (2008). *Nudge: Improving Decisions About Health, Wealth, and Happiness*. New Haven, CT: Yale University Press.
4. Noah Brenner (2010). Judge denies stay in moratorium ruling. *Upstream*, 24 June.
5. Richard Seymour (29 March 2012). *A Short History of Privatisation in the UK: 1979–2012*. http://www.theguardian.com/commentisfree /2012/mar/29/short-history-of-privatisation
6. Philip Angeli (27 March 2014). *DOE Approves LNG Exports to Non-free Trade Countries*. http://www.dlapiper.com/en/us/insights /publications/2014/03/doe-approves-lng-exports/
7. http://energy.gov/fe/services/natural-gas-regulation/lng-export -study
8. Reuters (4 March 2014). *China to "Declare War" on Pollution, Premier Says*. http://www.reuters.com/article/2014/03/05 /us-china-parliament-pollution-idUSBREA2405W20140305
9. Ibid.

10. Ibid.
11. According to US Energy Information Administration.
12. Christina Nunez (22 October 2013). *Harbin Smog Crisis Highlights China's Coal Problem.* http://news.nationalgeographic.com/news/energy/2013/10/131022-harbin-ice-city-smog-crisis-china-coal/
13. https://itunes.apple.com/us/app/china-air-pollution-index/id477700080?mt=8
14. http://www.dlacalle.com/green-energy-costs-rise/ and http://www.renewableenergyworld.com/rea/news/article/2014/01/german-energy-minister-proposes-cuts-to-renewable-subsidies-industry-reacts
15. Mary Harris Jones (1925). *The Autobiography of Mother Jones.* Chicago: Charles H. Kerr.
16. *Coal Statistics.* http://www.worldcoal.org/resources/coal-statistics/
17. *GDP Growth (Annual %).* http://data.worldbank.org/indicator/NY.GDP.MKTP.KD.ZG
18. http://www.iea.org/newsroomandevents/pressreleases/2013/december/name-45994-en.html
19. *Improving Efficiencies.* http://www.worldcoal.org/coal-the-environment/coal-use-the-environment/improving-efficiencies/
20. CBS News (12 September 2013). *China to Ban New Coal-Fired Power Plants around Beijing over Pollution Concerns.* http://www.cbsnews.com/news/china-to-ban-new-coal-fired-power-plants-around-beijing-over-pollution-concerns/
21. CAAC Clean Air Alliance of China (April 2013). *"Twelfth Five-Year Plan" on Air Pollution Prevention and Control in Key Regions.*
22. Environmental Protection Agency, *Particulate Matter (PM) Research.* http://www.epa.gov/airscience/air-particulatematter.htm
23. CommodityOnline (20 March 2014). *Coal no Longer King, but Getting Damn Cheap.* http://www.commodityonline.com/news/coal-no-longer-king-but-getting-damn-cheap-58287-3-58288.html
24. Francisco Blanch (2014). Another bad year for king coal. *Global Energy Weekly*, 20 March.
25. *Spark Spread.* http://www.investment-and-finance.net/derivatives/s/spark-spread.html
26. *The Economist* (12 October 2013). *How to Lose Half a Trillion Euros.* http://www.economist.com/news/briefing/21587782-europes-electricity-providers-face-existential-threat-how-lose-half-trillion-euros
27. The demand for electricity is not constant. It changes over time in response to intraday and seasonal drivers. *Baseload power*

demand is the amount that is needed at all times of the day, and has historically been provided by coal and nuclear, which are prevented from being easily shut down by lower running costs and technical issues. *Peak power demand* is the extra electricity required at peak times of the day or seasons, and has historically been provided by natural gas or hydro, which are easier to adjust. In hot countries, peak demand tends to happen around the middle of the day driven by industrial/business activity and air conditioning. In cold countries, the demand tends to be flatter across the day.

28. *The Economist* (12 October 2013). *How to Lose Half a Trillion Euros.* http://www.economist.com/news/briefing/21587782 -europes-electricity-providers-face-existential-threat-how-lose-half -trillion-euros

29. http://www.bloomberg.com/news/2014-03-14/merkel-s-green -push-blows-away-german-coal-power-profits-energy.html

30. National Renewable Energy Laboratory (March 2009). *Feed-in Tariff Policy: Design, Implementation, and RPS Policy Interactions.* http://www.nrel.gov/docs/fy09osti/45549.pdf

31. *The Economist* (12 October 2013). *How to Lose Half a Trillion Euros.* http://www.economist.com/news/briefing/21587782-europes -electricity-providers-face-existential-threat-how-lose-half-trillion -euros

32. Mark Fulton, Capalino Reid and Josef Auer (September 2012). *The German Feed-in Tariff: Recent Policy Changes.* http://www .dbresearch.com/PROD/DBR_INTERNET_EN-PROD /PROD0000000000294376/The+German+Feed-in+Tariff%3A+Re cent+Policy+Changes.PDF

33. Jacob Klimstra (21 November 2013). *Cogeneration and On-Site Power Production. Capacity factors, utilisation factors and load factors.* http://www.cospp.com/articles/print/volume-14/issue-6 /regulars/editor-s-letter/capacity-factors-utilisation-factors-and -load-factors.html

34. Fraunhofer Solar Energy. *Energy and Living.* http://www.fraunhofer .de/en/research-topics/energy-living/solar-energy.html

35. *The Economist* (12 October 2013). *How to Lose Half a Trillion Euros.* http://www.economist.com/news/briefing/21587782-europes -electricity-providers-face-existential-threat-how-lose-half-trillion -euros

36. Ibid.

37. Shayle Kann (3 June 2010). *The Global PV Market: Yesterday, Today, and Tomorrow.* http://www.greentechmedia.com/articles/read/the-global-pv-market-yesterday-today-and-tomorrow

38. According to US Energy Information Administration.

39. http://www.forbes.com/sites/williampentland/2014/02/19/stampede-of-investors-sue-spain-over-cuts-in-solar-subsidies/

40. According to US Energy Information Administration.

41. International Energy Agency (2012). *Key World Energy Statistics 2010.* http://www.worldenergyoutlook.org/media/weo2010.pdf

42. http://europa.eu/rapid/press-release_SPEECH-13-434_en.htm

43. http://instituteforenergyresearch.org/wp-content/uploads/2014/05/Hard-Facts-May-2014-Final.pdf

44. National Commission of Energy, Spain. http://www.minetur.gob.es/es-es/gabineteprensa/notasprensa/2013/documents/presentacion_reforma%20el%C3%A9ctrica120713_v5.pdf

45. Ibid.

46. Ibid.

47. European Wind Energy Association. *Wind Energy's Frequently Asked Questions (FAQ).* http://www.ewea.org/wind-energy-basics/faq/

48. European Wind Energy Association (18 January 2008). *Continuing Boom in Wind Energy – 20 GW of New Capacity in 2007.* http://www.gwec.net/index.php?id=30&no_cache=1&tx_ttnews%5Btt_news%5D=121&tx_ttnews%5BbackPid%5D=4&cHash=f9b4af1cd0

49. Capacity installed vs. expected productive capacity.

50. http://phys.org/news/2014-03-power-competitive-natural-gas.html

51. John Wihbey (11 November 2008). *Jimmy Carter's Solar Panels: A Lost History That Haunts Today.* http://www.yaleclimatemediaforum.org/2008/11/jimmy-carters-solar-panels/

52. William Pentland (10 March 2014). *Is Natural Gas-Fired Electricity An Intermittent Resource?* http://peakoil.com/consumption/is-natural-gas-fired-electricity-an-intermittent-resource/comment-page-1

53. International Energy Agency (2012). *World Energy Outlook 2012.* http://www.worldenergyoutlook.org/publications/weo-2012/

54. Keith Bradsher and Diane Cardwell (17 May 2012). *U.S. Slaps High Tariffs on Chinese Solar Panels.* http://www.nytimes.com/2012/05/18

/business/energy-environment/us-slaps-tariffs-on-chinese-solar-panels.html?pagewanted=all&_r=0

55. BBC News Business (2 April 2012). Solar Panel Maker Q-Cells to File for Bankruptcy. http://www.bbc.com/news/business-17587830

56. Daniel Lacalle (6 July 2011). *Solar Energy Stocks – The Debacle of Tariff Support Models.* http://www.stockopedia.com/content/solar-energy-stocks-the-debacle-of-tariff-support-models-58029/

57. Bloomberg: Average consensus of quoted solar companies.

58. Bloomberg: Estimated capacity vs. demand.

59. http://cleantechnica.com/2014/02/18/cost-of-solar-pv/ and http://www.bloomberg.com/news/2013-01-21/solar-costs-to-fall-as-reits-emerge-as-source-of-funding.html

60. *Renewable Fuel Standards (RFS).* http://www.epa.gov/OTAQ/fuels/renewablefuels/

61. Jim Lane (31 December 2013). *Biofuels Mandates Around the World: 2014.* http://www.biofuelsdigest.com/bdigest/2013/12/31/biofuels-mandates-around-the-world-2014/

62. Ibid.

63. Ibid.

64. Brent D. Yabobucci (22 July 2013). *Analysis of Renewable Identification Numbers (RINs) in the Renewable Fuel Standard (RFS).* http://www.fas.org/sgp/crs/misc/R42824.pdf

65. AgMRC (21May 2014). Ethanol Usage Projections and Corn Balance Sheet (mil. Bu.). https://www.extension.iastate.edu/agdm/crops/outlook/cornbalancesheet.pdf

66. National Governors Association. *Securing a Clean Energy Future: Greener Fuels, Greener Vehicles: A State Resource Guide.* http://www.nga.org/files/live/sites/NGA/files/pdf/0802GREENER FUELS.PDF

67. Karen Daynard and Terry Daynard (April 2011). *What are the Effects of Biofuels and Bioproducts on the Environment, Crop and Food Prices and World Hunger?* http://www.gfo.ca/LinkClick.aspx?fileticket=HKfOeU3cHTI%3D&tabid=139

68. Our own estimates.

69. Debashish Mukherjee, Akshat Seth, and Amit Saharia. (2013). *Winning in the Food in Emerging Markets: One Size Does Not Fit All.* http://www.atkearney.com/web/digital-business-forum/detail/-/asset_publisher/VMEx2L1PhjPS/content/winning-in-food-in-emerging-markets-one-size-does-not-fit-all/10192

70. Thais Leitão (17 October 2009). *Produção agrícola brasileira registra recorde em 2008 com alta de 9,1%.*
71. Daniel Azoulai, Henry Dunlop, and Brian Kuettel (20 December 2013). *Big Bottleneck: A Weak Transportation Network is Hurting Brazil's Once-hot Economy.* https://knowledge.wharton.upenn. edu/article/big-bottleneck-weak-transportation-network-hurting -brazils-hot-economy/
72. Keith Fuglie and Nicholas Rada (6 May 2013). *Research Raises Agricultural Productivity in Sub-Saharan Africa.* http://www.ers .usda.gov/amber-waves/2013-may/research-raises-agricultural -productivity-in-sub-saharan-africa.aspx
73. According to the FAO, 2013.
74. Monsanto (26 November 2012). *Do GM Crops Increase Yield?* http://www.monsanto.com/newsviews/pages/do-gm-crops -increase-yield.aspx
75. Ibid.

CHAPTER THIRTEEN

FLATTENER #10 – FISCAL, MONETARY, AND MACROECONOMIC FLATTENERS

Christians had a better chance against the lions than the American consumer has against OPEC.

Ed Markey

I spent the last weeks of 2012 busy with the launch of a new fund and travelling, visiting some of the most significant discoveries of the last decade, from Moccasin in the Gulf of Mexico to Jubilee in Ghana, through oil shale assets in Texas, and culminating in the most important annual meeting of the global oil industry, the Oil & Money Conference. An exceptional event, with the participation of people like the Secretary General of OPEC, Abdalla Salem El-Badri, the Saudi Prince Turki Al Faisal, directors of the largest oil companies, major financial institutions, and some investors.

It was evident by then that the internal disagreements among OPEC members were very real. Saudi Arabia had firmly set itself as the Central Bank of Oil, defending a well-balanced market, while Iran and Venezuela were taking a hawkish position towards production. The meetings of OPEC in Vienna since then have shown that the disagreements have increased because the oil price needed to breakeven differs more and more among members.

The "OPEC put"

The market often refers to the "OPEC put" as a price floor that will be protected by OPEC through production cuts. The perception among some participants is that the cartel plays the role of the "Central Bank of Oil" and can defend the price of oil at the level and for as long as they want, but the reality is very different.

The Swiss Central Bank can defend the floor of 1.20 against the euro by literally "printing as many Swiss francs as needed", because they are preventing the value of its currency from appreciating. But OPEC can only cut its production levels down to zero. That is, OPEC has "limited bullets" to defend the price of oil from going down. It resembles a central bank trying to defend its currency from depreciating. There are multiple cases where central banks have tried to defend their currency, and failed spectacularly, such as the run on the pound sterling by George Soros, where the Bank of England ran out of foreign reserves, or the collapse of the Thai baht that kick-started the Asian crisis.

In practical terms, OPEC will never cut its production to zero to defend the price. It will fold much earlier. First, zero oil production means zero oil revenues – no matter how strong the fiscal position. Second, the fields would incur some damage if production stops completely. Third, from a commercial perspective, they would be out of the market. Fourth, non-compliance would become an issue very quickly, thus penalizing those who comply.

At what level would OPEC stop defending the price?

Defending the price means a huge drop in output, a vast loss in market share, and unsustainable falls in revenues.

The loss of market share is a worrying consequence, and reduces the interaction and role of producers in the world markets. The rapid fall in political influence and significance, and the likelihood of further erosion, run counter to the fundamental precepts of producers.

At a certain point, producers move from a "defence of price" to a "defence of volume". This is a dramatic change in the dynamic of the oil market. A move from oligopolistic behaviour towards competition, which tends to lead to lower prices. The increase in production is required to maintain influence and increase revenues in a lower price environment. The transition can be drastic, but many producing countries have a tendency to "cheat" as they desperately need the revenues from oil. They want to create the impression that they are in control and can cut production, but in practice only a few large producers can. This is the reason why we see "cheats" on quotas constantly.

It is a mistake to think that OPEC defends a price that balances their fiscal budget ($100/bbl average) as these budgets are loaded with subsidies and unnecessary spending. OPEC will defend its position as a reliable supplier and price can be significantly lower.

The Btu that broke OPEC's back

Producing countries have become both used to and complacent about high oil prices. I remember back in 2005, when the Saudi Oil Minister Ali Al-Naimi was referring to $50/bbl as "too high, and out of line with fundamentals", implicitly blaming the "speculators". More recently, Saudi has indicated that $100/bbl would be a reasonable price. OPEC Secretary General Abdalla El-Badri said in 2014 that "supply is meeting demand and prices have been stable".[1]

And, in general, producing governments around the world have increased their government budgets substantially.

Walk around the streets of Tehran, Riyadh, Caracas, or Lagos and you will understand why OPEC countries need higher prices to balance budget. Massive subsidies and huge social and political spending are evident to any casual viewer, starting with the large proportion of young unemployed, living from government grants, to the countless government enterprises funded by oil revenues and the ludicrously low price of gasoline and services.

An APIC (Arab Petroleum Investment Corporation) study (http://www.apic.com/Research/Commentaries/Commentary _V7_N8–9_2012.pdf) has found that OPEC's breakeven price, that is the price of oil needed to balance the nation's budget, has soared from just $77/bbl in 2010 to $100/bbl in 2013.[2]

In Saudi Arabia, oil receipts account for 90% of government revenues, and directly account for 40% of GDP.[3] Riyadh is entirely dependent on oil for its economic and foreign policy, despite an increase in government-backed diversification initiatives. The government's diversification plan has focused on energy, power generation, natural gas exploration and petrochemical products, all connected to and funded by the oil industry.

Electricity, food, gasoline, housing and water are all subsidized, directly or indirectly, for Saudi's 28 million residents, who use the most oil per capita in the world. Saudi Arabia uses 40% more oil per person than the United States, and more than three times as much as Germany or France.[4]

Energy consumption in producing countries

Over the past few years, the domestic consumption of Saudi Arabia has increased on average by 8% annually,[5] which is larger than the supply growth, and has therefore decreased their net export capacity.

The increase in domestic demand is due to a combination of higher incomes, but also to subsidies, which shield consumers from higher international prices. Look at Venezuela for example, or Saudi Arabia, where gasoline is cheaper than a loaf of bread. As discussed, the large fuel subsidies "hook" consumers to the drug of "cheap fuel". Consumers are totally unaware of the true international prices of the fuel and end up consuming much more than they should or need.

Saudi has the highest domestic fuel subsidy per capita in the world, and the second largest in absolute terms ($43 billion in 2012), Iran is the largest ($61 billion in 2012) with a population almost three times larger, of 76 million people.[6] Saudi is selling oil domestically between $5 to $15 a barrel – a fraction of international prices.[7]

Saudis have been enjoying energy and power subsidies for decades. Saudi power-generating capacity has doubled in the past decade, partly for air-conditioning purposes, but it also takes energy to produce energy: pumps must be powered and vast quantities of seawater desalinated. "Aramco, the Saudi state oil company, sucks up nearly 10% of the country's energy output."[8]

Violent protests greeted Nigeria's attempts in January 2013 to raise the price of imported petrol. Only Iran, which had the most generous subsidy regime, has managed a big price hike – and it had a handy scapegoat in the form of sanctions.[9]

The vast majority of subsidies to fossil fuels come from the producing countries, such as Iran, Saudi Arabia, Russia, and Venezuela, who use these revenues to boost social and other costs, not just production. Large consumers such as China and India also have large fossil fuel subsidies in place, for social and inflation purposes.

While aimed at protecting consumers, subsidies aggravate fiscal imbalances, crowd out priority public spending, and depress private investment, including the energy sector. International energy prices have increased sharply over the past decade, yet many low- and middle-income economies have been reluctant to adjust their domestic energy prices to reflect these increases.

The resulting fiscal costs have been substantial and pose even greater fiscal risks for these countries if international prices continue to increase. In advanced economies, pass through has been higher, but prices remain below the levels needed to fully capture the negative externalities of energy consumption on the environment, public health, and traffic congestion.

The trend of demand growth, subsidies, and large social programmes is not sustainable and, little by little, has been increasing the breakeven price required to balance the budget. Furthermore, the higher breakeven increased the risk to lower prices as producing countries have a greater dependency on oil revenues, thus reducing their ability to cut production.

There are multiple reasons why crude oil prices may go down. One of them is the displacement of crude oil by other fuels, especially in transportation.

All these risks lead to the possibility of the incremental displacement, which forces producers to increase production, through what I call, "the Btu that broke OPEC's back".

Mortgaged future production

To make things worse, some producers like Venezuela have "mortgaged" much of their future production to China in the form of loans, adding to the tightening of the budget.

And to make things even worse, Venezuela is suffering from a lack of investment in the oil sector. In a way, "killing the goose that lays the golden eggs". Over time, oil production is not being replaced, as the money from the oil revenues is being used for other social programmes and keeps the population under control. But, as I always say, countries like Venezuela care for their poor, because every year they make many of them.

And removing these subsidies and social programmes can be extremely painful.

In the case of Venezuela, the depreciation of the bolivar (which as of the beginning of 2014 was trading at just 7% of its official exchange rate[10]) is already adding inflationary pressures to the economy.

Imagine what would happen if they lift the subsidies, and effectively "float" the price of oil. Inflation would skyrocket even further.

A default seems unavoidable, in my humble view.

The problem created by these self-imposed measures reminds me of how hunters catch monkeys in the jungle. You put a few peanuts inside a small hole in a tree. The hole is big enough for the monkey to put its hand in, but not big enough to take it out full of peanuts. Believe it or not, the monkey will not release the peanuts and will be "self-handcuffed" to the tree for the hunters to catch. Well, that's subsidies for you.

The paradox of plenty

Over the years I have witnessed first-hand the political and security problems that come with the "curse of oil", or "paradox of plenty".

In 1996, while visiting Nigeria, a massive shortage in gasoline led to riots and vandalism across the streets. There were massive queues of cars outside the service stations. Crude and products were being stolen from pipelines. As ironic as it was, one of the largest oil-producing countries in the world was not able to provide to its own population.

Over the years I saw countries like Venezuela, Iran, Colombia, Kenya, and Uganda benefit from the prosperity that came from the oil industry, but the same saw a massive increase in security threats and inequality.

Countries with the natural resources to be among the richest and most prosperous in the world, were instead facing enormous social unrest and political problems due to the "free money" that comes with oil.

Part of the problem was driven by macroeconomic forces. The "Dutch disease" is a well-known phenomenon that takes its name after the hardships that befell the Netherlands after it found natural gas, where the demand for the energy and the inflow of dollar denominated revenues led to a sharp appreciation of the currency. Non-oil-related industries become less competitive, and when the tide turns, the country is left vulnerable with no oil revenues and no alternative source of revenues.

Part of the problem is that many of these countries where oil was found often lacked a strong democratic and legal foundation. These geopolitical problems have also shaped the way in which the industry invests. Projects that would normally require 10–20-year timeframes are not often carried out due to political turmoil, lack of a clear and reliable legislation, property rights, security, and taxation and investment frameworks.

I remember one night in Freetown, Sierra Leone, when a friend of mine said "you better expect to recover the invested capital in two years – that is long term over here".

Over the years, I also saw examples of oil countries that had developed in an admirable way. Like Uganda or Ghana, where I was pleased to see that the "curse of oil" was being contained. And I remember walking down the beautiful streets of Baku in Azerbaijan, and seeing buildings that resembled Paris. Or how old and shabby airports and roads were being replaced by magnificent new airports and highways, with a much renewed fleet of cars. The countries remained exposed to commodity prices, but the creation of wealth was obvious.

The oil tax weapon

I contend that for a nation to try to tax itself into prosperity is like a man standing in a bucket and trying to lift himself up by the handle.

WINSTON CHURCHILL

Consumer governments addicted to oil taxes
The United States, Japan, Germany, the UK, and much of the OECD governments earn taxes from fuel consumers. And these taxes are very large.

In some cases they are exorbitant, and generate revenues larger than what the oil producer countries earn. Look at the

Netherlands, where the tax is over 65% of the retail price. Interestingly, often these taxes are somewhat "hidden" in the currency and units conversion. Most people in Holland are familiar with the price of gasoline in EUR/litre that they pay at the pump and the price of crude oil in USD/bbl, but they have absolutely no idea how they compare. Well, many would be shocked to know that they pay $373/boe.[11] And the picture is not that different across the OECD. It would be interesting to see the reaction from the public if OPEC educated consumers and started to quote the price of crude oil in USD/litre.

The original intention of the taxes was to disincentivize demand through higher prices. But over time consumers become used to higher prices which, as is often the case, had some unintended consequences. Indeed, higher taxes made the consumers less sensitive to changes in oil prices, which has historically contributed to the volatility in crude oil, as demand destruction requires much higher prices.

The consumer governments are "free riding" on OPEC. They often blame them for instability, but are taxing their domestic consumers and making a "bigger cut" than the producers themselves.

The problem is that the consumer governments are "hooked on oil taxes". They need these precious oil revenues to balance their stretched budgets and debt.

So what happens if natural gas or electric cars start to take away market share from oil products? Certainly, the consumer governments will look for ways to replace those oil taxes through natural gas or power taxes. This is easier when done at the "pump" or gas station, but how about recharging the car at home by simply plugging the car to the electric switch? If power taxes are increased, this will have an impact on all other uses of power. This conflict of interest explains why many OECD governments have cynically been promoting alternative fuels "on the surface", but not in practice. Look for example at the large subsidies for the car industry, or the subsidies to renew the fleet of cars and reduce the inventory of gasoline and diesel cars.

Either way, over the long run, these somewhat "hidden taxes" penalize consumer competitiveness. Unfortunately, there is very little that consumers can do about it. The "oil tax weapon" is very much in the hands of the governments.

Consumer governments hostage of oil subsidies

China, India, Indonesia, and many other net importers and consumer countries across emerging markets have historically subsidized oil prices for consumers through fixed regulated prices.[12]

So, when international oil prices are lower than the domestic fixed price, the mechanism acts as a regular tax (the consumers pay the government). On the other hand, when international prices are higher than the domestic fixed price, the mechanism acts as a "negative tax" (the government pays the consumers). It is often the case that the fixed prices are set too low, that is, the fixed price mechanism becomes "one-way negative tax".

The original idea of the subsidy was to "protect" consumers against volatility and inflation. But, yet again, the second-order effects are devastating. The subsidies make consumers totally insensitive to increases in international prices, they incentivize fraud and smuggling, they are bad for the environment, and they can spiral out of control as they deteriorate the current account, which can devalue the currency, and in turn increase the cost of energy imports and subsidies, thus creating a negative spiral that feeds on itself.

But there is a large difference between China and India.

In China, the subsidies are financed by budget surpluses. The oil subsidies are a "redistribution" of wealth. Not a good practice, but more manageable.

In India, on the other hand, the subsidies are financed by debt, by budget deficits. There is absolutely no justification. There is only a downside. These subsidies are suicidal. The consumer governments know it, and are slowly trying to remove them, but they are often caught in their own trap of inflation and social unrest.[13]

Government defence budgets

> Freedom is only provided by the military. Politicians just say words.
>
> GENE SIMMONS

> The need for a substantial American force presence in the Gulf transcends the issue of the regime of Saddam Hussein.
>
> PROJECT FOR THE NEW AMERICAN CENTURY

The United States has the largest military budget in the world, and by a very long way.

In absolute terms, the US military budget stands at $650 billion, larger than the next 10 countries put together.[14] Shocking.

In relative terms, expressed as % GDP, the US military budget is also the largest in the world, greater than Israel or China or Russia.[15] Also shocking.

Clearly, military is a big business for the United States, which not only holds a leading military position, but is also an engine of research and development of new technology.

Clearly, a large military is a very powerful defensive tool, a deterrent to attack. But the US military has also been a powerful "offensive" tool. Dark episodes such as Vietnam and Afghanistan were supported by "ideological" views. And on other occasions, such as Iraq (twice), the rationale had more economic interests – behaving as the "oil police".

But a more energy independent United States is less vulnerable to geopolitical crises. There is a lower incentive for the United States to defend its own selfish interests in oil-driven conflicts, when they are an oil and gas superpower themselves.

In fact, an energy independent United States opens the door to a significant reduction in government military spending to balance the budget and reduce its deficit.

But a less militarized United States may leave a gap. Will other countries defend their short oil position through war in the Middle East? How about China? Is a more powerful military in China a larger threat to the United States in the long run. Who knows?

Recent developments between Russia and Ukraine are bringing the United States to the forefront through its leading role in NATO. Clearly, geopolitics will continue to play an important role in global politics and economics. While the flattening, equalization, and globalization of the energy world can make consumers less vulnerable to geopolitical shocks, it does not make them indifferent or completely isolated.

Marshmallow behaviour

In the 1960s and 1970s, Stanford University researchers conducted a series of tests famously known as the "Marshmallow Experiment". In the studies, a child was given a choice between a marshmallow (or other treat) that he or she could have immediately, or two marshmallows if the child was willing to wait.

Years down the road, the kids who had been able to wait showed higher levels of development, both as rated by their parents and as measured by factors like SAT scores – suggesting an important link between delayed gratification and long-term success.

Most governments, driven by the desire of short-term results and re-election, resemble the child who can't wait. Debt and government spending is the easy answer for growth. One could agree that the political cycle is too short, that governments should have more time to make sure they are judged and incentivized to make the right long-term decisions. But a cynical answer to that would be "see how much damage they have done in four years, imagine if they stayed without the need for a re-election". Whether a government is able to continue for a second or third term in a row, or changes every four years, the main driver will remain as short-term behaviours.

I remember when I first moved to Singapore. I was the CEO of Asian operations. To get the job I had to be interviewed by the government. "Would you shut down your Singapore operations within the next 10 to 15 years, and run your business somewhere else?" was the question. "Wow", I thought to myself. I could see the huge benefits that "political visibility" gave the Singapore government. They only worried about doing the right thing. The risk of re-election was not part of the decision-making process, or at least that was the case in mid-2009. The latest elections have shown a growth in the "penalty vote" as inflation and the cost of living have notably increased. Time will tell if the risk of re-election becomes a bigger factor in their decision-making process.

Let's change the tax rules

In the early days of the industry, corporates were the only and dominant players in the exploration, production, refining, and distribution of crude oil. However, host governments became increasingly aware of their power, and progressively started to take a larger share of the revenues. Over time, the assets were nationalized and state oil companies took control, although they still depended heavily on the foreign corporates for the distribution of oil.

Yet, there is a clear risk of "wrong-way exposure". This is true not only for crude oil, but also for other commodities. Look at what happened in Indonesia in early 2014, where a large US mining group halted exports over a dispute with the government on a new tax scheme which unilaterally raised taxes from 25% up to 60% by the second half of 2016.[16]

The mining company says the tax breaches their contracts, although the government has hinted that it may review the tax if the company makes a firmer commitment on the construction and supply agreements for new smelters. That is, the government is "incentivizing" further investments through the introduction of a higher tax and penalty. These changes inspire very little confidence about the enforceability of contracts. More "marshmallow behaviour" for you.

Monetary experiments and the credit risk time bomb

Monetary experiments

> Paper money always returns to its intrinsic value – zero.
>
> VOLTAIRE

> Currency devaluation is merely a transfer of wealth from all of a nation's citizens to politically favoured industries . . . Furthermore, devaluation does not make a nation more competitive. It does nothing to spur increased domestic saving or external capital investment, which lead to the increased application of capital per capita, the only sources of increased worker productivity and the only sources of increased real wages.
>
> PATRICK BARRON

Black gold

"Taking monetary policy and stimulus out of the energy equation is wrong". I remember hearing these words as I witnessed the phantom cities in China, endless streets of empty buildings.

"Monetary policy disrupts and expansive measures give incorrect signals of demand that we, as humans, tend to overestimate as new paradigms". My friend reminded me of a figure: almost 75% of oil demand growth between 2000 and 2007 was the result of excess global credit.

During 2012 I received many questions by the media about "rising oil prices". But when I pointed to monetary factors and the devaluation of the US dollar as key factors, everyone shrugged. The relationship between oil and gold (the price of oil in gold terms) had remained stable even though crude oil had skyrocketed in US dollar terms from $50/bbl to $110/bbl.

Oil prices, adjusted for inflation, peaked in 1978. And this was true for many commodity prices, which responded to the monetary tsunami from central banks around the world in general, and the US Treasury in particular with trillions of dollars of monetary stimuli. Welcome to the "Bernanke era", where commodity prices were no longer driven by supply and demand fundamentals, but by a third driver: monetary factors.

The World Bank Commodity Index has multiplied by four since the beginning of the Bernanke era of quantitative easing.[17]

Printing money and more than a decade of lowering interest rates have created inflationary pressures on commodity prices, which have partially offset the deflationary pressures of technology and the learning curve.

Since 2001 the main central banks have added a money supply equivalent to $10 trillion. In the period between 2009 and 2013 alone, the US Federal Reserve created half of the money supply of its multi-century history.[18] The US monetary policy had a dual objective. Domestically, low US dollar interest rates incentivized consumption and investment, and disincentivized savings. Internationally, a weaker US dollar favoured the competitiveness and exports of US products, and disincentivized imports of foreign products. Even today, as the US Federal Reserve is "tapering" its quantitative easing programme, the monetary base continues to grow, albeit at a slower pace.

But a weaker US dollar would effectively depreciate the Chinese yuan (CNY) due to the fixed exchange rate set by the People's Bank of China (PBOC).[19] Ironically, the peg created significant tensions between these countries, and China was dubbed as a "currency manipulator" by US officials, yet it was the United States which introduced the extreme unconventional monetary policies under the disguise of domestic oriented measures, which were undoubtedly having an impact on the US dollar and therefore the rest of the world.

The risk of inflation in the United States was viewed as a low risk due to the slack in the housing, industrial, and labour markets. But over time, the "marginal benefit" of easing became less clear. The US Federal Reserve was forced to print much more in order to have a similar impact. Time will tell how much damage has been done in the process.

The risk of inflation in China was a completely different story. The artificial peg would create large distortions, which would result in the large accumulation of foreign reserves and extraordinary imbalances, such as the emergence of the shadow banking system. As of 2014, the PBOC and the Chinese government are taking proactive measures to gradually float the CNY and address the large imbalances in the system, but once again, time will tell how much damage has been done.

And since monetary policy is "contagious", Japan, Europe, Switzerland, the UK, and many more credible central banks are providing unprecedented levels of monetary stimuli through all possible channels.

As a result, central banks around the world have engaged in a race to the bottom, "currency wars", altering the monetary base and looking to "depreciate their way out" of their economic problems.

In this environment, asset and commodity prices are no longer a function of supply and demand alone. A third factor, monetary policy, has been an inflationary driver to commodity prices in the US dollar, through what I would call the "Monopoly effect", in reference to the famous board game, where the players receive more and more money to spend on the same limited amount of houses.

In addition to the monetary excesses, governments around the world have provided massive additional fiscal incentives. In 2008 alone, China put in place a $585 billion stimulus package[20] that undoubtedly translated into additional infrastructure demand.

All these measures increase the demand from China, contributing to the tightening of the energy complex and higher commodity prices in US dollars.

The race to the bottom

We are in a period that will be studied in the future in business schools because of the obstinacy of repeating the same formulas that created the crisis over and over again.

Japan's Prime Minister, Shinzo Abe, said that with the dollar above ¥85, "companies that haven't been paying taxes until now can pay taxes" because a weaker yen lifts profit. Really? Or is it a case of exporting at no profit because planning was made at an unsustainable yen exchange?

Is devaluation a good idea? The defenders argue that "it *improves* competitiveness", or that "debt *disappears* as the currency in which it is denominated loses value", so they can "start again".

Really? That simple? Well, no. Because the fundamentals of the economy do not change, and we have sunk the credibility of governments and the financial system. This pyramid scheme does not work without confidence.

First, low rates, disproportionate spending in high-risk assets with poor results, impoverishment, and useless stimulus plans. The consequence is more debt and low productivity economies. The solution, according to our governments? Repeat it. "Stimulate to combat unemployment".

To "repeat" such a "successful" formula, governments have to steal from the pocket of savers: taxes, depreciation, and manipulation of the cost of money. And, of course, unemployment doesn't fall ... certainly not because of government intervention. Textbook financial repression version 2013.

The generational debate

Shall we take the pain now, and effectively impact the current value of our assets and savings? This would bring the valuation of assets to its true level, giving a better chance to the young people entering the economy, but hurting the elderly through lower savings.

Or shall we "inflate our way out of the problem"? This would preserve the notional value of the assets and savings of the elderly, but would slowly dilute the problem and hurt the young entering the economy.

Clearly, governments around the world prefer to "kick the can" down the road. A formula that we have used over and over again, and that only leads to larger and bigger crises. Depression version 2014.

Inflation is a relative term. My inflation is different from yours. Daniel had triplets. Diego had twins. And both of us can tell you that nappy inflation was a consideration during a period of our lives. The kids have grown now, and nappy inflation is no longer part of our lives, but it is for other people. Likewise, food, education, and electricity may impact the inflation basket of people differently.

Central banks use a convenient and arbitrary basket of goods and services to determine what the official inflation is and set the pace at which pensions grow, for example. Other forms of inflation, including financial inflation, housing and asset inflation, become more "qualitative" inputs. Official inflation is therefore another tool, subject to the overriding rule that "the government can change the rules anytime".

The monetary time bomb of credit risk

One effect of this currency war is the pursuit by investors of yield at any cost to compensate for the fear of the loss of value of money. That is, less interest accepted for higher risk.

According to Bloomberg, the demand for junk bonds and debt of troubled countries has soared to the levels of 2007. Companies on the verge of bankruptcy issue bonds with demand exceeding supply by 10 times.

Unemployment doesn't fall, but inflation rises

It amazes me to read that some people think that monetizing debt creates jobs.

Unemployment is reduced when economic activity recovers, when we see real private investment. However, when we create a monetary bubble the effect is counterproductive, because money is invested in short-term financial assets.

The risk-return of productive real economy investment is simply unaffordable compared to that of liquid financial products. Central banks are penalizing investors for being conservative, but these, in turn, do not put money to work for 15 years, and less so in real assets, until they see a secure environment and growth opportunities. Therefore money goes to the place that central banks are going to support until their final defeat: financial risk assets.

In the meantime, economic activity is contracting. That is why the velocity of money collapses. There is little trust in a system that represses and creates fake money. Inflation increases, even if it is disguised in official figures.

Structural problems are not solved with bubbles. They are perpetuated and increased by them.

"Beggar thy neighbour"

As the US Federal Reserve's Charles Plosser said "beggar-thy-neighbour policies would not be healthy". The main risk of massive devaluation is impoverishment and stagnation, added to the fall of productive investment.

Europe competes with Japan for global exports. A brutal devaluation of the yen means a drop in exports of the EU to Asia. If we add the ongoing devaluation of the dollar, the effect is simple: the US exports inflation, because 75% of global transactions are made in dollars.[21] The currencies of emerging countries soar, commodities, especially energy, remain high and, therefore, global imbalances are exaggerated.

Surprisingly, the common view is that Europe should participate in this crazy war.

We frequently hear that the euro crisis is all Germany's fault, which refuses to turn on the money printing machine. We hear things like "it's criminal that Spain has 26% unemployment just because Germany doesn't want more inflation"... as if we have learnt nothing from the 1990s' competitive devaluations. It doesn't work.

Yet despite the efforts of the ECB to increase its balance sheet, reaching $2 trillion ... we just do not see the euro devalued. Why? Europe, and Spain, Germany and Italy in particular, have improved their exports due to a policy of "internal devaluation" – reduce costs and wages, and selling at dollarized prices. This means that a large part of the recent years' export success, up to 80% according to Goldman, comes from selling in dollars or equivalent.

Germany knows that the vast majority of transactions in euros are made between EU countries. Therefore, to try to artificially devalue the common currency has the risk of being like a shot in the foot. Inflation in the Eurozone could spiral alarmingly. It has happened many times in the past. In the EU offices in Westminster they are well aware of this. I have often talked about this mess but, unfortunately, there are a few who consider forcing inflation a "lesser evil" and that "it would not hurt to try".

High risk and volatility

Currency wars may have had a very remote strategic sense when they were not global and concerted, when there was confidence in the global political and financial system, and when central banks remained independent and used conventional policies instead of printing machines.

But today none of those conditions apply. Unconventional policies are now commonplace. Raising the bet that "next year all will improve" has led to massive loans creating a bubble in futures and derivatives that generates a systemic risk if there is a correction, which in turn makes it impossible to stop the printing machine, otherwise the banking system will collapse.

The central banks' balance sheet is like the cockroach motel. What goes in does not come out.

Central banks have stopped sterilizing and now must continue to implement unconventional measures to sustain the perennial sovereign credit bubble driven by unsustainable spending.

Money supply is increasing by about 6–7% per year globally,[22] which is creating inflation in commodities, and exporting inflation to developing countries that cannot compete in global currency wars, creating more poverty that ends up affecting everyone. The most important thing is that the velocity of money is collapsing and that means that the economy does not recover, because the message that is launched is "do not worry about investing in real assets and invest in risk". It is creating a monstrous bubble in bonds.

Countries are printing money to deal with a debt that is very difficult to repay but it continues to grow because the disposable income of families and small business profits decrease because states increase the tax burden and fail to reduce spending. Financial repression is negatively impacting economic growth and consumption.

Considering the slowdown of recent years in advancing trade liberalization and the slow growth of world trade, there is fear that in some countries we begin to hear protectionist proclamations. Hopefully there is only the threat and not anything tangible.

A structural problem of debt and spending, lack of growth and de-industrialization is not solved with cheaper debt and devaluation. The solution is innovating and growing the high-productivity areas. That does not happen when we print money and manipulate interest rates. It encourages borrowing, mal-investment and maintains declining zombie sectors.

The solution is precisely what everyone seems to want to avoid: cleaning an exhausted system and replacing low produc-tivity sectors with technology and high productivity, selling in dollars or equivalent.

The complacency phase

A great civilization is not conquered from without until it has destroyed itself from within.

WILL DURANT

We are currently in a phase of complacency that ignores the accumulation of debt and the creation of fake money as uncomfortable anomalies, until it explodes. And it does, make no mistake. What we do not know is when, but we know how. Abruptly and painfully. We've seen it many times since 1789, when France was trying to solve a problem of spending and debt by printing paper money without justification.[23]

There are positive indicators, most global economies are in an expansion phase, although at a modest pace well below the potential.

But these positive elements do not mask that the hole of debt is growing faster than any indicator of GDP, corporate earnings, fiscal revenues or industrial growth. The hole in the United States exceeds $17 trillion dollars.[24] It is a formula that should not be copied for three reasons:

- First, the policy to increase and monetize debt, as we have seen in the US or UK, does not reduce the need for massive budget cuts or solve the problems of growth. In fact, it is precisely the dependence on a debt pyramid model that creates the bubbles that then lead to crisis and cuts. If we don't allow the system to clean up, we perpetuate problems. Since 1981, the US has increased its public debt by 1560%, while the population grew by only 35%, to generate an increase in real GDP for every dollar of additional debt of less than 0.24%.[25] In the rest of the Western world the figures are similar. All Eurozone countries have a public debt that exceeds two to three times its revenue. A spending pyramid with a diminishing base to support it.
- Second, the credit and stock market bubble is created by low interest rates and printing money which generates an "illusion of growth" leading to poor investment decisions, increasingly short-term and risky.
- Third, the middle class disposable income and corporate profits are reduced by tax increases, lack of productive investment, economic uncertainty and systemic risk. The recovery is delayed by "trying to prevent" a drastic solution to the debt hole with clear market principles. Bankruptcies where needed and conversion of debt into equity where possible.

The risk of bankruptcy is essential for the market to function, to reward the good managers and clearly establish the penalty for bad investments. However, when we add the placebo effects of printing currency, low rates and bailouts we destroy the principle of credit responsibility, generating perverse incentives, exaggerated risks and the credibility of the entire system sinks.

But central banks continue to destroy currency and add borrowing . . . For nothing, because they forget that the population and GDP will not grow enough to finance this spending spree we created.

Divergence between the economy and financial markets

Many mention the strong performance of the stock market as a leading indicator of the recovery. In my opinion, stock markets and risk assets discount four effects:

- First, the fall of the weighted average cost of capital (WACC) by lowering interest rates, intervention, and aggressive policies of monetization – yes, loans from the ECB are also "back door" monetizations. When the WACC falls, corporate profits stagnate or worsen and stocks go up, and vice versa. See above as an example of WACC moves in Spain.
- Second, inflation risk.
- Third, destruction of currency and negative rate risks. Thinking zero interest rates are not enough? There is already talk of the possibility of negative interest rates. Savings, when currencies lose value and rates collapse, turn to risky assets.
- Fourth, the current news is bad, but not "much worse". I tend to follow and analyse over 150 global macroeconomic data, and when the incremental negatives ease, the economy is bad, but is depleted of "surprise negative indicators." This effect is the "illusion of recovery." For example, if GDP grows 1.2% but consensus estimates 1%, it's an "illusion of improvement".

"Do not fight the central banks"

The often-repeated "do not fight the central banks" is true, but we sometimes forget that governments and their banks are reactive, not proactive, and despite calls for "unlimited measures", resources are not unlimited. Debt is ultimately paid by citizens in a scheme with less ability to lend, fewer taxpayers, and more dependent on decreasing disposable income.

What markets fear is that fundamentals remain poor. The absence of aggressive negative news does not reduce the accumulation of credit risk, the banking problem, and deteriorating corporate earnings.

When safe havens are more expensive than what you try to protect

Capital preservation through safe assets is impossible with global financial repression.

The problem for investors is that global monetary policy pushes risk up as the economy deteriorates. The "shelter" -keeping money in deposits- becomes too expensive. So this market becomes a good bet but a bad investment, because we are creating bubbles which are pricked faster and faster, as the illusion of "value" is diluted as quickly as it is created. There is no value when returns remain below the cost of capital.

We must avoid bubbles, and to do that we have to understand how they are created.

The bubble machine

When all states are determined to create inflation and inject liquidity unsupported by fundamentals, it encourages a bubble in the beneficiaries of that cash: political spending and zombie companies, those that should have gone bankrupt but remain "alive" with eternally renewed loans because realizing a loss would create too big a hole for the banks. It discourages cleaning the system, because "too big to fail" becomes the norm. No need to be efficient and productive. Companies just have to be fat. Not strong, but fat.

When the unconventional monetary policies become standard, bubbles are created everywhere at both ends of the risk spectrum, from the United States, Germany and sovereign "low risk" countries to companies and troubled states at the "high risk" end. A 0% interest for US or German bonds is as unjustified as receiving only 5% coupon from bonds of companies or countries at the brink of collapse. And this creates an "oversupply" of debt with negative marginal returns. Economies do not improve.

Let's not spoil such a "successful" formula. With it comes an excess of risk that leads to extreme volatility in financial markets that are not supported by fundamentals. The central banks, of course, do not go bankrupt, because they get paid by us and our grandchildren. They perpetuate their "unconventional" actions that are now common, ruining its citizens via inflation and devaluation. But while supporting excessive government spending and stock markets, they create a "feeling of wealth" – I love that term – when nothing really happens. Yet central banks may lose credit and make their paper worthless. We seem to be in that race.

These bubbles are pricked with a "demand shock", when the flow of new participants disappears or dries up and competition for capital becomes fierce. And when it happens, it is very aggressive. Then the pyramid scheme stops working altogether. Enjoy it while it lasts.

Financial flows. Let's blame the speculators

> A speculator is a man who observes the future, and acts before it occurs.
>
> BERNARD BARUCH

In many interviews and television programmes I have debated the role of speculators and financial markets. What I find interesting is that in the minds of most people, a "speculator" makes commodities rise without a reason, yet when the price of commodities falls, no one mentions financial markets. Funnily enough, these same people tend to blame speculators for stock market falls, not for the rises. Speculators tend to be blamed for the move that affects us in a negative way.

"There is absolutely no relationship between price and supply and demand. Crude oil is not worth more than $50 a barrel based on fundamentals" said the Saudi Oil Minister Ali Al-Naimi in 2006 as he justified a surprise production cut from Saudi Arabia. "The reason for the cutback is simple. People are not asking for oil".[26]

Indeed. Consumers were not asking for oil. They were asking for gasoline, diesel, and kerosene, and in very large incremental quantities. But by then the bottlenecks in refining capacity were very evident, and pumping more sour heavy crude oil would increase the glut of residual fuel oil even further, effectively reducing the value of Saudi's heavy sour crude. The refineries were in control, something that neither OPEC nor Saudi Arabia had anticipated.

And the consumers were proving to be very price insensitive. The fuel subsidies in China, India, Indonesia, Malaysia, Nigeria, Venezuela, and many other countries, including Saudi itself, meant that domestic prices for consumers remained constant, despite the massive pick up in international prices. There was no market-based mechanism to incentivize demand destruction across emerging markets, so the burden of adjustment fell entirely on the OECD consumers, who in turn were somewhat isolated from the prices due to the high taxes. A rule-of-thumb calculation after the fact showed that a 100% increase in prices would result in a 2% decrease in demand.[27] Anyone surprised why prices rallied towards $140/bbl, and jet fuel towards $200/bbl in 2008?

Instead of accepting the dynamics of the market, Al-Naimi went on to blame the speculators. "The oil price is determined by the multi-billion dollar market that brings together oil companies, traders, investment, and hedge funds. These bubbles are pricked with a demand shock, when the flow of new participants disappears".[28]

The impact of financial flows has been analysed and debated at length. In the following sections I will share some of the main arguments for and against the role of speculators, along with my own personal opinion. What is clear is that blaming the speculators tends to be the easy answer to explain the apparent disconnect between prices and fundamentals. Yet, with the benefit of hindsight, things become clearer and as was the case in the example above, everyone could see why prices reacted the way they did and were indeed reflecting fundamentals. The problem is that fundamentals were not well understood at the time.

Politicians and regulators pass the blame

Regulation is part of the game and impacts prices. There are times when regulation is well designed and complements market forces. And there are times when regulation is poorly designed and disasters happen. Quoting Larry Summers yet again, "Policies that aim to thwart market forces rarely work, and usually fall victim to the law of unintended consequences".[29]

What is cynical is that politicians and regulators tend to blame speculators for the problems they have created themselves.

Look at the California power crisis, for example, which many people view as a failure of deregulation. With a detailed analysis, the Chairman of the Federal Energy Regulatory Commission said "the California crisis was a failure of regulation".[30]

Or corn prices. During the super-cyclical run up in prices in the 2000s, most commodities were making historical highs, from crude oil, to coal, to natural gas, to copper, to corn. Correlations had notably increased, which was often used as an argument to justify that speculators were driving prices. And of course, high fuel and food prices were generating inflation and increasing the risk of financial stability.

Once again, politicians and regulators were quick to blame the speculators. "Food inflation, how dare they?" Corn was considered too expensive and would impact the poor the most and increase inequality.[31] How cynical.

The main reason why corn prices were going up was the surge in demand for corn-based ethanol in response to both high energy prices and the regulated mandates. Corn, which had traditionally been "food and feed", had become "food, feed, and fuel". The incremental demand had to be accommodated by incremental supply and demand destruction. Since we could not "print corn", prices went up substantially. The market had no choice.

In 2012, following an acute drought in North America, the price of corn reached historical highs above $8.30/bushel, 400% higher than in 2005. "The speculators are taking advantage of the situation. We must reduce their futures risk limits. They are responsible for the pick-up in food inflation". Yet, that year over 40% of the physical harvest went to ethanol to "feed" the car.[32] The quantities were mandated by the government as "fuel" forced the demand destruction of "food and feed" via high prices. It was the cattle and hogs who had to change their diet, not the car. By mandate.

As is often the case, regulation and mandates are not flexible enough to adjust to special circumstances. The risk of supply shocks in agriculture should not come as a surprise.

Once again, the high prices were a fair reflection of fundamentals. It is just that the rules of the game had changed and the fundamentals included mandated quantities to be devoted to ethanol. But the government, far from taking the blame itself, passed the blame onto speculators. Much easier, I suppose. And public opinion, often half-educated and misled by the media, added to the fire.

Causality

Do spot prices converge to futures prices? Or do futures prices converge to spot prices?

Causality analysis by Merrill Lynch Research shows that futures prices converge towards spot prices, and not the other way around.

In simple terms, spot markets reflect the current market conditions in terms of demand, supply, inventories, and storage. Preventing any manipulation, spot prices represent the "true price" of a commodity as per the then prevailing fundamentals. The ultimate participants are the consumers and producers of the physical commodity.

Futures markets reflect the equilibrium between buyers and sellers of a given commodity for delivery in the future. As time goes by, futures prices will converge towards spot prices reflecting "non-arbitrage" constraints. That is, there is no "free lunch". The participants in the futures markets include consumers, producers, and speculators, who play an important role in providing liquidity as a "financial bridge" between the consumers and producers. As per the work from Keynes, investors will be incentivized and compensated by a "risk premium".

Market manipulation

Regulators play a critical role in the protection of market participants. All markets are at risk of manipulation. Equities, bonds, currencies, and interest rates have all had many instances of fraud and price manipulation. But commodity markets, due to their physical nature, are particularly vulnerable.

A typical form of market manipulation is a "physical squeeze", where the buyer takes physical delivery of a large position, forcing those sellers who are unable to fulfil their obligations to buy back in the market at a much higher price. This is a dangerous game, and often the speculator gets burnt in the process.

In February 2014, during a speech titled "Speculators and Commodity Prices", Commissioner Bart Chilton said: "it's high time to kick it in gear and use the one tool we have to appropriately address high oil and gas prices. You can't turn on the television or the radio without hearing about record high gas prices, and yet the CFTC has not yet been able to implement Congressionally-mandated position limits to put the brakes on excessive speculation in oil and other commodity markets".[33]

In his speech, Mr Chilton provided a long list of articles and used a specific example to support his argument.

However, as the CFTC itself found after its studies, "as a whole, speculation does not seem to destabilize futures markets".[34]

In my view there is a danger of taking the concept of "speculative premium" out of context. Financial futures on commodities do not move the price, they reflect the movements of the physical market. A trader is exposed to such moves, but does not cause them. Let's assume that prices are in equilibrium at $100/bbl. News emerges that tensions are increasing in the Middle East, and there is a 20% probability of major escalation that could send the prices to $150/bbl, and an 80% chance that nothing happens. The futures price of oil will react and "price in" $10/bbl (that is, 20% of the $50/bbl potential increase). The premium is reflecting the weighted average of future possible outcomes. Producers and consumers are free to act on those prices. The realized spot price in the future will reflect the then prevailing fundamentals. In the meantime the market is simply trying to do its job. Unhedged consumers will pay spot prices, irrespective of what futures do.

Investor blow-ups

One extreme of the impact that investors can have on volatility and prices are financial blow-ups, when investors have accumulated large positions which they are forced to liquidate, often in very thin market conditions.

But history is also full of examples where corporates and banks have created similar circumstances. Speculative "hedging" by gold producers in the 1990s is a good example, where they were forward selling significantly more production than what they were able to produce, incentivized by the steep contango and the negative outlook.

Long-Term Capital Management

You may remember Long-Term Capital Management (LTCM), which despite having Nobel prize winners Myron S. Scholes and Robert C. Merton, suffered one of the largest blow-ups in hedge fund history, losing $4.6 billion in four months.[35]

LTCM suffered losses as traditional relationships and correlations broke down, leaving it with extremely leveraged positions. The "implied worst case" based on historical relationships turned out to be a mild forecast, and the "realized worst case" was much worse than anticipated as correlations broke down and liquidity dried up and the "size of the exit door" narrowed, increasing the cost of liquidating the position.

In short, the tail risk they were running was much larger than what their models would have predicted. As per Murphy's Law: if there is something wrong that could happen, it *will* happen, and LTCM capitulation created significant stress to the financial system.

Amaranth

I have also seen the other extreme. When risk models are correctly representing the size of the risk but are overruled.

This was the case in the largest blow-up in natural gas trading by a hedge fund called Amaranth, where the head trader, when challenged about the potential exposure of his positions, allegedly responded to his risk and management teams: "that number is mathematically correct, but will never happen".

Models that are too complex may look more accurate, but this is a well-known fallacy. They look accurate by construction, because they have been calibrated to fit the *past*. That is, the variables and coefficients are able to explain the past with extreme certainty. We just need enough variables and coefficients. For example, we could probably predict the temperature in Miami based on a formula that links the results of football teams with coefficients. We would be "reverse engineering" an explanation for the temperature in Miami using some variables. The fact that we can "fit" outcomes to a formula does not mean that it will work in the future. The field of econometrics is fascinating and an extremely powerful tool for decision making, but like any other science, needs to be used sensibly.

Just like you would not let a plane do the whole route in "auto pilot" without a human pilot on-board, it is advisable that quantitative modelling is complemented with qualitative risk management.

In my experience, simple models can often be more effective than complex ones. The objective is to identify the key relationship and variables.

Value at risk

During my trading career I have seen traders incur losses that were much larger than what any model would have predicted. Part of the problem is overconfidence and overreliance on complex models.

Value at risk (VaR) is the most widely accepted tool used to measure the risk of a monetary loss, and in my view it is much to blame for many of the financial blow-ups we have experienced. Strictly speaking VaR measures the minimum expected daily loss with 95% degree of confidence. In practical terms, I like to view it as the minimum daily loss that is expected to happen at least once within the trading month (a 95% confidence interval is equivalent to a 1-in-20 chance, which is approximately the number of trading days in a month excluding holidays).

VaR has extensive limitations and must be used with full awareness of those limitations.

I realize the following contains a great deal of technical language from the risk management world that may not be easily understood or followed, but this is precisely my point – complex models are not necessarily better.

The ensuing discussion about VaR identifies areas where the modelling can "go wrong" and result in much greater losses than we would have anticipated.

First, VaR estimates minimum losses within one day subject to a two-standard deviation move, but in practice those daily moves could be much larger. Even if we have a "stop loss" order that will close out the exposure once the VaR threshold is reached, the realized loss can be much greater if liquidity is poor, which is often the case for large moves. For example a $1 million VaR position could lose $5 million in just one day.

Second, even if the daily moves stay within the VaR estimations, it is possible that these moves happen more than once a month. I have seen many instances where the market is "limit up" or "limit down" during several consecutive days, which means the risk cannot be closed out. As a result, the cumulative losses can be much larger than initially predicted. For example, a position can suffer five consecutive daily losses of $1 million per day, adding to $5 million.

Third, the model requires statistical inputs – the "small font" of the model.

Some people use "historical volatility" (that is, the past observed standard deviation of the distribution of prices) to estimate future risks. This has the potential to create "black-swan" events because periods of low *realized past* volatility can create the perception of low *future* risk, which can be a fatal mistake, as the size of the positions and the losses can be much, much larger. Look for example at the Chinese yuan, a currency that has been pegged and closely managed within a tight trading band versus the US dollar for many years. But the future may well be very different, with a wider trading band or even a free floating currency. As a result, using historical volatilities has some shortcomings that may lead to large risks.[36]

On the other hand, some people use "implied volatility" to estimate future risks. That is, the expectation from the market. In my view, using market inputs is a much better approach, although it is far from perfect. Here, once again, there is significant room for surprise. The supply of volatility in the market from corporate hedgers for example may underestimate the risk. Or unpredicted events such as a natural disaster or war that were not priced in can also result in much more volatile moves (and losses) than initially anticipated. The problem is that implied volatility is a forward-looking measurement that requires manual input and may not exist in a liquid and transparent way for many markets. On the other hand, historical volatilities can be computed using more accessible data such as historical prices. As a result many models rely on historical input for volatility.

Fourth, the model requires input for the "term structure". Short-term volatility may be different from long-term volatility. Once again, more data input is needed.

Fifth, the complexity of the model grows exponentially as we add multiple assets. The model requires extensive correlation inputs for the "portfolio effect". The "covariance matrix" once again faces the issue of "historical correlations" or "implied correlations". These are even less transparent than implied volatilities. Yet, they are a key input to understand the overall risk of a portfolio. For example, the correlation for small moves may be low ("noise") as the two assets move up and down pretty much on their own, subject to normal market conditions. But what happens when we are faced with "hostile markets" such as a Lehman Brothers event? Well, correlations tend to increase significantly. That is, the equity markets in the United States, Japan, or Europe, which day to day may move on their own, are likely to move in the same direction. So, in practice, the model may predict low VaR as it benefits from low correlation and "portfolio diversification", but when these "tail events" happen, the risk literally explodes and so can the losses.

I do not expect you to follow all the above, but the discussion hopefully makes the point that modelling financial risks is extremely complicated. The models are helpful. Risk limits are necessary. And their application and limitations must be well understood.

Notes

1. Wael Mahdi (8 April 2014). "OPEC's El-Badri says crude prices stable". http://www.bloomberg.com/news/2014-04-08/opec-s-el-badri-says-crude-prices-stable.html
2. Rowena Caine (15 August 2014). "FACTBOX – Oil prices below most OPEC producers' budget needs". http://uk.reuters.com/article/2014/08/15/opec-budget-idUKL6N0QL1VY20140815
3. *Economic Commentary* (August–September 2012). "Fiscal break-even prices revisited: what more could they tell us about OPEC policy intent?" http://www.apic.com/Research/Commentaries/Commentary_V7_N8-9_2012.pdf
4. US Energy Information Administration.
5. Ibid.
6. Ibid.
7. Wael Mahdi (27 December 2012). "Saudi Arabia must review its oil subsidies, former adviser says". http://www.bloomberg.com/news/2012-12-27/saudi-arabia-must-review-its-oil-subsidies-former-adviser-says.html
8. *The Economist* (31 March 2012). "Keeping it to themselves. Gulf states not only pump oil; they burn it, too". http://www.economist.com/node/21551484
9. Ibid.
10. *Gulf Times* (14 March 2013). "Venezuela looks beyond US to China as customers". http://www.gulf-times.com/business/191/details/345682/venezuela-looks-beyond-us-to-china-as-customer
11. OPEC data, NARECO Advisors, Bloomberg.

12. International Energy Agency (June 2009). *Petroleum Prices, Taxation and Subsidies in India.* https://www.iea.org/publications /freepublications/publication/petroleum_pricing.pdf

13. Ed Dolan (13 August 2013). *Why Fuel Subsidies are Bad for Everyone.* http://oilprice.com/Energy/Gas-Prices/Why-Fuel-Subsidies -are-Bad-for-Everyone.html

14. Central Intelligence Agency. *The World Factbook: Military Expenditures.* https://www.cia.gov/library/publications/the-world -factbook/rankorder/2034rank.html

15. The World Bank (2013). *Military Expenditure (% GDP).* http: //data.worldbank.org/indicator/MS.MIL.XPND.GD.ZS

16. John McBeth (10 February 2014). *How to Kill an Industry in Indonesia.* http://www.atimes.com/atimes/Southeast_Asia/SEA -01-100214.html

17. Commodity Price Index 2009–2012.

18. Fractional Flow (24 May 2014). *Central Banks' Balance Sheets, Interest Rates and the Oil Price.* http://fractionalflow. com/2014/05/20/central-banks-balance-sheets-interest-rates -and-the-oil-price/

19. Ibid.

20. Frederik Balfour (9 November 2008). *China Unveils Major Stimulus to Economy.* http://www.businessweek.com/globalbiz/blog /eyeonasia/archives/2008/11/china_unveils_m.html?chan=top +news_top+news+index+-+temp_news+%2B+analysis

21. International Monetary Fund.

22. *The World Bank. Money and Quasi Money Growth (Annual %).* http://data.worldbank.org/indicator/FM.LBL.MQMY.ZG

23. Richard Ebeling (1 July 2007). *The Great French Inflation.* http: //www.fee.org/the_freeman/detail/the-great-french-inflation

24. http://research.stlouisfed.org/fred2/series/GFDEBTN/

25. Hayman Capital Management (15 November 2012). *The Central Bankers' Potemkin Village.* http://snbchf.snbchfcom.netdna-cdn .com/wp-content/uploads/2012/12/Kyle-Bass-Hayman-Investor -Letter-2012-11.pdf

26. James Hamilton (8 July 2006). *Questions Remain about Saudi Oil.* http://econbrowser.com/archives/2006/07/questions_remai

27. NARECO Advisors.

28. James Hamilton (8 July 2006). *Questions Remain about Saudi Oil.* http://econbrowser.com/archives/2006/07/questions_remai

29. Lawrence Summers (16 February 2014). *America Risks becoming a Downton Abbey Economy.* http://www.ft.com/intl/cms/s/2/875155ce-8f25-11e3-be85-00144feab7de.html#axzz32xxVuATv

30. http://www.cbo.gov/sites/default/files/cbofiles/ftpdocs/30xx/doc3062/californiaenergy.pdf

31. David S. Jacks (March 2013). *From Boom to Bust: A Typology of Real Commodity Prices in the Long Run.* National Bureau of Economic Research.

32. Ibid.

33. US Commodity Futures Trading Commission. (2011) *Speculators and Commodity Prices.* http://www.cftc.gov/PressRoom/Speeches Testimony/opachilton-41

34. http://www.cftc.gov/ucm/groups/public/@swaps/documents/file/plstudy_03_cftc.pdf

35. Franklin R. Edwards (1999). Hedge funds and the collapse of Long-Term Capital Management. *Journal of Economic Perspectives,* Spring. http://www.gsb.columbia.edu/faculty/fedwards/papers/Hedge_Funds_&_the_Collapse_of_LTCM.pdf

36. Victor Golovtchenko (21 March 2014), *Two-Way Yuan Volatility Makes USDCNY Trading More Attractive.* http://forexmagnates.com/two-way-yuan-volatility-makes-usdcny-trading-more-attractive/

CHAPTER FOURTEEN

IMPLICATIONS AND OPPORTUNITIES IN THE FINANCIAL MARKETS

Price is what you pay. Value is what you get.

WARREN BUFFETT

Winners and losers

During the Gold Rush, most would-be miners lost money, but people who sold them picks, shovels, tents, and blue jeans (like Levi Strauss) made a nice profit.

As discussed throughout this book, there will be large winners and losers from the current energy revolution, but the opportunities are not "one-way directional bets". It is the same as with the internet revolution.

The key trends and themes identified within the book need to be implemented efficiently. There are simply too many cases of "good idea, bad outcome" where the vehicle, be it a commodity future or an exchange traded fund (ETF),[1] or an equity, did not behave in the way we anticipated.

The following sections focus on educating and teaching you "how to fish" instead of sharing some recommendations based on a snapshot of the market and "giving you the fish fished".

Long-term success is about capital preservation. Much of the focus is on making money, but over the years as a hedge fund manager I can tell you that the most successful investors and traders are obsessed by "not losing money". And using a golfing analogy, long-term success is as much about "making birdies" as it is about "avoiding bogies and double bogies".

As experts in energy equities and commodity derivatives, we have no bias, and we recognize the importance of the small details for successful implementation. During the following sections we will discuss some common mistakes and misconceptions, with the hope that we will save you money first, and make you money second.

Think against the box

I joined one of the largest hedge funds in the world after years in the corporate world. The interviews were extremely detailed and covered many areas, not just my knowledge of markets and the energy sector, but also personal information. When I finished, I was completely sure I had failed. One month later, I received an offer.

From what I was told, their decision to choose me from among the other candidates, despite being older and having fewer years' experience in the City, was what they called an ability to "think against the box". Not only were they looking for someone who thought "out of the box" and could come up with different ideas, but also for someone who actually thought contrary to the status quo.

When we understand that the major economic players have three principal characteristics, it becomes easier to understand the reality of economic cycles. They are sellers (seeking to sell a product), reactive (they manage things once events have occurred), and, above all, they hold an optimistic view of the future. Hence the overriding importance of thinking "against the box". It's about identifying inconsistencies and cyclical changes, or at least understanding the level of risk to which we are exposing ourselves and studying the possible solutions to problems.

Natural gas, winner in volume, not necessarily in price

As discussed previously, I believe natural gas will be one of the winners of the energy revolution. "Shall I buy the natural gas ETF, then?" people ask, to which my answer has historically been "No, I would not buy the natural gas ETF". Two big reasons:

1. Natural gas will be a winner in volume, but not necessarily in price.
2. The US natural gas ETF is a lot more complex than it looks and has historically been a "financial weapon of wealth destruction", as I will discuss in detail in a later section.

To be clear, there will be times when the US natural gas ETF is an attractive and efficient way to express a bullish view on natural gas prices, and there will be times when it is not. But before you buy it, you must understand what is inside the "black box", the risks that you are taking, which are not the simple directional bet most retail investors believe they are making.

Before we go into that, let's have a more generic view about the relationship between commodity prices and commodity equities, as well as some key considerations when investing in both.

Commodity versus commodity equities

Commodity prices (e.g. the price of crude oil) and commodity equities (the price of, say, Exxon) are different. Yet, there are many investors who express a bullish view on crude oil via oil equities, or via gold equities, and so on, but there are many reasons why the valuations can diverge, and occasionally even go in completely opposite directions.

Look at crude oil versus oil equities, for example. It is perfectly possible for oil prices to go up significantly and the oil equity valuation to collapse. How is that possible? Well, the higher the oil price, the greater the risk of higher taxes, expropriation, or even nationalization. Think of Repsol in Argentina, or BP in Russia, or many others, all examples of "tail risk" and "wrong-way exposure". But there are many other risks that can lead to price divergence, such as strikes, supply disruption, hedging policy, leverage/financing, currency risks, and even environmental disasters (ask BP again . . .) that will impact equity valuations.

As a rule of thumb, less than one-third of the equity prices can be explained by the underlying commodity. The rest, that is, more than two-thirds, is driven by "other factors" that have nothing to do with the commodity price.

These relationships are dynamic, not static, and can be extremely unstable at times. Investors must be very mindful when looking at past or realized correlation and performance because the "future is not what it used to be", as my mother always says.

Bet against the losers

"I would rather buy a *good* asset at a *fair* price, than a *fair* asset at a *good* price", famously said Warren Buffett, the billionaire value investor who looks to buy stocks that are underpriced and sell them once they become overpriced.

"I see the stock market as a business partner. Sometimes he is too pessimistic and wants to sell his part to me. Sometimes he gets overly optimistic and wants to buy my part". Warren is totally unemotional about investing. When the value of an asset increases beyond what he believes is fair, he sells it.

But why not take advantage of opportunities when the market is overvalued?

As a friend of mine says, "making money via longs is work, making money via shorts is pleasure".

Traditional investors have always had a "long bias". They "buy stuff". They may identify opportunities that they view as overvalued, but most investors lack the tools and expertise to implement or take advantage of the situation.

Historically, retail investors would liquidate their positions into cash, and wait for value to return. But professional investors were able to borrow the overvalued asset, then sell it, and wait until the price goes down to buy the asset and repay their loan. And there are many other alternatives, such as selling futures or buying put options, but these are often outside the comfort zone of most investors and often come with their own risks and considerations. More recently, the market has developed financial instruments such as ETFs that provide short and even leveraged exposure to down markets in a simple and cost-efficient manner.

Having the flexibility to capture value through long exposure to undervalued assets or short exposure to assets can add significant returns to the portfolio.

The shorts and relative value strategies

As a natural expansion from the above, investors can enter into *simultaneous* long and short positions. The investor is no longer betting on the direction of the market, but rather on the relative valuation of two assets.

For example, an investor may believe that natural gas is undervalued and crude oil is undervalued. Or go long on an oil equity producer and go short on another oil producer. The possibilities are unlimited.

In the stock market where investment recommendations are predominantly positive, where stock market corrections are considered "anomalies" and upward moves are deemed "fundamental", where the mantra of "do not fight the central banks" is almost a religion, there are fantastic opportunities to generate incremental returns via short positions.

There is a fundamental reality that shorting an asset has asymmetric risk against us since the maximum profit on a short is capped at 100% but the maximum loss is unlimited.

But the goal when entering a short position is not always for prices "to go down", but to finance a long position and reduce volatility. And once you have found that stock you love, where you see a huge potential but also a high level of volatility and significant market risk, you can fund that position with a good short.

The quality of the profit and loss (P&L) is often expressed as a Sharpe ratio, which in simple terms describes the return above the risk-free rate generated per unit of volatility. The Sharpe ratio can be approximated via the information ratio (IR). For example, a manager making 15% pa with 30% volatility has an IR of 0.5 (15%/30%). Another manager, making 30% return with 15% volatility has an IR of 2 (30%/15%). All else being equal, the manager with the higher Sharpe or information ratio is preferred. The P&L is "higher quality". Yet, many people often ignore the risk and volatility part and focus only on returns. Not a good idea, as we will discuss in more detail later.

Back to the shorts, the ability to mitigate volatility is part of the success of investment. It helps remove undesired risks and noise, as the "long noise and short noise" cancel each other. That's why the best thing you can find are those gems of shorts that are set to underperform their peers.

Forget the ECB, the Bank of Japan, the Federal Reserve Bank, and the Bank of England. There is a very clear reason why certain companies tend to underperform their benchmarks: value destruction through the investment process. These are companies that are "running to stand still", spending money to generate lower returns. These are the jewel shorts, which in a bullish market environment, create "short on strength, never buy on weakness" opportunities.

How to identify a good short for the long term

When I read an analyst report, there are three sentences that put me on alert that the company may be a good short candidate with value-destroying qualities: "it is a good company", "fundamentals have not changed", and "dividend yield is high".

First, "it is a good company" is irrelevant when it comes to generating superior returns in the long run, which is what you want when you buy a stock. It is important to distinguish between industrial companies and financial investments. A "good business" can be a great company to send a CV and work for, but that does not mean it will generate higher returns, shareholder value, or grow margins.

Second, "fundamentals have not changed", which in my experience usually means that the company lives off the memories of a glorious past and legacy assets but the forthcoming results will be poor for many quarters.

Third, "dividend yield is high". I am extra careful when the dividend is unsustainable and hides balance sheet risk. The dividend is deducted entirely from the stock price. It should be noted that, on many occasions, that dividend is paid with debt or – worse – in shares. A high yield usually hides low growth, very mature businesses, and diminishing returns. Of course, there is a golden rule . . . when a stock exceeds a 7% estimated dividend yield as shares collapse, usually you will see afterwards a cut in shareholder remuneration.

Value traps

A stock is considered to be a "value trap" when it appears to be cheap because it trades at low multiples of earnings, cash flow, or book value, but in reality it is not. There are cheap stocks because they deserve it.

They tend to attract investors who are looking for a bargain, but the low valuation may imply that the company or the entire sector is in trouble. Often, a value trap appears to be such a good deal that investors become confused when the stock fails to perform.

Value traps tend to destroy shareholder value through megalomaniac "diversification" acquisitions, which analysts and management always consider "small", or through large capital expenditure programmes with very poor returns.

But these are companies that through the process of making acquisitions and investing become "fatter" not "stronger". They become destroyers of value where the executives in charge of the different divisions or businesses are consumers of budgets, not managers to improve profitability.

Similarly, there are stocks that are expensive and deserve to be so. Companies that create true value become more expensive without the need for acquisitions or mergers, they are expensive because they are more profitable, stronger, and because they focus on what they actually do well.

Value trap examples abound and tend to be concentrated on what governments call "strategic sectors", that is, where uncontrolled spending and investing in political ventures is typical – are often semi state or privatized firms but with huge cronyism – where managers are not entrepreneurs, but VIP employees appointed by governments and where the goal of the managing team is to remain in their positions, not create shareholder value. It is common to see the top executives of these firms receive a gigantic fixed remuneration but very few own shares – or very little stock – of the company compared to their personal fortune.

Indeed, the misalignment of risk taken, exposure to the shares, and objectives between shareholders and management team is a critical factor in identifying a value trap.

In the energy sector, just like the dotcom bubble, overly optimistic assumptions for growth, profit margins, and cash flows can lead to disappointment. And when reality catches up and the bubble bursts, "value traps" often emerge with a "growth mirage" that tends to justify the high multiples based on elusive targets and unrealistic expectations.

The vicious cycle of value traps

Value trap companies tend to be "pro-cyclical". That is, they buy high when the market is "hot" and sell low when debt drowns them. Acquisitions are made at steep multiples for alleged "growth" markets or to "diversify" (generally, when they have to diversify it is because something is wrong with their core business).

Value trap companies always "invest" late. These are companies with multi-billion capital expenditure plans but almost always targeted at copying what their leading competitors do, creating a bubble in which everyone participates . . . until it explodes. Value trap companies make investments via committee based on optimistic estimates where corporate advisers are afraid to deliver bad news to management teams. Where "yes-sir" internal policies reward mediocrity and cronyism. Using the shareholders' money in ventures where PowerPoint slides justify any optimistic expectation. And afterwards come the downgrades of the company's own estimates . . . the profit warnings, the capital increases, and convertible bonds . . . without costing anyone their job.

Value trap companies tend to use excessive debt. This vicious cycle tends to lead to excessive debt as "growth" disappoints and margins deteriorate. The process starts with justifications (such as "we can afford it"), and continues with shareholder-dilutive actions (such as convertible bonds, issuance of preferred stock and hybrids) and ends with write-offs, dividend cuts, and capital increases at rock-bottom prices.

Once these companies have destroyed several hundred billions in value (in the EURO STOXX alone €150 billion between 2007 and 2010), they start again. Back to acquisitions "to grow" and press "reset".

There will always be some CEO who will say that the "shares do not reflect the real value of the company", that the "new plan is different and very realistic" and that "fundamentals have not changed". But there is a reason why these segments of "strategic semi-state-owned cronyism" stocks have underperformed their respective sectors year after year.

The value trap of "big oil"

I had been working in an integrated oil company for almost a decade, and I was reading about why the large telecoms had become value trap investments and why the energy sector was different. I kept hearing about "value", "growth", "next year will be different", and "market perception is unjustified".

When I joined the financial market industry, I came to the realization that the large cap energy sector had gone ex-growth. It became clear how the fundamental changes across the energy world would invariably end up disappointing growth expectations, from profit warning to profit warning.

The decade had seen enormous mergers across oil, gas, and utilities. The "large discounts to net asset value", "opportunities to create synergies", supported by vast amounts of detailed analysis from corporate bankers. But the disappointing results of these giant mergers and acquisitions would only become evident over time, after many years of justifications and excuses. The sector had generated an average of 13% ROCE when oil prices were around $11/bbl, and despite a 10-fold increase in prices to $110/bbl, the ROCE remained unchanged at an average of 13%. Growth had disappointed year after year but capex had continued to rise, eroding the benefits from higher commodity prices.

It was obvious to me that "big oil" was not a good way to play the oil price, yet many investors were implementing their bullish views through them.

One reason for the divergence between oil prices and oil producers is taxation.

In most countries, the "host government" keeps an increasing share of the revenues as the oil price goes up via a combination of restrictive taxation and "profit-sharing agreements". In some cases, the host government can keep up to 75% of the revenues above a price of $100. Not the kind of participation that some investors might have expected. The host governments have been able to "get away with it" based on simple demand and supply (more majors bidding than contracts available). The average price realization of their crude oil basket for the oil majors has fallen to $65–$68/barrel from $100.

Another reason for the divergence in valuations is natural gas.

Most of big oil's mid-term growth strategy is heavily weighted towards natural gas. This has helped big oil companies generate returns of 33% in "legacy assets", but much lower, close to 10%, on new projects. Therefore, to reinvest cash generated at 33% in projects that generate 10% destroys shareholder value, as the multiples reflected by the share price are implying higher expected returns.

Another reason is the cost of reserve replacement.

The industry invests on average 30% of its capitalization to replace its reserves. This is why the sector "does not work". The multiples "seem cheap" (low price to earnings, high dividend yield), but in a sector as capital-intensive as energy, what really matters is the cash-flow generation. Free cash-flow yield has fallen year after year from 7.0% in 2003 (when oil was at $30/barrel) towards a very poor average of 3.7% in 2013 (when oil was at $100/barrel). Since depreciation of assets is still lower than the capital invested, the real price to earnings (the economic PE) is much higher. If we add that such investments can hardly generate any growth, it adds to the sector problem: "running to stand still".

And of course, diversification does not add value to shareholders.

Another typical argument is that mega oil companies are trading at prices far lower than the sum of their parts. Not necessarily true. A conglomerate discount is justified when the generation of returns of some of the parts is much lower than the core business. For example, one of the major listed companies invested annually 15% of their capex in non-core areas, namely refining and power, which generated an ROCE of 5.5% between 2001 and 2010, much lower than the expected return for the core business. It should not be a surprise that from a valuation perspective, these activities subtract value to the core and higher yielding activities.

And large reserves do not mean value.

The valuation of big oil based on reserves is not valid, unless the company, like some independents, was for sale. If, in addition, it appears that these companies acquire new reserves to replace those consumed, the value of the conglomerate does not exceed $4/bbl (proven and probable) until it starts generating cash. That is the reason why big oil trades on traditional profit–earnings ratios, enterprise value/debt-adjusted cash flow (EV/DACF), and free cash flow yield.

And finally, the argument that big oil pays a great dividend. Right. But it is also true that if free cash flow falls, as we have discussed, much of that dividend is paid with additional debt. So it is difficult to see that dividend as increasing in US dollar terms, unless we consider that debt is too low. And at first glance, it seems like it. With 20–30% debt to capital (equity) on average, companies seem to have very little debt, but if we add working capital requirements, and turn to the equation "free cash flow = operating cash flow – capex – dividend", it is difficult to be positive, as these dividends are not anywhere near as enormous as they may look. Remember that almost none of the large cap oils covers the dividend with cash flow after capex below $80/barrel.

The value trap in European utilities

A similar case is happening with the European electricity sector which has been one of the worst performing sectors in the

2008–2012 period due to the weight of the major integrated companies, which have all the features of a "value trap":

First, the returns of the companies are "seized" when governments need money. Indeed, from Germany to Italy (the cynically called "Robin Hood tax"), power companies are perceived by governments as public service entities, available to tap the capital market to make huge investments in the long term, but not allowed to generate returns above what governments consider "adequate", which is a paltry 8% ROACE on average. At the end of the day, the governments think, they can always make capital increases (more than €30 billion in 2008–2012) and start all over again. A sector where companies invest hundreds of billions per annum for 25-year projects but where the rules of the game change every four or five.

Second, the European utilities have been "running to stand still". Part of the huge number of mergers and acquisitions that we have seen between 2004 and 2007 came from the objective of these groups, several semi-state owned, seeking to generate returns outside their country because the profits in their home market will always be limited. But the results end up being as disappointing as the domestic.

Third, the European utility sector trades "optically cheap". The sector trades at an average of 7.2 times 2015 EBITDA[2] and dividend yield of 4.5–5%. It seems very attractive to those seeking an investment in the "long term", right? Careful. The EBITDA multiple is actually closer to 9 times if "clean" estimates, removing the free carbon dioxide permits, are applied. And more importantly, after the wave of mergers and acquisitions and re-gearing, the WACC has increased, something that companies do not acknowledge.

And be careful with the estimated dividends. First, because we have already seen cases in which the dividend is paid by the investors themselves through scripts, capital increases disguised as "opportunities for growth". Also remember that such a capital-intensive sector needs to maintain a pristine credit rating to access the bond market. With returns confiscated and an average three times net debt/EBITDA, the sector does not generate enough free cash flow to undertake the committed investments, pay dividends, and reduce debt.

Fourth, the reserve margin management. The sector has delivered the keys to the reserve margin management and investment decisions in new generation capacity to their governments, who are delighted to see overcapacity, and the industry, with the risk of seeing no growth, prefers to invest in the hope that someday they will be remunerated for the investments.

Fifth, poor management. Except for honourable exceptions, it's worth highlighting the low quality of management teams, with a history of investing billions at the peak of the cycle and then selling at the lows, and their poor exposure to the share price (minimal ownership of directors in the shares). After all, how can an investor trust a manager who owns almost no shares in their own company, is incentivized to buy anything that moves to "grow", and having to invest long-term, have such a poor long-term track record? Additionally, I would highlight the low interest that governments have in the share price of their own investments, which is not aligned with the minority holders.

It is interesting to see in this environment that the worst performing stocks tend to be the most recommended by analysts, with over 80% of "buy" recommendations. I always say it: "In a bull market you don't need analysts and in a bear market you don't want them".

The only utilities that are doing well are the ones showing financial discipline, focused on return on capital employed (ROCE) and "anti-government rebellion". The rest are a waste of money.

Look for scarcity

In the physical commodity markets, contrary to common belief, commodities with lowest *demand* growth tend to be the ones that experience greatest price appreciation. On the other hand, commodities with the highest *demand* growth tend to perform worse.

The reason is simple: scarcity. For example, crude oil and copper are commodities that have experienced low demand growth. Why? Because there was not enough supply to satisfy the demand. As a result, prices must go up to incentivize demand destruction, substitution, and incentivize incremental supply.

Look for bottlenecks

Bottlenecks can be viewed as "temporary scarcity" and tend to generate explosive "boom and bust" behaviour. For example, coal is a very abundant commodity. There is certainly no shortage of coal reserves around the world. But during the run up in prices in the 2000s, surging coal prices reflected the logistical bottlenecks across the supply chain.

Bottlenecks tend to cause a "domino" effect. High prices incentivize exploration and production. A railway or alternative transportation needs to be built to accommodate the growth in volumes. Then the export port tends to be expanded to allow for more ships and higher volumes. In turn, more ships might be needed to support the increase in global trade. The importing ports also require the ability to handle higher volumes, which then need to be transported to the final consumers. Any bottleneck along the process has the potential to translate into higher prices, which provide the signals and incentives for the market to clear it.

But be careful. Bottlenecks are temporary. They offer attractive tactical opportunities, but they are not structural. The bottlenecks are eventually cleared. And so the cycle perpetuates, through a boom and bust, and rarely through a continuous and steady investment process.

Bottlenecks and scarcity in the stock market

The global oil and gas capex has recently accelerated to $720 billion per annum, a trend that in my view is set to continue.

The oil services sector is well positioned to benefit from this trend, but the winners are a few chosen ones.

Oil services companies are the key to maximizing the performance of the fields and avoid expensive delays and technical problems. They generate spectacular returns of 25% ROCE and higher. The myth that these returns are unsustainable and that cuts in capex will reduce them dramatically has been proven wrong in the post-Macondo world. Safety and reliability is worth every dollar.

New contracts are being awarded to the more efficient, aggressive, and flexible service companies. And if anything has been demonstrated in the 2008–2009 period, it is that, despite the large drop in oil prices, oil service costs did not fall more than 15% over the same period. This is the proof of the power of this sector over its customers. Competition is relatively low, barriers to entry and specialization are very high, and oil companies (clients) do not jeopardize safety and efficiency to save a little money.

Also, it's worth mentioning the companies that specialize in large complex projects. Among the latter, Halliburton and Schlumberger have proven their ability to carry out giant projects from Saudi Arabia to Nigeria and generate very strong returns.

For the uninitiated investor, I would recommend focusing on the following three characteristics:

- First, the ability to maintain or increase prices to customers and increase its order book. This is a highly specialized industry and the weaker players die quickly.
- Second, avoid semi-state owned and over-diversified firms that often face execution risks, or are too dependent on one customer.
- Third, focus on independent and well-capitalized companies with expertise in a specific segment that is of interest to predators. From my point of view, these are the deep-sea drilling and seismic companies.

The service sector is an area for investors with risk appetite who want exposure to oil prices, as one of the few sub-sectors that generates double-digit growth and high margins in the oil world. As the world continues to need more than $700 billion annual investment in oil and gas, and I think we have many years ahead like this, oil service industry leaders will maintain the capacity to increase margins and orders.

Another key bottleneck and source of value for investors is exploration, where independent companies have consistently outperformed large majors in success rate and quality of portfolio.

Cherry picking in exploration is critical but in my view these companies are attractive for two reasons.

- First, there are very few independent companies with attractive natural resources, which makes them almost inevitable "targets" for predators.
- Second, their exposure to high-potential exploration assets causes the values to move upwards and downwards faster than other sectors. These are also companies where there is only one objective: to find and monetize reserves. No plan for 50 years, no political strategy, no obligations towards the media. And they fall as well when they do not deliver. According to Wood MacKenzie, between 2007 and 2013 independent companies worth $155 billion have been acquired.

For the uninitiated, let me briefly explain how they are valued.

Independent explorers buy assets with an attractive potential for exploration, drill them and, once they are assured that the wells are commercially viable, either they develop the portfolio or farm-out to big oil. Normally they keep a series of wells that will ensure production, access to financing and cash, and use the financial resources to explore more and sell again. The key factor to value for an investor is the history of exploration successes. It is not the same to trust companies with 77% exploration success track record against those with a much lower track record.

The independent companies are valued on an estimate of their core net asset value (NAV) and an estimated percentage of future exploration success on their portfolio of wells. A percentage assigned by the market depending on the geology and seismic interpretation. Then, as they start conducting their exploration programme, the market assigns value to the reserves encountered, or subtracts it from the pre-estimated value given to those assets if what they find is a dry hole (non-commercial).

If you are interested in the sector, pay attention to companies with little debt and exposure to areas of strong interest for predators, but also to those with better opportunities to acquire and explore reserves in attractive areas: West Africa, North Sea, gas in the United States and Gulf of Mexico.

In shale gas in the United States always look for companies with low costs and an intensive exploration programme. Obviously they are exposed to a complex environment of gas prices, but focusing on low-cost producers in attractive positions to make alliances or mergers is critical.

These are stocks that are highly correlated to oil and gas prices, but also very exposed to the credit environment, as they have to maintain a very low level of debt while financing large exploration programmes. These are stocks to buy when there is a point of entry, either a capital increase to finance a drilling programme or the announcement of a non-commercial well of low relevance before an intensive and attractive programme of exploration. A sector that is not suitable for risk-averse investors or fans of dinosaurs with high dividend yield.

In the renewables sector there are no such obvious bottlenecks, the sector moved quickly to create significant spare capacity driven by government incentives. The main area of bottlenecks and pricing power that we see in the long term is polysilicons and downstream light-emitting diodes (LED). Brian Chenel of Digital Lumens explained it perfectly: "A broad consensus is emerging here that intelligent, connected lighting will be the next big area of innovation. As we continue to approach the practical limits of device efficiency and cost, it is software, built on top of commodity hardware, that will drive the next wave of lighting market disruption. Whether it's new business models built to deliver light as a service, biophilic lighting that can help improve our quality of sleep, or simply the radical energy efficiency that next-generation intelligent systems can deliver, it is clear that the near future of LED lighting is about a lot more than just making photons".

Technology, again, drives competitive advantage.

The illusion of dilution

You cannot print commodities. Sounds simple, but the physical nature of commodities results in a completely different dynamics to commodity equities, commodity bonds, or even commodity currencies.

Equity instruments can be issued on demand or for necessity, as was the case during the Lehman crisis, when the financial sector was forced to issue billions of new shares, effectively diluting the value of the existing shareholders.

It is the same with debt. Corporates and governments can borrow and issue new debt by as much as the market may be willing to lend them. Pick your choice. The list of heavily indebted governments and corporates is immense. Leverage is a time bomb though.

And the same with currencies. The aggressive monetary policies and "printing" of money has an undeniable dilution effect on the value of a fiat currency. Look at Japan, with over a "quadrillion" yen in debt and aggressive monetary policy.

I also find funny how investors look at the "cent stocks". In Australia, many new equity issues are priced at $0.01/share. Believe it or not, investors view the price as "cheap"! The company wants to raise $100 million in capital, which means they will issue . . . 10 billion shares!

And it was the same thing during the Lehman crisis. The banks were forced to raise capital via share capital increases, which in some cases more than doubled the amount of outstanding shares . . . Yet, some investors viewed the stock as cheap relative to historical valuations "pre-dilution".

This will never happen with a commodity. A barrel of oil is a barrel of oil. However, the dilution can take different and dangerous forms.

One way or another, the important consideration is that commodities and other commodity-related instruments are different. Expressing a commodity view via commodity equities can result in major disappointment. And vice versa. The basis risk between them is too high as investors incur many, often undesired, exposures to their original intentions.

Let's have a closer look at commodity investments.

Rolling futures, commodity index, and ETFs

As Albert Einstein said, "It you can't explain it simply enough, you probably don't understand it well enough", to which I would add "If you don't understand it well enough, don't invest in it".

The following section is critical in order to understand the performance of commodity future based strategies, which are commonly used by retail and institutional investors.

Total returns are not spot returns

The performance or commodity indices and rolling futures strategies tend to be referred to as "total return", which is composed of "spot returns" and "roll returns".

"Spot return" accounts for the directional movements (up or down) in crude oil or natural gas front month futures. The spot return is very intuitive. It is what most investors "think" they are buying. But unfortunately it is impossible to replicate.

"Roll return" accounts for the benefit or cost of not taking physical delivery of natural gas. The roll return is not intuitive and generally not well understood. It is not constant, it changes over time reflecting market dynamics.

The roll return is of critical importance for natural gas, and also for crude oil, agriculture, and any other commodity where seasonality and storage play a role in pricing. In the following section I will try to explain it through a few different angles.

The Goldman Sachs Commodity Index (GSCI) was created in 1991 with the view to provide a benchmark for commodity allocations. The GSCI is composed of a diversified basket of front month futures that are rolled to avoid physical delivery. The weighting is based on "consumption and production weighted" where the weight of crude oil is larger than, say, silver. This is comparable to an "equity market cap" where the weight of Microsoft or Apple may be larger than a smaller market cap name.

The crude oil ETF

In 2005, my colleague Francisco Blanch published a note called "Sticky Contango". Until then, crude oil was thought to "belong" to backwardation. Many analysts used Keynesian arguments to defend a structural backwardation based on the fact that producers were willing to sell future production at a discount in order to secure fixed prices. But the world was changing, in 2005 the

risk was increasingly more biased towards higher prices and the
report argued the case of "structural contango" where consumers should be willing to pay a premium to secure fixed prices.

The implications from the report were enormous, as it challenged the return profile of the main commodity indices. A
structural contango would mean "negative carry" for commodity
indices. While many dismissed the report, Francisco and his
team became first movers and introduced a new generation of
indices that would avoid the front month rolling, in an effort
to reduce the negative carry. The new indices also looked at
providing exposure to "downstream" commodities such as
refined products, instead of crude oil.

It was only one year later when people started to realize
what we were talking about. Crude oil was up 15% on the year,
but the GSCI was flat. How was that possible? Well, the answer
was the negative carry due to the super-contango and storage
dynamics.

The new generation quickly expanded to agriculture and,
of course, US natural gas, possibly one of the worst horror
stories in the commodity index world.

Mind the natural gas ETF
Contrary to what many people believe, the natural gas ETF does
not hold any physical natural gas. If it did, it would have to
deal with the nuances of storage, insurance, and financing
among others.

Instead, the natural gas ETF buys front month futures. That
is, it is equivalent to buying natural gas for delivery on a
"future" date. In this example, one month. So, by design, the
ETF gives the buyer exposure to the prices but without taking
physical delivery.

As the front month contract comes closer to expiry, instead
of taking delivery of the natural gas, the investor "rolls" the
future into the next nearby future contract. In a way, the

investor is "kicking the physical delivery-can down the road". But there is no "free lunch" here, so whoever is taking the other side will pass on the cost of storage, insurance, and financing in the roll.

As discussed, the roll yield can be positive or negative. It depends on the market conditions. The important thing is that it can be very large, potentially creating a significant divergence between the performance of spot prices and the ETF. As discussed, the average cost of rolling natural gas has been a negative carry of 30% pa compounded. This is huge.

On day one, the investor pays $100 and receives one share of the ETF. The $100 are invested in US Treasuries, which will pay, say, 0% interest. At the same time, the fund buys $100 worth of natural gas futures. Let's assume the front month, say the March contract, is $5/MMBtu. Then the ETF will effectively buy 20 MMBtu. So far so good.

As time goes by, and the March future approaches expiry, the ETF will sell March and buy April. Let's assume that March is still at $5/MMBtu and let's assume that the second nearby future contract is at $5.125/MMBtu, which in the commodity lingo would be $0.125/MMBtu contango. Our $100 worth of March futures now can buy only 19.5122 MMBtu (100 divided by $5.125). That is, we have been able to buy less units of natural gas. Last month we had 20 units, now we have only 19.5122 units. This is the cost of not taking physical delivery.

As another month goes by, let's assume that April is trading at $5, effectively the front month price (what you can find on the *Wall Street Journal* or CNBC) has not changed over the past two months. March used to be the front month at $5, and now April is the front month and is also worth $5. Optically, "nothing has happened". Those consumers and producers buying and selling physical natural gas have not observed any difference in the price.

However, the ETF investor is starting to suffer from the negative roll yield. His $100 that during the roll had bought him 19.5122 units of gas are now worth $97.56, which is a loss of approximately 2.5% during one month.

If the shape of the futures curve remains unchanged (front month $5 April and second nearby $5.125 June), the $97.56 will now buy 19.04 units of June futures. The problem comes again if the June futures "roll down" towards $5 and the July futures remain in contango at $5.125, as the $97.56 effectively become $95.18, which is a loss of 4.82% in just two months and with "no price change", as it is still at $5.

If you continue to process over many years, it is easy to see how your $100 have become $5.

The roll yield in natural gas has been so extreme, that over the long run the shape of the forward curve has been a more important factor in determining the value of the ETF than the actual price of natural gas.

Complex, I know, but important.

In April 2007 the United States Commodity Fund launched the first-ever Natural Gas Exchange Traded Fund approved by the SEC for distribution to retail (small) investors. The website describes the product as: "The United States Commodity Funds LLC is the manager of exchange traded securities designed to track the movements in the prices of different commodity futures".

In April 2008, one year after the launch, natural gas broke through $10 for the first time. Front month natural gas prices were up over 30% since the launch. What a shock it must have been when their broker told them that the ETF they bought for $100 was worth $90, down about 10%. How was that possible? Natural gas was *up* 30% and the ETF *down* 10%?

And it got worse. As I am writing this, the price of US natural gas was down 40% since launch, but the ETF was down 95%. Yes, $100 invested in US natural gas would be worth $5 today.

Well, the answer is storage costs which are crystallized as negative carry through rolling futures in a contango or super-contango market. While the roll returns can be positive (rolling in backwardation) or negative (rolling into contango), unfortunately for natural gas investors it has been extremely negative (more than negative 30% pa) and during long periods of time.

So, the performance of the natural gas ETF is not as straightforward as it sounds. It depends on both the spot returns as well as roll returns.

I looked through the 169-page prospectus (legal document) supporting the US natural gas ETF, and I could not find any clear explanation or disclosure of these risks. I am sure it is there, somewhere, but I could not easily find it.

Are all commodity indices and ETF the same?

No, they are not. And before investing in the ETF, no matter how popular, you must try to understand what you are buying. And if you don't understand it well enough, I suggest you do not buy it to avoid any surprises.

One consideration is whether the ETF is backed by rolling futures or physical. As discussed, the crude oil ETF and the natural gas ETF are based on collateralized rolling futures. Some others, like the gold ETF (GLD), are backed by physical gold.

If the ETF is backed by rolling futures, it is important to understand the potential risks and order of magnitude of the roll return. In that sense, there is no limit to backwardation and therefore no limit to positive carry. On the other hand, the danger comes from the risk of super-contango, when storage is full. This risk is less for "solid" and "unseasonal" commodities such as coal and aluminium. The risk of negative carry increases significantly with "non-solid" or "seasonal", such as agriculture, crude oil, and natural gas.

A game of skill and luck

In the short run, market prices reflect the actions, expectations, and emotions of market participants, often based on limited and incomplete information. There is plenty of "noise" and randomness in the behaviour of short-term prices. New trading platforms and many more players are adding to the noise. Yet, it is human nature to try to explain and rationalize them.

Shortly after I joined an investment bank in London, I was sent to New York to complete a three-month programme focused on financial markets. We were about 50 young analysts and associates from all over the world. It was a highly competitive environment, where the heads of our desks back home were monitoring the grades closely. Financial markets were new for many of us, and every other morning the group was asked to discuss the latest developments in the markets. One morning the teacher asked a Japanese colleague: "Hitoshi-san, why did the Japanese yen go up yesterday?", he hesitated for a second and replied: "More buyers than sellers?" The class broke up in laughter. The teacher felt insulted. As top graduates from some of the best universities in the world, we were expected to come up with a more "profound" answer. Something that would "rationalize" the behaviour of the market. But what looked like a rebel answer, was deeper than it first looked. In the very short term (the next few minutes) the price behaviour is extremely random, pretty much a 50/50 chance of going up or down. The odds dramatically improve over the long term, but in the short run prices are very random. The teacher and most of us at the time did not fully appreciate the sarcastic depth of Hitoshi's answer. But accepting the randomness of the market is one of the most important basic rules of the game.

In the long run, the short-term "noise" tends to even out and valuations tend to converge towards fair value.

Phil Ivey is thought to be one of the best poker players in the world. Yet, over one single hand, I have decent chances of beating him. Over a single hand, the cards we get are random and luck is more important than skill. But my odds decrease significantly as the number of hands increases. And over the long run (thousands of hands), the noise and randomness tends to even out. My probability of beating Phil decreases significantly with the number of hands we play. Over the long run, skill takes over. Luck averages out. True for poker. True for trading and investments. And true for most things in life!

In that sense, investing and trading are closer to poker than to chess.

Chess is a game where both players have full information and there is no element of randomness or luck involved. But in investing, no matter how good you are, there will always be some element of randomness and luck.

For example, someone might have developed a bearish fundamental view that global natural gas prices would go down due to the shale revolution. To take advantage of this, they could have "shorted" the futures with the view to buy them back at a lower price at a later date. And then Fukushima happened. Who could have predicted that?

There is no such thing as "certainty" when it comes down to financial markets. Static views and "high conviction", when combined with high leverage, can be a lethal combination.

It is human nature to try to model, forecast, and predict the future. Spreadsheets and other complex modelling tools make it simpler than in the old days, when we had to do the calculations by hand. Everyone can build a model and extrapolate conclusions into the distant future, by simply dragging the mouse down and copy and pasting cells. This "channelling effect" can result in overconfidence about our ability to predict and control the future, as described by Nicholas Taleb in *Fooled by Randomness*.[3] Modelling tends to oversimplify reality, and has severe shortcomings as we try to establish relationships and probabilistic outcomes across "known unknowns", often ignoring important "unknown unknowns".

Profits and stops

"You make and lose your money when you get out, not when you get in". Yet, many investors spend most of their time thinking about when to enter into a position.

Very few determine upfront where they are going to get out. That is, setting a "profit taking" and a "stop loss" level. The lack of discipline can be a fatal mistake. Most investors show plenty of "improvisation" in the exit, which often results in profit taking too early, and taking losses too late if ever.

As a rule, you must set a profit and stop upfront. And stick to it.

I remember the first position I ever took. I was long gold futures. The market was going down. I was very emotional about it. "The market is wrong, it is going up". Eventually, the market reached my stop loss, I was upset and told my boss that I wanted to "double up" the position, that is, to buy more. He told me, "sure, but you have to sell the position you have first, and then you can buy it again". I complained, "why? I am going to cross the bid-offer and pay the commissions twice!", and he said "just do it. . .". And so I sold the futures, took the loss. And then, something magical happened. Suddenly buying gold did not look as appealing as before. "I will wait", I told my boss, who smiled and walked away. It was then that I understood the negative power that emotions can have in your investment process, and how discipline can help you overcome them. I lost money that day, but the lesson was worth it and paid many times over.

Perfect timing

When it comes to investments and trading, there is a saying that goes: "timing is everything".

Perfect timing (consistently sell at the highest price, and/or buy at the lowest price) is practically impossible. Just like catching the bus, sometimes we are early, sometimes we are late, and sometimes we are "just in time". Timing the entry and exit of positions in the markets is similar, and can be heavily impacted by randomness. One needs to accept the reality that we will most likely be too early or too late, and prepare for it.

In financial markets, unlike taking the bus, being too early can be even more dangerous than being too late. Most experienced traders look to "trade the rebound", and "try to avoid catching a falling knife". In our view, the process has already started and is unstoppable, but that does not mean oil prices will only go down and/or will not make new historical highs. Anything can happen. Investors must accept this reality, and prepare for it.

The crystal ball

To illustrate the importance of timing, let's assume you have a crystal ball that can predict the future with 100% accuracy and certainty. And let's assume that the crystal ball tells you that crude oil will be at $35/bbl by 2020. Given that crude oil prices are currently above $100/bbl. What would *you* do?

Most people would be tempted to go sell crude oil futures, right now, and in large size: "*at the end of the day, I know I am right. . . I just need to wait and make a ton of money, right?*" Well, it does sound like "free money", but this is not necessarily the case. In fact, *high conviction* (and at the extreme, 100% certainty) can be fatal. Part of the problem is that high conviction trades tend to be implemented in larger size than normal and kept for longer than they deserve. The combination can be fatal. As Keynes famously said, "the markets can be irrational for longer than I can be solvent". A basic and important reminder that investing is about *making money*, not about *being right*.

What the crystal ball did not tell you

The crystal ball told us – with the highest degree of conviction – where the price *will end*, but rarely tells us the *path that prices will follow* to get there. For a given starting and ending price, say $35/bbl and $100/bbl respectively, there are literally infinitely many possible paths that prices could follow. Most likely, the path will not be a smooth straight line, but rather a volatile path with spikes and troughs along the way. This is particularly true for volatile assets such as crude oil, often rocked by macro or geopolitical risks.

Why does the path of prices matter? It matters because it will determine the buffer the investor needs to stay in the trade. The price may end at $35/bbl (as correctly predicted by the investor) but what if losses – at some point during the life of the trade – were so large that you were forced to liquidate and *stop loss*?

The worst-case scenario

A golden rule of investments is "know your worst-case scenario". Most investors do not think about this enough *before* they enter a trade. Often because we are blinded by our high conviction or simply because of lack of discipline and trading technique.

I remember a dinner during the Lehman crisis, when one of my best friends told me he had bought some financials that were trading at the then historical lows of $25/share. It was still early in the crisis, with a fairly polarized view between those who thought it was "the end of the world" and those who thought the crisis was blown out of proportion and financials offered some great opportunities. I was in severe pain via my own shares in Merrill Lynch, and asked my friend naively: "what do you think is your worst case scenario of the trade?" Influenced by my wife's ultra conservative view of the world, I said that: "my worst-case scenario is I lose the full value of the shares", which sparked an "interesting" debate. "That will *never* happen. Citibank will *never* go down. . .". And they were right!

My gloomy and pessimistic outlook raised some concerns, but the follow-up worst-case scenario raised a few laughs. I guess I sounded like a depressed crazy lunatic, to which my answer was "When I mean *worst case*, I really mean *worst case*, not how bad *you think* it can get. I know it is unlikely, and I really hope I am wrong, but you cannot ignore it!"

There are two angles to this:

- First, "what is the worst-case scenario for this individual trade?" The answer was full loss of capital. No matter how unlikely, the true worst case was the entire $25/share. In order to reduce the worst case, disciplined investors have a "stop loss". The other, more loose, risk management rule is "only invest what you can afford to lose".
- Second, "how would the rest of your portfolio (and income) behave if the worst case of this investment materializes?" The Lehman crisis impacted everyone, across all sectors. My friend, like many other great professionals, was made redundant during the following months. A scenario where the share prices of Citibank (and other financials) collapsed was unlikely but it happened.

Concluding Remarks

And in the end the love you take is equal to the love you gave.

The Beatles

I have always liked this joke that an old friend of mine from Exxon told me once when we were stranded in Nigeria:

A seasoned oil executive goes to heaven and St
Peter tells him, "Sorry, the quota of oil men has been
surpassed, you must go to hell". The guy says, "If I

convince some of the oil men that are currently in heaven to go to hell, will I be able to come in?" St Peter says "Sure". So the oil man screams "There has been a huge oil discovery in hell!!!!" Suddenly, thousands of ex-oil sector angels flood towards hell in a stampede. St Peter sees that the oil executive follows them down to hell and shouts, "What are you doing? You don't want to come to heaven?" And the man replies "Are you kidding? What if the rumour is true, and there is oil in hell?"

The energy industry is pro-cyclical. Never forget it.

Energy is everything. Without it there is no industrial and economic growth.

It is the mother of all battles and will not end. It is the war between consumers and producers to reach an equilibrium of interests and win the competitiveness game that leads to prosperity and growth. It is constantly ongoing, because it is an essential part of the development of humanity.

This battle is as much about energy security of supply as it is about cost. It is about global interdependence between countries and at the same time an inherent need to control the variables that affect the supply of energy of each individual state regardless of the overcapacity or tightness of the global marketplace.

The mother of all battles is as much about technology as it is about resources. The quest for affordable, abundant, and clean energy.

As discussed during the book, similar to the internet broadband during the late 1990s and early 2000s, it is possible that overcapacity may grow to a point that margins will be depressed as prices converge towards variable costs.

Large capital expenditure acts as a barrier to entry. But once built up, it acts as a barrier to exit. And, given the nature of the cost structure, excess capacity will continue to operate as long as it can cover the variable marginal costs.

The biggest winners of the energy revolution may well also be the consumers, who will have access to more and cheaper energy.

Energy disinflation is a source of stimulus too. One of the most important results of the shale gas revolution is the savings to US consumers on power and gas bills. Assuming the average household pays about $100–$150/month for power and $85/month for natural gas, between 2007 and 2014 these bills have fallen dramatically, saving around $700–$900/year.

Investors must beware, this war is fought globally but with a distinct nationalistic viewpoint. As such, things like economic return and overcapacity tend to be ignored by governments when providing incentives.

In this book we have outlined the armies, the battlefield, and the weapons, but the key is to understand that this is no "one-way bet".

There will be big losers and winners.

And the key is to follow capital expenditure. Where is the money invested? What are the incentives? And what is the risk for investors when governments intervene? Especially when there is no consideration of return on investment.

The losers will likely fall aggressively on the bait of government incentives and short-term price signals.

The winners will be those that ignore fashionable trends and favour good old return on capital as their key guideline – without ignoring policy.

The losers will likely see credit as an opportunity to expand balance sheets and get fatter, not stronger.

The winners will be those who understand that their peers are pro-cyclical and will fall over and over again into the trap of oversupply.

The losers will expect policy changes to solve their strategic mistakes.

The winners will understand that overoptimistic demand assumptions should not drive investment.

Losers will wait for the cycle to turn.

Winners will understand the nature of the cycles and keep their options open.

More importantly, winners will understand that governments on either side of the resource and technology spectrum will always favour overspend and security of supply over profitability. Governments need energy companies for their political aspirations, and assume their support has to be eternal and unconditional, but energy companies tend to underestimate oversupply and cycles.

In the end, energy will continue to be about displacement of the least competitive.

And the last barrel of oil will not be worth millions. It will be worth zero.

The end game will be about cheap and readily available energy for all consumers. The alternatives are real and plentiful.

Prices and technology will continue their relentless flattening of the energy world.

A new energy regime that gives a more equal opportunity for the wealth and prosperity of nations is closer than we may think.

The battle rages on.

NOTES

1. An exchange traded fund is an instrument, structured as a fund, quoted on an exchange which replicates the performance of an index.

2. EBITDA stands for Earnings Before Interest, Taxes, Depreciation, and Amortization. It is often used to analyse and compare profitability between companies and industries because it eliminates the effects of financing and accounting decisions.

3. Nicholas Taleb (2004). *Fooled by Randomness*. New York: Thomson /Texere.

FOR A COMPETITIVE EUROPEAN ENERGY POLICY

"Industry will gradually lose its competitiveness if this course of increasing subsidies is not reversed soon",

Kurt Bock, CEO of BASF

Europe, like the US, needs to exit the crisis through competitiveness and security of supply.

Europe must change an energy policy that has forgotten companies and households with the objective of being "the greenest of the class" without paying attention to costs and competitiveness.

European companies and families cannot continue to bear the costs of planning mistakes and subsidy generosity, because the situation is dramatic.

In Europe, electricity costs are, on average, 50% higher than in the USA, the costs of industrial gas are almost 75% higher. This is the difference between an energy policy that promotes efficiency and replacement through low costs, and Europe's policy of promoting forced substitution through subsidies.

European companies are among the ones paying the highest prices for electricity and gas in the OECD.

The "green" policies and the development of renewables have allowed wholesale electricity prices to fall; while at the same time, with the addition of fixed costs and subsidies, consumer prices have skyrocketed. This is an error that destroys jobs and business and needs to be tackled urgently.

The European Union is responsible less than 14% of CO_2 emissions in the world, but 100% of the cost. Interestingly, despite the green policies of the EU, the United States, since 2005, has reduced CO_2 emissions by 12%, to 1994 levels, which is a more significant reduction than Europe's.

All these problems result in lower industrial production, increased offshoring of companies, difficulties to compete and, of course, lower employment.

For these reasons, the energy policy of the European Union must comply with the principles of safety, diversification and competitiveness.

Keep betting on renewables without passing the bill to businesses and families. Subsidies must be changed to tax incentives, as in the US. This prevents planning mistakes when estimating demand, subsidies and costs as the tax incentives are only provided when demand is real through agreements with consumers (PPAs, power purchase agreements). Every year I hear that solar will be competitive next year. And every time I hear it, the electricity bill goes up. After nearly a decade of subsidies, solar and wind technologies promoted by many leading European companies are competitive and at grid parity in some countries, without subsidies. To continue to demand subsidies in mainland Europe is at the least suspect.

Addressing the problem of overcapacity . Europe cannot be "green" yet subsidize inefficient coal technologies, pay unnecessary capacity payments, or maintain excess capacity, with reserve margins above 17%. And all of these paid for by consumers.

Replacement, not accumulation. Europe cannot allow for new generating capacity when it is consumers who pay for the accumulation of excess capacity. The new generation capacity has to come from replacement, and the change should be done at lower costs.

Solving the problem of security of supply, developing local energy sources - shale gas, oil, renewables-, as well as improving interconnection between European countries to use "hubs" to reduce dependence on Russia and other countries, using the various -almost idle- storage facilities and regasification terminals.

Do not demonize technology in a regional and ideological way. Consumers should be aware that replacing all nuclear and gas power with renewables would increase electric bills by three or four times.

Electricity prices in Europe in 2003 were among the lowest in the OECD and today they are some of the highest. Why? Because the final consumer bill was loaded with all kinds of fixed concepts. In Spain more than 62% of the typical electricity bill is accounted for by regulated costs, taxes and subsidies. The European average is 54%.

Europe's energy policy cannot be about "not in my garden". Pretending to eliminate nuclear power plants when most countries continue to support a few is ridiculous. In France, a large number of nuclear reactors has led to the lowest power prices in Europe and a safe, reliable and competitive nuclear power supply is one of the reasons why tariff prices have not soared. Another reason is that France did not jump to subsidize tens of thousands of Gigawatts of expensive renewables in early stages of technological development. As long as nuclear power is competitive, efficient and safe, Europe must continue taking advantage of it.

The challenges faced by Europe in its energy policy are enormous. But the opportunity is exciting, and the foundation to make Europe a competitive, self-sufficient world power is already in place.

Technology replacement should be achieved through lower cost, the same way that crude oil very rapidly replaced oil derived from other sources (eg whales). Not because a decision was undertaken by a committee, but because the cost of exploiting the first resource was lower.

The mistakes of 2007 began with optimistic estimates of demand growth, with errors of up to 35%, and thus it transpired that, for the first time in history since the industrial revolution, governments chose to incentivise the most expensive technologies. Europe's decision to substitute cheap energies for expensive ones have cost many lost jobs and industries.

Security of supply must be achieved, also, from a flexible and diversified energy mix which must be cheap and efficient. Not via subsidies, but through the tax incentives that prevent "fake demand signals" and prevent overcapacity.

Energy is the cornerstone of the future of Europe. Sinking competitiveness would likely worsen the crisis. Europe has the tools, using all technologies, to ensure an abundant and cheap energy supply. Anything else would bring it to repeat the mistakes of 2007.

The Oil Price War: Another Chapter in the Mother of All Battles

At the end of December 2014 oil prices fell to $70/bbl (Brent), the lowest level in five years, after OPEC decided to maintain production in its November meeting and prove to customers that they are the low cost reliable supplier. Market estimates fell sharply on the perceived glut in the oil market.

This drop was not about lack of demand, but about excess supply. While consensus estimates had been coming down, both GDP and oil demand figures were still in positive territory.

Despite reducing previous optimistic estimates IEA still estimates an oil demand growth of c0.8% for 2014. The supply demand balance, though, is bearish as production is expected to grow c3% in 2015, and –what is most important– coming mostly from non-OPEC countries. The US, in particular, is the main driver of non-OPEC demand growth. This means that the "call on OPEC" –the amount of oil needed from the cartel to balance the market- falls to 29mbpd from 30mbpd. This is a small, but very important decrease, which reduces the geopolitical risk premium that prices have enjoyed.

In their reference scenario, OPEC estimates that oil demand to 2019 will rise, on average, by 1 million barrels / day annually. This leads to the supply / demand balance showing a very healthy excess.

It's not just shale oil driving non-OPEC supply higher ... on the demand side renewables and efficiency have made a relevant dent on global oil demand and this is likely to continue.

By now it is not a secret. "We're in a real price war" were the exact words of Eulogio del Pino (CEO of Venezuelan oil company PDVSA), after Saudi Arabia and Kuwait decided, in a surprise move, to reduce prices to their customers instead of tightening supply. Price wars have happened in the past (notably 1986) and they tend to last longer than what market assumes.

Iran, in turn, has announced that OPEC could maintain prices of $60/barrel for several years and the oil minister of Kuwait commented that it was unreasonable to expect a reduction in OPEC output because it would be "ineffective".

This is a multi-purpose price war, as the 1986 one was. And in my view it has various "targets":

- Curb the shale oil revolution. OPEC seeks to regain market share against the US, which produces more than Saudi Arabia now, thanks to the shale revolution. By letting prices fall, the higher cost producers would –in theory- suffer and end up withdrawing from the market.
- This move also may seek to destabilize Russia's economy, which needs $100/barrel to subsidize their huge military

modernization budgets. Russia is an uncomfortable non-OPEC country that was instrumental in reducing Saudi Arabia's "Central Bank of Oil" role in the last seven years.

–   It is a battle against renewables. Despite solar costs falling c70% in two years and wind being competitive against fossil fuels in some OECD countries, a $60/bbl oil price brings renewables to being prohibitively more expensive than oil.

–   It is a war against electric and natural gas vehicles. With the price of gasoline in the US down to $3.0 a gallon, it is no longer easily economically viable to replace a fleet of gas vehicles to natural gas or electricity alternatives.

A good friend in an oil producing nation once told me: "When oil prices fall, we lower costs; when the subsidies fall, they go bankrupt". And this price war seems to be exactly about a show-down of who can maintain the most competitive position.

All these alternative technologies we have mentioned in the book have surged under the view of a "high oil price for longer", and –apart from the myth of peak oil– partially justi-fied by the argument that OPEC needs high prices to balance their budgets. This argument of "budget needs" disregards that up to 60% of the budget of these countries comes from entirely discretionary "social" subsidies, and a lot of wasteful spend.

The consensus view of "OPEC breakeven" at $100/barrel is not even remotely the cost of production or extraction, which is closer to a range of $ 35-70 per barrel according to industry estimates. Many unnecessary expenses are included in consen-sus breakeven prices.

What we are seeing is a race to see who survives at the lowest price, similar to the one seen in the US in 2010 when cheap gas killed most inefficient solar and wind operators.

New oil producers (*shale* and *tight oil*) in the US are now in the same stage of competition. They have to be more efficient and cut costs. The same will happen with renewable companies used to price power at the marginal high end. And Russia and Venezuela will have to limit their expenses.

According to JP Morgan the average oil price needed to generate a return of 10% in the US is closer to $65/barrel. The IEA estimates that 82% of US shale oil is viable at $65/barrel as well. As you can see, the price war may last longer than what many commentators expect.

It is also worth noting that producers are not counter-cyclical. As we saw in 2008, when oil fell to nearly $30/bbl, very few stopped producing. Costs are reduced, capex is cut and productivity is enhanced instead.

With a market of an excess supply that is almost structural in nature thanks to the shale revolution, this war is going to test many engineers and generate many efficiency improvements.

– Renewables will not stop because of low oil prices as they are policy driven, not price-driven. Germany is installing 6GW of solar despite 17% overcapacity and China is increasing solar and wind capacity. These are the two largest markets for renewables and they are not slowing down.
– Once oil prices reach below-10% IRR level, many oil producers simply produce to generate cash.

Low oil prices can mean a very relevant stimulus for the economy and consumer spending. Except in Europe. Almost 50% of the price consumers pay for gasoline are taxes. The price of gasoline (95 octane) is mainly tax (48%), the cost of the basket of oils purchased by the country (43%) and 9% is the approximate margin of marketing and refining.

A weak EUR/USD as well as high taxes are preventing consumers from enjoying low USD denominated oil prices.

So who benefits from the fall of oil? It is primarily the US consumer, who does not have to bear the burden of taxes that European consumers suffer under.

In the US, in December 2014, according to the AAA, the price of a gallon of gasoline fell to $3.0. The lowest level since 2011. Given that an average American family spends on average $ 2600 a year in gasoline / diesel, the result of this price reduction is equivalent to an improvement in disposable income of $ 500 (some estimate up to $700) a year per family unit. In fact, the price is a daily stimulus of 1.8 billion to the US, almost 660 billion per annum, according to Brean Capital.

If oil falls $10/bbl for a sustained period of time, it can boost the global GDP by +0.4%, according to the FT.

On the investment side, the main impact from low oil prices in energy tends to be that there are few winners. Mainly relative winners in the lower cost - higher margin space:

- Producers cut spending. After 10 years of steady growth, 2015 could be the first year of negative capex growth in the industry. JP Morgan already assumes a flat capex for the industry. This means lower backlog and weaker pricing power for services companies. These are traditionally the first ones to see margins down. According to Bloomberg, analysts are reducing 2015 North American rig count expectations by -15% year-over-year to 1,582.
- Dividends are at risk. Many supermajors need $85/bbl to pay dividends in cash, with a dividend cover below 30% at $70/barrel. The warning signs appear when they begin to pay dividends by way of debt.
- Refiners win as the feedstock is cheaper and margins improve. If energy demand and the economy strengthens, low cost refiners benefit from lower prices.
- Relative winners are renewables that have done their homework on debt re-structuring, benefit from a market immune to oil price shifts and driven by policy in countries with low sovereign debt.

– High yield suffers and the most indebted exploration and production companies will face difficult times.

The first battle in a drawn out war has just begun. Consolidation, balance sheet strength, divestments, efficiency and technology are the weapons. And the opportunities are enormous.

INDEX